CONTENTS

WHERE HAVE ALL THE HOMELESS GONE?

DISLOCATIONS

General Editors: August Carbonella, *Memorial University of Newfoundland,* Don Kalb, *University of Utrecht & Central European University,* Gerald Sider, *The Graduate Center & The College of Staten Island, CUNY,* Linda Green, *University of Arizona*

The immense dislocations and suffering caused by neo-liberal globalization, the retreat of the welfare state in the last decades of the twentieth century, and the heightened military imperialism at the turn of the twenty-first century have raised urgent questions about the temporal and spatial dimensions of power. Through stimulating critical perspectives and new and cross-disciplinary frameworks, which reflect recent innovations in the social and human sciences, this series provides a forum for politically engaged and theoretically imaginative responses to these important issues of late modernity.

Volume 1
Where Have All the Homeless Gone?
    Anthony Marcus

WHERE HAVE
ALL THE HOMELESS GONE?

The Making and Unmaking of a Crisis

Anthony Marcus

Berghahn Books
NEW YORK • OXFORD

First published in 2006 by

Berghahn Books

www.berghahnbooks.com

© 2006 Anthony Marcus

Library of Congress Cataloging-in-Publication Data

A catalog record for this book is
available from the Library of Congress.

British Library Cataloguing in Publication Data

A catalogue record for this book is available from the British Library

Printed in the United States on acid-free paper

ISBN 1-84545-050-7 hardback
ISBN 1-84545-101-5 paperback

PREFACE

This monograph emerged from an extended process of personal, professional, and sociopolitical revolution and evolution. However, there were a few primary moments and principal people that provided a foundation and context for themes taken up in the following chapters.

The primary research began in 1989 on New York City's "gentrifying" Lower East Side, when I convinced two colleagues who were also first year PhD students at the City University of New York (CUNY) to join me in a "research practicum" on housing loss and community activism. I had no idea at the time that any of this early research would enter my PhD thesis, become part of my later academic work, or form any part of a book written many years later.

Professor Leith Mullings provided intellectual support, professional contacts, and the academic credit points necessary to justify the huge amount of time that was taken out of our reading, writing, and discussing what counted as the anthropological canon at CUNY in the late 1980s. I remain grateful for her support and that of my two research colleagues in this first research project, Walter Ewing and Alfredo Gonzalez.

It is, of course, the case that the processes that yielded an American homeless crisis and the group of researchers who studied it was accretive and preceded, by many decades, my first days annoying tent dwellers and their neighbors and elected officials in Tompkins Square Park in 1989. However, if there is one moment that I would hold as the formative point when theory, history, and lived experience came together to create something new and dramatic that set the context for this monograph and the experiences that led me to research and write it, it was the first Tuesday in November 1980, when Jimmy Carter was voted out of the White House after one term. Though many of Carter's policies, such as his federal cost cutting and intensified cold war anticommunism that ended the Keynesianism and geopolitical détente of the Nixon years were indistinguishable from those of his successor, Ronald Reagan, this seemingly smooth evolution belied what was an ideological and political revolution.

At the time I was a first year undergraduate and knew little about politics, ideology, and the state. However, I, and my freshman friends, who were all liberal democrats, understood, along with much of the rest of the country, that there were big changes in the air. From the moment that Jimmy Carter undermined the west coast electoral process by making his concession speech in advance of the polls closing, the auguries were fearful. Like the eighteen-year-olds that we were, we took the opportunity to get drunk and held a "wake for democracy." The discussion focused on social concerns such as the end of the countercultural lifestyles and idealistic radical politics which had, since the late 1960s, been a birthright for many late teens. First and foremost, there were drugs, rock-and-roll music, and the sexual revolution that we were all looking forward to. We envisioned an army of Bible thumpers, moral majority conservatives, and public health officials concerned with the spread of herpes returning us to the 1950s.

The moral majority, in fact, came to our campus that year, and it was not long before "young Republicans" in suits and ties and dresses and pumps emerged from the shadows and filled university campuses across the nation with political arguments about the evils of affirmative action, multiculturalism, abortion, premarital sex, homosexuality, and welfare. There was a feeling among many of my professors and fellow students that the world of popular protest, countercultural lifestyles, attenuating moral codes in cinema, timid US foreign policy, and leftist idealism that had been the harvest of the post-Vietnam years was suddenly ending. The night of long knives that was the Reagan Revolution had arrived and we were suddenly all dressed up, with nowhere to go.

Some of us "fought" and some of us "switched," but public life and politics were changed forever. When I returned to New York City in 1984, after spending a year in Africa, my ideo-moral concern about the increasing belligerence of US foreign policy, the antilabor offensive that had broken the air traffic controllers' strike of 1981, and Reagan's outrageous social revanchism came to be dwarfed by shock at what had happened to the city in which I had grown up. It looked worse than many of the cities I had seen in the third world. Beggars and ragged mentally ill "street people" filled the sidewalks, housing problems had reached a point of visible crisis, and disease seemed to be everywhere. New York became one of the centers of the HIV epidemic and people feared contracting tuberculosis and other preventable diseases in crowded subway cars and public buildings. Nobody knew when their local firehouse or school would close, and the president was assuring the country that ketchup was "a vegetable," while cutting funding for school meal programs and the teaching, learning and research that those meals were supposed to support.

New York City had, of course, had its own night of long knives during the fiscal crisis of the mid 1970s. However, the combination of almost a decade of decay, a predatory and compassionless Republican White House, and an equally abusive Democratic Party in New York City, and the broader vision that comes with viewing home through the eyes of adulthood pulled me strongly in the direction of studying and advocating against the terrible depredations of the Reagan Revolution.

There were many oppositional liberal issues that emerged during this period that seemed to be defined by the distance between Michael Moore's first film, *Roger and Me*, about the destruction of Flint, Michigan by the closing of a General Motors factory and *Red Dawn*, Golan and Globus's late cold war tale of a high school football team's successful guerrilla campaign against a Soviet, Cuban, and Nicaraguan invasion of the United States. However, the issue of homelessness came to be one of the key outcome assessment indicators for the Reagan Revolution. This was so much the case that Ronald Reagan was forced to sign into law the 1987 McKinney Act that apportioned billions of dollars for study of and care for "the homeless." It was in this environment of declining support for nearly everything but the homeless that my scholarly attempts to understand and confront the Reagan Revolution developed.

Despite the virulent anti-Reaganism that drew me into studying the homeless from an anthropological perspective, this work is neither another attempt to write a nostalgic epitaph for the, previously reluctant and later failed, US welfare state, nor is it an angry attempt to "set the record straight" after the beatification of Reagan that emerged in the wake of his death in 2004. Though I continue to view the Reagan revolution as a profoundly negative period in U.S., hemispheric, and world politics, this book is in a much more fundamental way an attempt to draw a balance sheet on the political and ideological opposition to Reaganism between 1980 and 1992. Since homelessness was primarily a political construction that developed in and around the Democratic Party and yielded a research and policy agenda that heavily favored and was favored by liberals affiliated with social and political projects in such Democratic Party strongholds as New York, San Francisco, and Boston, this book is far more concerned with assessing the strengths and weaknesses of the opposition than with delivering more superfluous nails into the Reagan coffin.

A project such as this one, which is based on a PhD thesis, necessarily draws on the help and consideration of many people, most of whom do not even know they are helping at the time they are helping. My first debt of gratitude has to somehow be paid to my informants. I hope that those who do see this volume will, in some way, recognize themselves and their words in these pages and appreciate what I am trying to do. I must also thank my doctoral committee, Michael Blim, Ida Susser, and Gerald Sider. It was Ida who first offered me work studying homelessness, Michael Blim who gave me the courage to finally write about what I had seen, and Gerald Sider who has been there at every important step in my professional life both encouraging me and contesting nearly everything I say: a rare and potent scholarly cocktail. Beyond these core mentors many others have influenced me and contributed to this manuscript. Discussions with the late Del Jones were crucial to my thinking about the intersection between poverty, public policy, and race in America and my work with Ralph Miliband gave me tools for thinking about the relationship between the state and public policy.

In the field, I benefited from the help of my colleagues on the McKinney Act project that employed me. They were Kostas Gounis, who provided an anthropological take that was very different from my own, Paul Colson, who provided the view from Public Health and Social Work, and Brenda Roche, who helped me stay on top of whatever was happening on the project. There have been too many colleagues who have contributed to this manuscript to name all, but I must start with my father, Robert Marcus, who died in October 2000, but managed to read the first draft of the manuscript during the summer of 2000. His suggestions and criticisms were absolutely foundational to the product that emerged. Even now, he remains my first and most important colleague.

Other colleagues who sacrificed their time to read, listen, and make helpful suggestions are Sharryn Kasmir, Charles Menzies, Winnie Lem, Katherine McCaffrey, Suleyman Khalaf, Mary Patterson, and Gavin Smith. Finally, Dr. Alfredo Gonzalez, my collaborator in fieldwork, stands far above the rest for his intimate participation in the research and analysis. We shared the joys, dangers, and fears of fieldwork, as well as a lot of adventure. Our many discussions of what we saw together often made it difficult to separate out his work from mine. It was Alfredo who led the fieldwork for my first research project on gentrification on the Lower East Side and then helped guide me through three years studying homelessness for the federal government.

Of course, my ability to finish both the PhD thesis and the monograph depended on the help, support and guidance of many friends and family, in particular, my socialist grandmother Mary Weisstein, my dear friends Michael Weinstein and Andy Dawson, my sister Abigail Marcus-Hong, and my ex-partner Mary Lennon.

I am grateful to all those at Berghahn Books, who have helped bring this manuscript to press. In particular, Dr. Gus Carbonella who believed in my work, Dr. Don Kalb, who not only believed in my work, but helped shape major sections of some of the early drafts as part of his work with the journal FOCAAL, Marion Berghahn, Michael Dempsey, and Catherine Kirby.

Finally, it is impossible to imagine this manuscript without the love and support of my companion, Jo Sanson. When Gerald Sider informed me that I had passed my dissertation defense, but would need to hire someone to move every comma in the manuscript from where I had put it to where it belonged, she stepped up with her editor's pen. Later when I wanted to turn it into a book, she read several drafts, covering page after page with ruthlessly critical commentary and useful suggestions for improvements. However, more than being a great editor and a clear-eyed co-thinker, she gave me the love and courage to face all those pages covered with black ink from my desk jet and red ink from her editor's pen.

INTRODUCTION
Where Have All the Homeless Gone?

Where Have All the Homeless Gone?

For a decade from 1983 to 1993, homelessness was a major public concern in the United States. It was big business in social science, social policy, and national news. In 1987 the United States Congress passed the Stewart B. McKinney Homeless Assistance Act, which set aside one billion dollars for research and support programs designed to help the homeless. In 1990 discothèques across the United States rocked to a summer hit about a homeless woman, while anthropology, sociology, public health, and social work departments offered semester-long classes devoted to studying this population. Community groups and advocacy organizations fought politicians over homeless policy and ordinary citizens named homelessness, along with crime and the economy, as a major concern.

This widespread concern for the homeless suddenly began to wane in 1993. People stopped identifying homelessness as a major issue, public expenditures for homeless relief decreased, and media coverage of homelessness steadily declined. Despite all this, housing affordability indexes continued to drop in most major urban areas, per person space densities continued to rise, and the number of people seeking public shelter held steady or increased (U.S. Census 2004). Despite the billions of dollars spent on homeless research and services during the late 1980s and early 1990s, there has not been a time over the last decade when a nocturnal tour of the streets and subways of New York City has not revealed large numbers of people without proper housing. Studies by the National Law Center on Homelessness and Poverty (2004) suggest that there may actually be more people without proper housing in the first years of the twenty-first century than there were in the days of the 1980s homeless crisis.

Today, little is said or published about the homeless and few cite homelessness as one of the major public concerns. Although dramatic rises in housing loss have been noted for major cities in the United States since the economic downturn that accompanied the election of George W. Bush in 2000, homelessness still does not garner the press coverage or general outrage it did during the homeless crisis of the 1980s and early 1990s. In fact, homelessness often goes completely unnoticed, now. Always a good bellwether of the winds of public opinion and concern, the 1988 *New York Times* annual index devoted almost 200 inches of space to articles about homelessness, while the year 1999 had less than 20 inches. The steady decline in coverage of the homeless by "the newspaper of record" began in 1993, the year Clinton came into office. There has not been a year with 50 inches since 1995. The homeless crisis passed, while the homeless remain.

If any lesson is to be learned from the failure of homeless policy in the 1980s and 1990s to solve the problems it sought to address, it is necessary to understand not only why so many people lost housing, but also how the "homeless crisis," which garnered so much attention, was sociopolitically made and unmade with so little resolution. The ideological question of how "the homeless" took center stage in urban public policy during the 1980s then disappeared like so many Bobbitts, Buttafuocos, and O.J. Simpsons during the 1990s is ultimately a question about how poverty, public policy, and "difference" are socially constructed in American political culture.

This book, based on five years of participant-observation fieldwork among underhoused nonwhite populations living in extreme poverty in New York City in the late 1980s and early 1990s, as well as a brief return to the field in 1997–98, suggests answers to these two questions by looking at the way the homeless crisis was socially constructed by public policy makers, social scientists, and those whose job it was to provide homeless relief. It is the argument of this book that mass housing loss in urban America during the 1980s came to be defined as a "homeless crisis" due more to a set of peculiarly American misunderstandings about poverty, race, and social difference combined with conflict between the Democrat and the Republican Parties than to the actual rising housing costs, declining employment opportunities and reduced social services that forced thousands of people into the streets of American cities.

The social problems that drove men and women to beg for change or just pass idle days in public could have been understood and addressed in a variety of concrete, holistic, and empirically defined ways, leading to practical, substantive, and easily assessed policies. It could have been viewed as a crisis of affordable housing, in which rising housing costs throughout newly gentrifying older center city areas were creating mass housing loss among families with few economic resources. In such a scenario state policy might have been oriented toward a variety of housing policies and tax code changes designed to help the displaced, those in danger of displacement, and everybody for whom housing was problematic. Such a broad housing policy directed at the overall state of social housing could have had both ameliorative and prophylactic value for a variety of related urban social problems.

The problem also might have been identified as an employment crisis for those at the bottom of a changing economy. The mass displacements in which old sectors of the economy were replaced by new ones with different work regimens, different career trajectories, and different required skill sets has been documented by scholars from such fields as industrial organization, political science, sociology, and community psychology. The millions of families that were immiserated by this changing economy in the 1980s had traditionally relied on wages from unionized public sector employment and relatively unskilled industrial labor. They could no longer rely on this sector as union participation shrank, and older industries moved to the third world and the non-union "sunbelt" or reduced relative wages by employing immigrants who were able to live on less or draw on the combined incomes of large kin groups. Such a scenario could have yielded concrete and easily assessed public and private employment programs designed to improve both employment opportunities and the skills of the displaced and those in danger of displacement, as well as overall expanded social support for the unemployed.

The health care and educational aspects of the crisis could have been managed through concrete, definable, and practical remedies. The 1980s was a period in which public mental and physical health crises emerged in older urban areas. From the recrudescence of nineteenth-century diseases connected to poverty, such as tuberculosis, amoebic dysentery, and malaria to newer poverty-linked diseases such as AIDS, many of the poorer urban areas came to look like public health disaster zones. A rhetorical statistic cited by many during this period was that Central Harlem had the same infant mortality rate as Bangladesh. I remember times when a trip to work in the morning required stepping over a beggar with untreated elephantiasis. Far too often many of these problems were identified with the vague impressionistic term homelessness and were confronted through reactive measures addressing the almost ethnicized group that was embodied by this term.

Instead of narrating this synergy of crises as having been caused by its constituent social policy elements and attacking each part with concrete remedies designed to address such broad and holistic concerns as social housing, working class employment, or public health and education it was identified with an atomized group of individuals, the homeless, who were designated to receive a new form of totalizing public assistance. This was a group whose social difference was defined by a vague set of impressionistic signifiers that were often racially biased and never clearly specified, making effective social policy problematic. Following past urban poverty crises, the debate over the homeless developed into a mirror image of the "culture of poverty" debate. Scholars discussed how the homeless fit into other categories of poor people without ever settling on exactly who it was they were discussing.

In this book, I will interrogate the social categories and theoretical assumptions upon which these debates rested. Using data from the lives of those designated as homeless, those employed to provide services for them, and those who studied them, I will show the ways in which American political culture, U.S. urban poverty scholarship, and institutional constraints, have reified folk categories of social distinction like "homeless," "underclass," "inner-city," "welfare queen," "black family," "other America," etc. These invidious categories, which define and delimit success and failure, have tended to obscure rather than clarify the causes of poverty in America. Most importantly, the use of such vague and invidious categories and the rarified intellectual terrain upon which the debate over poverty amelioration has occurred, has impeded developing real solutions to this terrible problem, wasted vast sums of money, and ground down both the people who have suffered from these many social problems and the people who have made it their career to try to help them. By demonstrating the wide chasm between the actual lives of the hundreds of people I met on fieldwork and the social assumptions that underlay public policy, social science and homeless relief services I will critically assess the poverty relief programs that America has struggled with for the last forty years.

Bees, Ants, Neanderthals, and Humans

Every human collectivity in the history of the world has had a certain number of people at any given moment who either are not able to actively contribute their labor to the surrounding society or are not expected to contribute. There are also planned and unplanned periods in every person's life when working is not expected or encouraged. From the intense period of socialization and learning that has come to be called childhood to professional rites of passage such as law and medical school to periods of mental and physical illness, the immediate aftermath of childbirth, and old age, every human life is expected to be a combination of periods of work and nonwork. Even the poorest third world societies expect that there are times when people do not work. The vacation has become a recognized right, even in countries with the most extreme work regimens like Japan, the United States, and Mexico. Premodern European peasant societies had their several score saint days per year and a variety of systems for providing support to those who had become too old to effectively labor. Archeological remains at Shanadar IV in Northern Iraq suggest that our distant Neanderthal relatives also expended energy and resources caring for the old, the sick, and the damaged.

Since not everybody in a society will work every day of his or her life, states, which are the primary administrator of modern economy and society, are forced to produce policy to address this fact. The United States, like most of Latin America, for a variety of historical and economic reasons, has had a far more problematic relationship with its non-working populations than its European cousins have during the last century. In the 1990s the United States saw its longest and possibly most profitable period of economic boom in history. This has tended to obscure the view of poverty in America, leaving the sixty million who remained in poverty far less noticed and fuelling an orectic ethos that has marginalized such traditional social science discussions as the "feminization of poverty," "crisis of the inner cities," and "the underclass."

With the passing of the post–cold war economic boom, such discussions may once again become important and social policies addressing those who cannot support themselves through wage labor may repeat many past mistakes. The same political forces that convinced America in the 1960s that there was an "other America" submerged in a "culture of poverty," marketed the underclass in the 1970s, and promoted homelessness as a national crisis in the 1980s remain an important part of American politics. It is likely that once the current hype over "war against terror" subsides, new policies may emerge that repeat the errors of the past. It is for this reason that we need to take a careful look at the birth, rise, and decline of the last major poverty crisis of the twentieth century, as it was lived by people who lost housing, and those who cared for them, studied them, made public policy for them, and profited from them.

Research Methods

The research for this book was conducted over a five year period from the late 1980s to the middle 1990s. My first forays into research on the homeless were in 1989, when I joined a research practicum as a graduate student in the PhD program in anthropology at the City University of New York Graduate Center. This practicum was composed of two other students, Alfredo Gonzalez and Walter Ewing, and led by Professor Leith Mullings, who at the time was specializing in studies of urban poverty. Our fieldwork sought to examine the causes of the urban riots of the summer of 1988 in Tompkins Square Park, a small open space at the center of Manhattan's Lower East Side, as part of a broader look at the political and ideological response to the assault on the "reluctant" American welfare state.

During the nearly nine months that my two research colleagues and I tramped around asking questions of people on the community board, local religious leaders, neighborhood old-timers, recent arrivals and local business owners the question of "the homeless" arose in nearly every interview. "The homeless" also came up every time the three of us sat in Dr. Mullings's office and discussed our fieldwork and where it was leading. There had been a sizable contingent of people who regularly slept in the park who had participated in the riots, and a wide variety of our informants from anarchist squatters to the local police had an opinion about the role of these homeless park dwellers. I became fascinated by the importance of the moral discourse that emerged around this small, powerless, and relatively unimportant group of people. They seemed to be the moral pivot around which discourse was crafted about what had happened on that hot summer night when protesters and police on horseback fought a running battle on the streets of the East Village. In 1990, while living in the East Village, I witnessed smaller, but still fierce riots in Tompkins Square Park, as well as an extended conflict between police and community activists over an abandoned public school that had been occupied and renamed, "the ABC Community Center." In all such incidents, the homeless, despite their relative unimportance to what had happened seemed to be at the discursive center of the conflict.

In the winter of 1990, I was offered a job on a three-year McKinney Act funded demonstration project called Critical Time Intervention (CTI) designed to change homeless behavior and improve the chances of retaining permanent housing for the mentally ill. CTI tested an experimental weekly social work intervention designed to help create new community ties for 110 mentally ill homeless men who had been placed in transitional, usually psychosocially supportive, housing. One of the key goals of this project was to develop an efficient form of social remediation that would prevent men who had been homeless from engaging in "homeless specific behaviors" that they may have learned at the shelter. The most important of these behaviors was the desire to return to the familiar environment of the shelter.

I was one of two staff ethnographers, along with Alfredo Gonzalez from the previous project, hired to track and interview participants in the study. Since we were both planning to use our research for a doctoral thesis, we each took a half time post, in order to give ourselves plenty of time to follow up interesting research opportunities and contacts outside our responsibilities to CTI. I moved my home and all my belongings from the East Village to an apartment near Columbia University that was a short distance from the shelter in Washington Heights and many of the transitional housing facilities on Manhattan's Upper West Side. The research project involved studying the 110 men over three years. Each of the men in the study was "placed" in a variety of community based transitional housing, including natal family homes, unsupported Single Room Occupancy (SRO) hotels, supported SROs and "intensive supportive community residences," which were much like small-scale psychiatric hospitals. It was our job to develop a rapport with the subjects before they left the shelter, keep track of them in the community, and locate them when they disappeared. Each month for eighteen months we went out to their placements to administer a paid interview that recorded the places they remembered sleeping during the month. We were randomly assigned men who were in both the control and experimental groups and it was our job to reconstruct each man's month to determine how many nights he had been homeless. A CTI social worker would regularly visit each of the experimental group members over a nine-month period and we were to chart behavioral changes during the intervention and for nine months after the intervention had ended. There were new subjects entering the study every month. Finally, our primary ethnographic goal was to make a qualitative assessment of the effectiveness of the CTI intervention.

In preparation for these interviews, I spent several months passing entire days and evenings hanging out in the shelter, drinking beer with shelter residents in neighborhood doorways, parks, and bars and talking to clients at Community Support Services (CSS), the shelter mental health unit where research subjects were recruited. My informants were adult males of all ages of either African American or Latin American descent.

Because many of my informants had problems that made placement difficult, and their new housing was by definition transitional, I found myself following their tracks to prisons, other states, psychiatric hospitals, and even a homeless resettlement camp in rural upstate New York. I lived near several of the major placement facilities and saw many of my informants far more frequently than the once a month that was prescribed by the study. As I developed a rapport with some of them, I found myself having breakfasts with them at local diners or visiting them in jail. Several of them continued to occasionally reenter my life in one form or another long after the study had ended. Remarkably, neither my ethnographic companion and collaborator, Alfredo Gonzalez, nor I lost a single informant in our three years at CTI.

Since I was assigned fifty-five research subjects to interview over the course of three years, I had a fairly large selection of people and personalities with whom I could spend my own personal research time. I quickly discovered that many of my informants' mental illnesses were either extremely mild, largely situational, or part of a duplicitous strategy between client and social worker to obtain social service resources that were only available to shelter residents who had been diagnosed as mentally ill. These men, who were described by social workers as "higher functioning" became the "key informants" upon whom I most heavily depended for data and occasional help interpreting it.

A few of the fifty-five had mental illnesses or developmental disabilities that were severe enough that it was quite difficult or impossible for me to develop a rapport with them. Sometimes I gleaned insights into their lives through contact with neighbors and family members when I was unable to gain direct entry into their often solitary and bizarre worlds. With some of the fifty-five men I was responsible for tracking, I never got beyond the distances created by the American caste color system, and there were some informants who simply never liked me. However, I had several "key informants" over the years who argued with me, gave me support and friendship in the field, and shared good times. I sometimes accompanied them on their forays into illegal activity and often experienced danger side by side with them, in the often heavily armed world of the Washington Heights drug economy.

However, I made no life-long friends and never reached the point of acceptance and integration that Clifford Geertz describes in his "Notes on a Balinese Cockfight." Though I once spent a night sleeping with homeless people at the Staten Island Ferry Terminal as part of Kim Hopper's study of the U.S. Census's attempt to count the homeless in 1990, I never spent a night in the shelter or slept in a park or on a train. This would have seemed like pretension to most of my informants and it seemed like unnecessary ethnographic pyrotechnics to me.

Organization of the Book

Nearly every serious book written on the homeless begins with a definition that is used throughout the book. This book is similar in that chapter 1, entitled "Who Are the Homeless Really?" is about the problem of defining the homeless. However, instead of seeking a workable definition for the homeless based on some pragmatic or humanitarian consideration, I suggest that the very task of defining the homeless may have prefigured many of the problems with public policy. It is one of the central contentions of this book that the issue of definitions is one of the chief reasons why the billions of dollars spent on homeless aid seem to have done so little to resolve the problem.

One of the key reasons that a homeless crisis could appear and then disappear so quickly without any resolution or denouement is that the group that was identified as the subject of policy may not have really been a salient group. Without a clear definition of the target group or problem, designing policy becomes something like looking at a set of clouds floating through the sky: the angle from which they are regarded and the amount of sky in the field of vision determine the shape that is seen. Without agreed-upon boundaries and definitions, social science becomes no more than a series of exercises in imaginative description. In attempting to answer the question "who are the homeless, really" I have looked at who they said they were, who the researchers who studied them said they were, and who the ordinary people who shared city streets with them thought they were. It is in the interstices between the vastly different views of the many people who developed research and folk definitions for the homeless in the 1980s that the real nature of this group of people can be found.

Chapter 2, entitled "The Good, the Bad, and the Ugly: The Performance of Homelessness," addresses the specific and particular intersection of race and gender that challenges African American men in poverty. The public political representations of African American men were a highly contested discourse that directly impacted on the homeless crisis and became one of the focal points for public policy discussions in 1980s America. The 1988 presidential election largely turned on the discussion of an African American "ghetto super-predator" named Willie Horton. The problem of African American masculinity and gender socialization has long been a core aspect of discussions of both poverty and social deviance in American life. The homeless debate was no exception. This chapter pulls together some of the themes in these discussions and suggests ways that the homeless crisis was a part of this larger discourse, during the 1980s on poverty and inequality in America.

Chapter 3, entitled "New York City and the Historiography of Homelessness," is a critical review of some of the historiography of the homeless crisis. In identifying homelessness as a major site of public policy, scholars and politicians offered differing historiographies of mass housing loss in America that often related to their theoretical and methodological foci. By critically reviewing some of the historiographies of homelessness this chapter contextualizes and situates the homeless crisis of the 1980s in broader conflicts over politics and social inequality and provides a view of the ways in which different political conjunctures yield different types of housing crises.

Chapter 4, entitled "The Poverty of Poverty Studies," continues from Chapter 3 in locating the rise of a homeless crisis of the 1980s in the broader politics of American society. Through a historical review of the theories that underlie academic poverty studies this chapter identifies some of the central methodological assumptions that contributed to making the homeless crisis of the 1980s different from previous crises of inadequate social housing. Locating these assumptions in the intersection between national politics and academic policy research, this chapter offers a critique of the instrumental use of social science to fine-tune the U.S. government poverty bureaucracy.

Chapter 5, entitled "Shelterization: In the Land of the Homeless," examines the way homeless shelters often provided a key stage upon which the drama of a homeless crisis could be played. As early as 1981 Baxter and Hopper observed that it was very difficult to define, locate, count or help homeless individuals in the places where their problems had developed, limiting homeless studies to observing shopping bag ladies and ragged men at a distance (Baxter and Hopper 1981; Hopper 1992, 1995). Social science and social remediation that focused on homelessness required a real physical environment in which to study and engage the target population. The shelters provided the perfect location for such studies. As such, some researchers were tracked into studying in shelters where the homeless were plentiful and easy to study in a way that enabled the fulfillment of obligations to the government agencies that funded research. Concentrations of peripatetic individuals who often had little in common besides their use of the shelter were described and discussed as part of a bounded self-contained environment that often meant more to the researchers than it did to those without housing. As such, some researchers ended up studying the shelters rather than their occupants.

Chapter 6, entitled "Doin' It in the System," looks at the ways in which the social service system that was built to manage the homeless crisis structured the lives of its clients. Though the system was set up with the goal of rehabilitation and reform for these men's disintegrating lives, for many of them, the very structures that were designed to aid them in getting back on their feet and finding some satisfaction in life, impeded or blocked their progress. The rules and understandings of the system that had been set up to deal with the problem of homelessness put social worker and social workee into a frequently conflictive relationship over my informants' attempts to create a feeling of home in facilities that were designed to be transitional, often causing more harm than good. This chapter discusses the strategies that my informants used to negotiate the difficult path through the homeless bureaucracy.

Chapter 7, entitled "The Black Family and Homelessness," looks at the way discourses on African American family and kinship figured into the homeless crisis. The comparison between immigrant and African American family structures presented by Daniel Patrick Moynihan in his 1965 report to President Lyndon Johnson remains the most popular folk model for explaining success, failure, and mutual aid in poverty. Despite being savaged by social science in its first two decades and largely ignored in the last two, the Moynihan model, intensified by contemporary immigrant success narratives, informed many discussions of "the color of homelessness" and the problems of kin networks stretched thin by poverty. As such, explanations and remedies for the problems that created homelessness must, at the least, take into account the real or imagined differences between Euro-American and Afro-American kinship networks.

Chapter 8, entitled "Housing Panic and Urban Physiocrats," is somewhat different from the other chapters, in that it draws on field research from the Tompkins Square Park area and attempts to draw out some of the concerns facing ordinary New Yorkers who lived through the homeless crisis, but were never either designated "homeless" or paid to give care to or research individuals so designated. Looking for the perspective of "ordinary New Yorkers" in a neighborhood that was so bohemian, oppositional, and marginal that it spawned the Broadway musical *Rent* is, of course, counterintuitive. However, in the hothouse environment of the gentrifying East Village, many of the broader social concerns and tropes that fuelled the homeless crisis were forced to the surface, consciously articulated by the community, and distilled for public consumption. There were few places in New York City where the homeless were more frequently discussed, and it was perhaps the one neighborhood where actual "grassroots" activism around homelessness flourished outside the institutional confines of the welfare academic complex. As such this neighborhood was something of an exception that proves the rule: even in the unique situation where there is some small group of people who self-identify as homeless and have community ties, the homeless reification tends to melt away upon close inspection.

The final chapter, "American Thatcherism: The Making and Unmaking of a Crisis," presents conclusions that can be made about the rise and fall of homelessness and the future of poverty amelioration programs. As the United States government continues to pare away the generally unpopular and largely unsuccessful poverty programs that developed out of the New Deal, the Great Society, and Richard Nixon's post-1960s crisis management programs, very little is being created to replace them. The many well-intentioned statements about volunteerism, charity, and community values that became popular during the Clinton era have proved to be threadbare, even during the post–cold war economic boom period. However, the potential necessity for emergency management that looms on the horizon presents what amounts to a social planning gamble that will inevitably prove far more costly in both economic and human terms than the money saved by "ending welfare as we know it." By pulling together a final balance sheet on what was one of the most important and well funded poverty policy crises of twentieth century America, it is my hope that this book can make a small and historically informed contribution to a reemerging discussion of the causes of and remedies for the problems of the roughly sixty million Americans who live at the economic and social margins of society.

Chapter 1

WHO ARE THE HOMELESS, REALLY?

Who Are the Homeless, Really?

In the summer of 1993, as I neared the end of my contract as staff ethnographer on a massive three-year federally funded demonstration project on homelessness, I faced the difficult task of turning thousands of pages of research data into a doctoral thesis. Throughout my three years on the job, friends, neighbors, in-laws, and just about everybody I met at any social gathering had asked me the same question, "Who are the homeless, really?" When I came to write up my work, I discovered I still was not any closer to answering this simple question, despite having passed three years with hundreds of "homeless" and learning many of the most intimate details of their lives.

When I approached my colleagues on the project with this question they were unhelpful. "It's a stupid question. It's someone without a home," one said. Another more thoughtful colleague told me that he had worried about this at first, but eventually decided it was more important to try to figure out what would help them the most. He pointed me toward Peter Rossi's book that describes the homeless as one part of the "extremely poor" (Rossi 1989) and some public health literature on the question. One of my professors at the University told me not to worry so much about definitions, "just pick one you are comfortable with and write about the people you met," she said, and "stay close to the ethnography."

As my concern turned to despair, I returned to the literature on homelessness and poverty and looked for others who had worked on this same problem. There were numerous books about the homeless, each with a different definition. Some authors had no concern for the problem of definitions (DeHavenon 1995; Dinkins and Cuomo 1992); others used the first pages of their work to qualify their subject and explain that the term "homeless" wasn't fully adequate to describe this subgroup of the "extremely poor," "working poor," or "underclass," (Blau 1992; Hopper and Hamberg 1984; Jencks 1994; Rossi 1989). Since it was as difficult to find someone who self-identified as homeless as it was to find a self-identifying yuppie, all the studies relied on objective rather than subjective categories. However, nobody could agree on an objective definition, making comparative discussion and substantive conclusions difficult. Nobody could agree on how many nights sleeping publicly were necessary to make someone homeless. Nobody believed that two nights or even ten nights in a year were enough to define someone as homeless, but some researchers believed that living situations in which someone regularly spent a night or two a week in a semi-public place constituted homelessness. Then there were people who never slept publicly but had no place of their own. Kim Hopper (1991; 1995) called these "the pre-homeless," another subgroup to study, discuss, and possibly provide service to.

Nobody was even sure what constituted sleeping publicly. Was a top landing of an apartment building public? Was a basement laundry room after closing time public? What if there was a locked closet in the laundry room where bedding and personal belongings were stored and a key was supplied by the superintendent in exchange for unpaid maintenance and cleaning duties? I had informants who lived in shacks in a garden. Did their homeless status change when electricity was run into the shack and they were given keys to a toilet and shower room in the community center next to the garden? Then there were squatters in abandoned buildings and people who lived in shacks under the highway. Furthermore, nobody was sure how to count three families living in a three-bedroom apartment. Did their status change if sisters headed all three families? What if there was a brother who lived in the living room and was registered at the shelter as an escape for when a sister's boyfriend became violent with him?

For many of my colleagues, being registered at a shelter was what counted. However, we all knew people who registered with the shelter to obtain free meals and keep their personal belongings there, but never slept there, preferring a girlfriend's house. Similarly, we all knew people for whom the shelter was an extra bedroom. They kept their belongings at parents' houses, ate meals with family, and took showers at home, but went down the block to the shelter to sleep at night because there was a lack of space or because a same-sex lover lived at the shelter. Many housing situations depended on being registered at the shelter in the event of occasional problems or uncertainties.

Finally, as is usually the case with studies of poverty in America, the race question was never very far below the surface. I had found whole networks of white ethnic blue-collar types living in the interstices of the suburbs and edge cities around New York. Generally well versed in using the system and sometimes registered at a shelter, many of these people exhibited the homeless life in every way down to the ratty clothes and street corner begging, but they were rarely included in the category. I also discovered networks of young, often college educated white Americans who had spent nights sleeping in train stations, on roofs, in parks, and on friends' floors because of economic problems and housing conflicts. However, for most people at the time, a black twenty-three-year-old casual cocaine user trying to become a writer and bouncing from bad housing situation to bad housing situation was "homeless," but the same person in white skin was merely without housing.

Since none of the work of experts had helped answer my questions and most amelioration projects were failing, partially, I sensed, due to confusion over who was to be helped, I turned to nonexperts. A 1990 *New York Times* poll had shown that 82 percent of New Yorkers saw homeless people daily (Fantasia and Isserman 1994). I decided to test exactly what it was that they were seeing. I had been collecting data on many of the underhoused people, the beggars, street salesmen, and mentally ill in my neighborhood (the Upper West Side of Manhattan) and in the one where I was doing much of my fieldwork (Washington Heights in Upper Manhattan). Over the course of a few months I took people I knew from these neighborhoods around in my car, or walked them through the streets and tried to discover who they thought was homeless.

They pointed to the bizarre looking middle-aged black men asking for change from passersby. Though I knew that they were longtime residents of the Single Room Occupancy (SRO) on my block, they presented an image of homelessness. The Vietnam veteran, with VA benefits that were higher than my salary, who sold secondhand books for extra money and in order to pass the time and have a sense of purpose was seen as homeless. Though he had never spent a night on the streets, he was black, passed his days on the street, and dressed in shabby clothes. There was an unbathed black woman dragging children behind her who also got the designation homeless, but she lived two blocks down in a large crowded studio apartment with her sister and her niece. No one pointed to the well-dressed Barbadian man with sharp creased brown pants and a stylish dress shirt sitting on a bench reading a paper on his favorite traffic island in the middle of Broadway. He was a shelter resident. The white man on crutches hawking videos, who slept in Riverside Park, the good looking young black man arguing in a shop, who slept in a basement uptown, and the Latina City University of New York (CUNY) student who worked in the supermarket and alternated nights at an aunt's home in Jersey City, the student government office at City College, and her best friend's bedroom (when there was no boyfriend present) in a shared apartment, all received no notice.

My colleagues had been unable to provide a scientifically justifiable objective definition of homeless and my friends and neighbors were equally perplexed about what a homeless person was, despite seeing them every day. They tended to use a folk category that described people with some combination of dark skin, poor grooming, inappropriate behavior, and little to do with the day except hang out on the streets. I went in search of help from my informants. I knew that they did not think of themselves as homeless, but I thought they might have special insights into what I was studying.

My informants were the only group that could agree on a definition of the homeless. "Why don't you ask the Spanish guy (director of the Community Support Services office at the shelter). He's the one who decides who stays in the shelter and who gets a place," snapped one informant, summing up the general sense about the category. Throughout fieldwork informants had expressed doubt or disgust toward my research category, but I had always disregarded what they said, often putting it down to race resentment or even mental illness. I went back to my field notes and began to revise my views of what they had told me.

Henry,[1] a middle-aged African American trumpet player who had lost housing due to a combination of professional failures and a bad crack habit, had teased me mercilessly throughout my fieldwork about being an anthropologist looking for culture among the homeless. "You the guy who studies culture," he'd say. "How come you can't teach me any of the traditional homeless songs so I can do my improvisations. You holdin out on me?" I was almost afraid to ask him his view on this topic.

I brought my doubts to an articulate older informant named Delaney who had been in the merchant marines for many years, but had lost housing after a mental breakdown. He later found a place in the sunny second story front bedroom of a boardinghouse in a beautiful historic brownstone in the Bedford Stuyvesant section of Brooklyn, owned by the daughter-in-law of an African American World War I veteran and his French war bride. There were a few other "select" older black men renting rooms there, some of whom had briefly passed through the shelter system. We sat in the sunlight on tall antique wooden chairs and he explained to me that I was studying black culture in its most degraded form. "You want to know about the homeless, study the social workers," he suggested, "they're the ones always talking about it." He compared my study to looking for Jewish culture in a concentration camp, "you want to understand the camp, study the damn Nazis."

I even had an informant who responded to an interview question about where he imagined being in five years by claiming that what social workers call homelessness is sometimes the last phase of youth for late teenage, early twenties urban black men. "It's kind of like you white folks and your frat parties," he said, "everybody goes around sleeping in big houses with a bunch of different people and they drink beer all the time instead of use drugs. I seen all that in the movies. We just ain't got the fancy cars and the wealthy daddies." He cited cases of people who had passed through periods without housing and a job, eventually settling down to the lower ranks of the steadily employed and disappearing from the view of social workers and researchers. At the time I merely noted it and moved on. How many of the men I had met might fit such a category of unestablished young black working-class men, and did this narrative of coming of age merely rationalize their misery, or did it give them something useful for survival, I later wondered?

As I saw the category of homeless "melting into air" many of these comments began to make sense. One of my informants, an African American in his late 20s who was too emotionally unstable for me to bring my doubts to, had once told me that he believed that the shelter was a giant intelligence experiment "to see how many niggers is stupid enough to enter. The guards, the big gorillas that sleep down at the other end, the crazy ones like me, hell even the shelter director don't know they fuckin with him. They can call us homeless or whatever the fuck they want, but it's just a bunch of poor niggers." As I looked back, I realized that in a strange and unconscious way he was voicing the same thought that virtually all my informants had: the concept of homeless was a weak abstraction imposed from above on people who may or may not have had housing and those whose job it was to manage the crisis. None of my informants were sure where and why they fit into my study, but they were all sure that "homeless" was not a useful category.

I approached the social workers, as Delaney and several other informants had suggested. They were busy preparing for the next research project and suggested that I was taking the ravings of the mentally ill too seriously. However, there was one who encouraged me to pursue my line of questioning. As he put it, "words are important because they appear on budgets. The word homeless is like triage at the hospital. When you have somebody who is about to freeze to death on the streets, after a knife fight with a family member or being burnt out of his apartment or just out of Attica (a state prison) you gotta find the guy a place to sleep and damn quick. But after a good night sleep, a shower and a cup of coffee, how ya gonna convince him that his problem is homelessness. Sure he needs to find an apartment, but maybe he has a bigger problem, like no job or nobody to take care of him until he gets on his feet. Maybe he just needs a new prescription for his meds. The guys are not stupid. Only an idiot could convince himself that being homeless is anybody's number one problem." He claimed that he had doubted the value of the concept of homeless for a long time, and as he became more frustrated with fitting men into the homeless model, his work life at the project became more untenable. He eventually resigned his position.

The Performance of Homelessness

As I continued to pursue a rigorous definition of what I'd studied, I found it ever more difficult to connect lack of housing and homelessness. Certainly, nearly all of the men I had spent my three years of research with were underhoused. Some of them had nowhere to go besides the shelter and continued to live in the shelter even when working long hours at the hodgepodge of temporary jobs that many of them strung together, in order to survive. Most, however, saw the shelter as one option among many possible residences. A day or two at the shelter might relieve conflict in a crowded apartment that they shared with friends or relatives. If trouble arose at the shelter a night or two on the subway might end a feud over money, drugs, or sex. Recently released prisoners usually found a few nights at the shelter a welcome relief from the dangers of unsecured basements and the pressures of taking up space on people's living room floors or trying to instantly fit themselves back into the lives of loved ones.

However, so much of New York City, during this period of rapidly rising housing costs was seriously underhoused and also approached housing flexibly. A very wide range of people in New York City during the 1980s engaged what might be called peripatetic, flexible, and unstable housing strategies. This included white students, recent university alumni, and people trying to break into an arts profession, as well as the long-term unemployed, mentally ill, physically ill, and recent arrivals from other states or foreign countries. Despite the fact that many of these people never spent a night in a shelter, they shared many housing strategies with those who had been designated "the homeless."[2] They were certainly not "homeful," but most of them could not have credibly been included in the category of "homeless." It seemed that the answer to the question "who are the homeless really" lay in the social role they filled and the social performance that was often necessary for their survival.

This sense that "homeless" was a very weak and abstract social performance, with little room to appropriate an identity was very clearly expressed to me when I briefly worked for Kim Hopper in his 1990 "S-Night" study that attempted to assess how accurate the U.S. Census was in counting homeless people sleeping on the streets and in public locations. In this experiment groups of students were sent out on the night when the U.S. Census takers were supposed to count the homeless. The students were dressed up in raggedy clothes and dispatched to locations known for having many homeless people. I was sent to the Staten Island Ferry Terminal at Whitehall street, where I was supposed to take my raggedy blanket and join the homeless people sleeping in a corner. I was expected to wait through the night to see who the census takers counted and how they counted.

The ferry terminal was one of the few places where I met white "homeless" people. During this long night we were pretending to be homeless, it was clear to the people who were actually living in the ferry terminal that Kim Hopper's research assistants were not used to "the life." Most of the people sleeping in the ferry terminal assumed that we were recent arrivals from some place in the Midwestern United States and, therefore unfamiliar with this strange world of sleeping in public and gaining help through "playing homeless." We received counseling from people around us on how to be more homeless and what roles were best for different situations, how to deal with police, teenage toughs, and so on. They were helpful and friendly, though amused by what they saw as an inability to look pathetic enough. One woman, who was actually white and seemed to be mentally ill, told my companion, who was coming along for the adventure and the $120, that "here in New York City, white people don't live like this. You should go back home to your parents." She explained the research project to this woman, who pestered us for the rest of the night about getting Kim Hopper to hire her. When the U.S. Census workers finally arrived, they instantly spotted a fraud and made sure to interview all the researchers, making it clear that they resented being spied on at work.

Such public performances of helplessness and misery are not uncommon to beggars, indigents, and those dependent on compassion and charity, the world over. However, the connection between homelessness, helplessness, and charity that those in the ferry terminal were making was only the thin edge of a huge wedge that makes up state poverty policy and social custom. This wedge divides individuals and the self through the assumption of the universal rights, obligations, and expectations of citizenship and the systematic denial of those rights to those who are trapped in the historical nexus between African descent and poverty. The following chapter addresses some of the specific issues around the public performance of homelessness and this nexus.

Notes

1. All names of informants have been changed to protect anonymity.
2. The study that employed me required all participants to have spent at least one night in the shelter. Since the project recruited from a day program in the shelter, virtually all participants had spent at least one night sleeping in the shelter. However some were no longer shelter residents, but were still in the day program and nonetheless were categorized as homeless. Finally, it was rumoured that a small number were recruited straight to the research project and had volunteered to spend a night in the shelter to fit the project definition of homeless.

Chapter 2

THE GOOD, THE BAD, AND THE UGLY: THE PERFORMANCE OF HOMELESSNESS

"When you got no money, no job, and nowhere to hide, you gotta be a stereotype. Good nigger, bad nigger, ugly nigger. I've been a good nigger and a bad one, but I never want to be an ugly one. They had me looking real ugly."

> Delaney, a middle-aged homeless man on why he left a community residence for the homeless against the wishes of his social workers

"I want to be one of those 'well spoken' black men. You know, the kind that white folks want to have around them. Ever hear the term 'hankie-head'?"

> Jeffrey, African American homeless man in his 30s on why he was carrying a copy of *Democracy and Education* by John Dewey

"Freddy Kruger, nobody ever fucks with Freddy Kruger. He just takes what he wants. He fucks up anyone that gets in his way."

> Michael, African American homeless man in his mid 20s on how he wants the world to see him

The Performance of Homelessness

For most of my informants the category "homeless" was tied to both the ritual humiliation that was required to receive resources from state social welfare programs or private charities and the management of black masculinity, which they often identified as one of the key problems in American society. As one of my informants, an early-twenties African American, once said to me, "black men are scary, we even scare each other lots of the time. If you're not working for some white guy, you have to be pretty ugly, tired and sad to get any help. Its prison or the shelter." For him, the shelter was part of something approaching a conspiracy to force him into public submission, humiliation, and admission of weakness. Delaney, who regularly read the NOI newspaper, *The Final Call*, informed me, in no uncertain terms, that "homeless" was about stealing African American manhood. He also saw fear of African American masculinity as being the genesis of the homeless performance, suggesting that a white dominated state offers the choice of being a criminal or a homeless person. Even those men who did not carry strong visible resentment connected to the intersection of race and gender suggested a similar understanding of the problems of "performing homeless." Henry, the trumpet player, often complained about the problem of the racial dimension of this required social performance, saying "you gotta act homeless, so the white folks will help you." Though Henry was not an angry or bitter person and seemed to carry little animosity toward Euro-Americans, he was positive that the performance of homelessness was centrally concerned with appearing harmless, weak, and pathetic. He like nearly all of my African American informants believed that underneath the concern and care directed at the homeless was a desire to maintain and affirm social caste distinctions between black and white. For him and most of my other African American informants, the issue of role models, role playing, and gender roles was a key issue connected to regaining a lost (or never known) control of their lives. Within this narrative discourse, "playing homeless" was the most difficult and unpleasant of all the major roles that were offered. It was what Delaney referred to as "the ugly" (see epigraph).

Though many of my informants used slightly different terms or slightly different primary public exemplars, they all frequently referred to the same three black male roles or what might in the 1960s have been called "ghetto personality types." I have settled on the typology used by Delaney. I frequently heard informants discuss how white people categorized black people into "good niggers" and "bad niggers." Delaney's addition of the phrase, "ugly nigger" (quoted in the epigraph) created a trio that seemed to encompass all the representations and interconnected mutual stereotyping that constituted the daily relations between white and black during my fieldwork.

The Good

I first met Jeffrey (quoted in the epigraph) when he came into the office I shared with another anthropologist for the first of his eighteen monthly interviews. I had been told that he was "well spoken" and a model client for the social workers. He was wearing casual dress slacks and a dress shirt and had a pleasant and outgoing manner. His bad skin and the big scar across his cheek contrasted with his slightly effeminate manner and gave him a disturbing rough around the edges look. As he sat down to chat with me before our first interview, I noticed that he was carrying a worn copy of John Dewey's *Democracy and Education.* I was curious and intrigued. It was not unusual for even my most disreputable informants to be interested in literature. The combination of a black consciousness and lots of time underemployed gave some of them the impetus and time to read. I had informants who were devotees of twentieth-century black fiction, history buffs who were always ready to talk about Martin Delany, Malcolm X, W.E B. Du Bois, and even Carter Woodson and there were always avid readers of *The Final Call,* the Nation of Islam's official newspaper. I even had informants who had cracked Martin Bernal's *Black Athena.* However, I had never had an informant who had shown an interest in Euro-American literature. An author as dry and dull as John Dewey seemed to be a particularly strange choice.

We chatted amiably as I explained the purpose of the study and where I fit into it. He spoke with little of the typically African-American dialect that has come to be known as Ebonics. He asked a lot of interested and intelligent questions about what the project was about: behavioral changes in homeless men; and what it was I was studying: the anthropology of homelessness and urban poverty. He looked a bit dubious, but he was very polite and somewhat reserved. As always I stressed the fact that despite my use of space in the shelter offices, everything we discussed was completely confidential and none of the shelter officials or social workers had any access to what I learned. He said he understood, but I assumed he was skeptical, since he could see that I was employed there.

Before we got to the dry and schematic interview that I was required to administer to each man I met, I wanted to find out about the John Dewey book. "I see you're reading *Democracy and Education.* You interested in philosophy?" I asked.

"It's the basis of knowledge, isn't it?"

"I guess so, I was never very good at it."

"It's challenging, but rewarding when you figure out what an author is saying."

"I know that Dewey was a pragmatist. Any particular reason you took up John Dewey?" I asked, hoping to find the answer to my riddle.

"I'm taking a philosophy class at City College and this week we are discussing the Anglo-American tradition: British positivism and American pragmatism."

"You like the class?"

"It's interesting stuff to think about. I like just being in the classes. It feels like I'm part of something exciting. I'm working on my degree you know. I can't afford to wait any longer, because I'm HIV positive. They must have told you right?"

He was testing me. I lied and told him that they didn't take me seriously enough to tell me more than the phone number and address of the SRO where he lived. I assumed that he did not believe me, but I figured it was a gesture to let him know that this was voluntary and I would respect his privacy as much as he wanted. As we started the interview I forgot about the book and tried to do my best to let him know how little stock I put in the interview. When it was over, I asked if I could come and visit him at his home the next time. He made some joke about home being the wrong word for where he lived. I told him I would take him out to lunch and we could talk a bit in a more comfortable environment. He agreed and I told him I would call him the week before I was coming. I paid him $10 for the interview and an extra $20 as a bonus for the first interview, shook his hand and watched as he went out the door.

When I got home that evening, I mentioned to my companion that one of the homeless men whom I interviewed was reading *Democracy and Education*. I made a comment about what a wonderful resource CUNY was for the poor and working people of New York City. She made some joke about resolving the homeless crisis by boring them to death, and then I thought nothing of it until I met Jeffrey again for his next monthly interview.

We went to a little Latin American diner near the SRO where he lived. It was nearly empty. I asked him about the philosophy class at CUNY and he told me that it was going well. Each month that I interviewed Jeffrey we talked a bit about philosophy, CUNY, and his attempts to find a job.

We never got very close but our interviews were always cordial and interesting. A couple of times we discussed my research. I was still struggling with the culture of poverty paradigm and I presented my concerns to him about whether to stress heroic adaptations to difficult conditions or the ravages of poverty on the human psyche. Like most of my informants at that time, he was pretty adamant about the ways in which poverty made one less human. The idea of heroic adaptations sounded wrong to him.

Somewhere around his sixth month in the study, I called him to meet for lunch in the Bronx and he said that he was going to be near my office for some kind of employment workshop. I agreed to meet him at the McDonald's on 169th Street and Broadway. When we met, he was carrying the John Dewey book again. We started eating and I asked him about the book. "You're not taking another class in Anglo-American philosophy are you?"

"No, I'm trying to impress some white folks," he said in a sort of offhand way. "I need a job and I want them to see me as one of those 'well spoken' black men. You know, the kind that white folks like to have around them." He looked at me in a more direct way than I'd seen before and asked, "Ever hear the term 'hankiehead'? Well today, I got to put on the handkerchief and beg for help."[1]

I asked him if he had a job interview. "Not a real job," he said. He told me about a government program that enables people on Social Security to do part-time work to get job training and earn the maximum allowable income, $74 a week. "What's the job?" I asked.

"Receptionist."

"You have to know John Dewey to be a receptionist?"

"Ya gotta be creative 'bout the handkerchiefs. Look at the mayor (black Democrat David Dinkins), he's the biggest hankiehead in the world, but his handkerchief's a yarmulke. Nobody would believe me in a skullcap. You just have to prove that you're harmless and all about the white man. What was the first thing you thought when I walked into your office last year? 'Why is that black man carrying a book by John Dewey?'"

I must have looked very uncomfortable and uneasy at being "caught" stereotyping him, because he burst into a trickster sort of laughter that was almost affectionate. I felt one of those Geertzian moments when you break through and become part of the "tribe." It was a false start, because it was probably the first and last time that he opened up to me in a genuine and warm way.

Jeffrey was hired as a receptionist in a hospital clinic and worked the full six months of the program. When the six months were up and the government money ran out, his supervisor applied for an extension. They gave him another three months then let him go when the money finally ran out. They apologized to him and told him that there was no money in the budget for new hires, but he was never sure whether it was something he had done, his scar, his skin color, or his criminal record. He turned it over in his mind many times as he looked for other work for "well spoken black men." There was none. He decided that he just looked too "ugly" and tough to get even a low-level white-collar job servicing people like himself. For this he blamed his time in prison. He worked temp as a security guard, being careful never to work on the books for fear of losing his benefits. When I last saw him, he had sunk into a deep depression, was being heavily medicated by the doctor at his transitional housing facility and had given up looking for a job. Too "experienced" to be "good," too tired to be "bad," he had become just a little bit "ugly" in the world of homelessness, mental illness, and the monthly government support that demands complete retreat and submission in exchange for food and a roof.

The Bad

Those who were young enough, "black" enough, and masculine enough generally preferred the other 1980s deviant male social performance of the ghetto: crackhead. Though many of them slept in the shelter and a variety of other semipublic spaces, crackhead was an alternative to being perceived as a loser. Being a Willie Horton style ghetto "super-predator" was far more appealing to most of my informants. It carried notions of danger, sexuality, super-masculinity, power, and self-reliance.

But playing a crackhead was often dangerous even for the strong. I lost my first informant at the shelter to this role. He was a well-dressed and articulate man living in the shelter who was murdered in May of 1991, in a drug deal gone bad. He was an early-twenties Jamaican man who had friends who saved space for him in the West Indian corner of the shelter. When I first met him, he had been living there for slightly over nine months. The path he took to the shelter is one that is not unusual. He had been working in a moderately high paying job as a janitor in an office building. He claimed that he was laid off during a budgetary shortfall, but I suspected that there might have been other problems. He passed through several much lower paying jobs, before he was finally evicted from the apartment he shared with a Jamaican friend who had come up from the island at about the same time.

His lack of financial solvency had gotten them both thrown out of their housing. They moved to the shelter and Robert became a leader of the "West Indian corner": a roughly twenty-bed section of the vast 600–700-bed shelter dormitory or "drill floor," demarcated by a wall decorated with postcards of the West Indies, a giant poster of Jamaican basketball player Patrick Ewing, and "beaver photos" of black women. Robert always dressed beautifully when he went out into the streets, paying one of the guards to keep his steam iron for him in a safe locker. He was well groomed and always concerned with having razor sharp creases in his clothes. As he put it, "If you're living in the shelter, you got to work extra hard to make sure no one knows you're living here. Besides I always liked to dress well before I moved here."

He was well respected and liked and had the authority to get two beds saved for him, whether he showed up to sleep or not. As he put it, "two beds give you some elbow room." While in the shelter he was registered with several employment agencies (this was a very common pattern) and had frequent temporary work as a security guard. He would often pass on information about day labor to his buddies in the West Indian corner. At one of these jobs he met a woman with whom he established a relationship. He never told her that he lived in the shelter, but gave her a phone number at the pay phone downstairs. After a couple of calls she figured it out, but they never talked about it. He kept his belongings at the shelter, where his friends guarded them for him. Some nights he slept at his girlfriend's place and some at the shelter. When I last saw him, he was beginning a second relationship, and spending only two nights a week at the shelter. He hoped that the security guard day labor would eventually turn into a permanent job and enable him to move out of the shelter and in with one of his girlfriends. But he was not optimistic. As he put it, "I never get noticed by the white guys. They know I'm smart, but they like to hire really big black guys."

At $5.00–$7.50 per hour there was little chance to make a real living on a part-time basis, and Robert supplemented his income with occasional drug deals that he never really explained to me. He was not well connected there either, which he ascribed to the fact that "you have to be Hispanic to make it in the drug business." On the night of 2 May 1991 he was shot to death two blocks from the shelter while involved in one of these drug deals. In his obituary in the local Washington Heights community paper he was listed as "a homeless person" who lived at the shelter.

Like playing homeless, being a crackhead offered more than a social category to be fit into by strangers; there were also material benefits: money, drugs, social networks, and sexual satisfaction. As Franklin, one of my closest informants in the shelter often said, "I get SSI for being homeless and crazy, but if it weren't for crack how would crazy poor fucked up guys like me get any pussy."

There were men who due to age, personality, religion or other factors were unable to switch between these three roles and permanently inhabited one social region. However, for most of the men whom I met in my studies, the border was permeable and was usually linked to survival. Most preferred to think of themselves as Willie Horton, rather than an ugly and broken homeless man, but none of these social roles or public representations fitted comfortably. They were symbolic suits of clothing that required terrible contortions to wear. Though work and public life always involves wearing clothing that acts as a personal prison, as members of the most economically marginalized sector of America's most famous subordinate caste/color category: African American, they walked a far narrower path than most people do and had far less ability to take control of their roles and tailor them to their own preferences.

Franklin, a key informant and collaborator in the field was a good looking, strongly built, medium height man in his early 20s who liked to say he had the black man's education: a year at City College studying literature and eighteen months at Fishkill (a state penitentiary) "studying criminology." He had a high-energy intellect and loved to talk. He had serious drug problems and a variety of clinical diagnoses that had entitled him to Social Security. He had been in and out of the shelter and prison, but usually lived with his sister, Ermaline, with whom he had a close but very conflictual relationship. His dream was to be a poet and a drug counselor when he was finished with his period of "wandering in the desert." He was the informant who best defined and explained the "bad nigger" archetype to me.

It was a sunny late winter afternoon and we were sitting on a heavy concrete park bench on Edgecombe Avenue at the precipice of the rocky cliffs that make Washington Heights, literally, the top of Manhattan Island. Stretched out below us in the canyon created by the Harlem River were the giant brick public housing blocks of the Polo Grounds Projects where the New York Giants baseball team had last played home games in the 1950s. Beyond the river was the Bronx, with its once beautiful lush forested hills sticking out here and there from amongst vast stretches of paintless concrete piled on concrete.

Franklin was smoking a crack pipe. As I smelled the slightly nauseating odor of crack smoke spreading out from Franklin's pipe, I wondered how safe I really was sitting there with a crackhead talking about black culture. What would the police do if they found us? Would Franklin turn on me if the police handcuffed us? How much could I depend on being a researcher to get out of trouble? What would happen to my job if anyone found out that I abetted Franklin in his drug use?

Franklin and I had first developed our friendship when I caught him smoking pot on the drill floor of the shelter. He had been worried that I would tell his social worker and he might be denied help. He was part of the experimental group and one of the directors of the project had interceded to make sure that he had maximum social security benefits, which he feared losing. I had offered to keep it quiet if he let me have a smoke. He was completely shocked that I would smoke with him and he enthusiastically passed me the joint as I sat down on someone's bed. I was very nervous about losing my job, but realized that this went to my basic credibility as an ethnographer. It was the only way to put distance between me and the people who managed his life. It had been a good decision. He became a key informant and a friend.

Our interview had started that afternoon in the McDonald's on Broadway and 169th Street. I plowed through the questions about housing and drugs knowing that Franklin was lying. He did not believe that there was any confidentiality in the study, he did not want anyone to know what he was doing, and he suspected that there was some kind of white supremacist plot behind the program. He always assured me that the two men who ran the study were closet white supremacists. I kept up the fiction of a formal interview, while he answered questions between bites of a Big Mac and fries. When he finished his lunch and I finished my interview, he proposed a trip to Edgecombe Park to do drugs.

Crack always made him talk; often hyper. He was a like a James Joyce novel; an eloquent and sometimes hard to follow stream of consciousness would emerge and I would try, like Notker the Stammerer recording the doings of Charlemagne, to keep a record in my head of the things he said. Today, the crack seemed to be making him slow and reflective, and I kept a mental record. I knew that what I missed he would correct in my notes at a later date.

"The secret of the black man is that he can't be nothing but a nigger in the eyes of a white man. That's the thing. There are good niggers and there are bad niggers. But you always gotta be something. When I go out on the street I'm no longer Franklin the poet and prophet. I'm Franklin the tough guy, the hard mother-fucker, the street nigger, who don't take shit from no one. You know that nigger: Shaft, New Jack City, Wesley Snipes, and Nat Turner rolled into one. He's the one that makes you into nobody and fucks you up, bad. He's got no history. He got no prophets and he got no soul. He's the goddamn Texas Chainsaw nigger that white people fear in their beds at night.

"You hear all kinds of stuff about police brutality against us black folks and its all true. I had a policeman with his foot on my damn neck the last time they arrested me. I couldn't breathe. All I thought was please god, don't let these peckerwoods kill me for jumpin' a turnstile. But you know what. You just look around you at all the trouble that the Spanish get into [immigrants from the Dominican Republic]. They walking down the street, cop stops 'em. They tie their shoes, a cop stops 'em. They wipe their ass and a cop tells 'em what toilet paper to use. Cops don't stop the bad nigger for nothing 'less they serious. They go up to a bunch a Spanish guys in a car and tell them some shit 'bout this or that. They insult their goddamn mama, but they see a car fulla bad niggers, they call for backup. They call in the goddamn national guard for a bunch of sixteen year olds. I can feel the fear in all those white boy cops from the suburbs when they look at me walking down the street.

"Ask any cop. He don't want to be bothered. He wants to get through the day easy. He got something going on with his old lady that night and he won't be bothering none of us niggers. He can always go and find some Spanish guy to shit on or some bullshit peddler from god knows where.[2] Problem is, it's the good niggers, the ones like Sharpton [an important black Democrat, usually viewed as a black extremist by white people in New York City] and Dinkins and Cosby [Bill Cosby, popular African-American television comedian] that get all the success. That's cuz white people don't fear them. They like to have 'em around like some kind of souvenir from the battle. The problem is when you stop thinking you're a man and start believing you're a nigger. There's guys out there that are really good at the bad nigger good nigger stuff and they forget what it's all about, which is freeing yourself. They stop dreaming and start believing that they're those stereotypes that white people give us. That's what prophets are for, to remind us that we ain't niggers."

He went on to tell me about Malcolm X, again. Malcolm X was his hero in life and when he wasn't trying to be a bad nigger, he was wearing his Malcolm X glasses and sporting a Malcolm X goatee. I had once made the mistake of challenging him, suggesting that Malcolm X had left an uncertain body of philosophy and a small organization isolated from both white and black political forces.

"You smoke and you hang out, but you just don't understand Malcolm. That's the black thing. Malcolm's the one black man that no matter how hard they try they can't ever make him a nigger. They can say he betrayed his people at the end. They can say he hated white people. They can say he didn't like the Jews. They can say whatever they want about Malcolm and they still can't make him a nigger. They can't turn him into a Nat Turner, rape yo mama Mandingo and they can't make him into Martin Luther King neither. I ain't sayin' nothing against Martin, but we've talked about that. He's everybody's favorite black man.

"Malcolm went to prison like me. Malcolm is the new model. When we are all Malcolm, there will be no more niggers, no more white folks, none of that shit. We'll just live and love and smoke reefer."

Franklin had given me as clear a portrait of the bad nigger as Jeffrey had of the good one. This was the mythic archetype of the black man who could not be caged into a role of caste/color submission. My informants pointed to rap stars like Dr. Dre, Ice Cube, and KRS 1, but their most animated moments were when they self-identified with movie characters. The most revered black man in film was Wesley Snipes, but far more interesting than the identification with real actors were the characters in movies that fed the fantasy of the bad nigger.

These characters and images were nearly all race neutral. From Franklin's mention of the 1970s classic cult movie *Texas Chainsaw Massacre* to the desire of Michael, the informant quoted in the epigraph, to be Freddy Kruger, the compassionless predator of dreams in Wesley Craven's *Nightmare on Elm Street*, the libidinal fantasy was largely without color. In a particularly strange version of this, Sean Connery's James Bond briefly came to be a bad nigger role model. Connery's Bond was a legend in gangsta rap culture and I heard occasional assertions during fieldwork that the Scottish actor "with a license to kill" was part black.

Good nigger/bad nigger was one of the central motifs in the lives of men I met on fieldwork. Because it was an issue of public presentation they saw it as intimately related to obtaining a job. Most of my informants believed that white people only saw two different kinds of black men when they were looking for employees, the good ones and the bad ones. Since most of my informants had little in the way of marketable job skills, had virtually no real resume, and were still looking for their first job well into their late 20s, when they went to look for work, they were marketing little beyond their identity.

One of my informants, a very light-skinned black man in his early 30s who occasionally worked as a security guard and dreamed of becoming a housing cop, summed up the general sense about how interactions with white employers should be approached. "If they want a black guy to work for 'em, it's gotta be somebody they can trust. They don't want a black guy who acts white. They'll never respect you and figure you're either a faggot or up to no good. I've worked places where they do nothing but make fun of some little black guy in a suit. They want somebody who can be a nigger, but be their nigger. It really hasn't changed much since the plantation days."

Everybody had a story to tell about an effeminate white-acting black man who had been badly mistreated at work because he did not demand respect as a black man. On the other side of the divide, there were always stories circulating about men who had been sacked because white supervisors feared supervising them and did not have the moral authority to look them in the eye and tell them what to do. It might be argued that this is the same problem that white male workers, particularly blue-collar types, face in finding and maintaining employment. The degree to which the problem of identity and role playing in the search for employment and respect represents a qualitatively or quantitatively worse problem for black men is unclear. However, there is little doubt that black men face far greater challenges in the labor market, making the subtle distinctions of identity and personality more demanding and the stakes of each encounter far higher. As Delaney frequently intoned, "black men walk the narrowest path."

The Ugly

Though my informants never referred specifically to "ugly" as a noun the way they did with "the good" and "the bad," it was a black male ghetto trope that frequently came up in adjectival forms, such as, "there ain't no homeless people here, just ugly raggedy assed black men." This trope is the one that David Dinkins and other liberal Democrats had used to counter the Willie Horton "bad nigger" image that George Bush and the Republican Party were promoting through much of the 1980s. In opposition to the Republican vision of a pre-oedipal mother-raping, father-stabbing jungle beast that demanded vastly expanded prisons and law enforcement, Dinkins and other liberal Democrats counterpoised the deracinated black man who had been thrown out of his home and forced to wander the streets in rags. This was the performance of homelessness, the black role model that all my informants feared the most. It was the one that gave them the fewest material rewards, the least room to appropriate an identity for themselves, and the greatest feeling of being in ontological free fall.

The "ugly" is traditionally the vision of an older black man who has become helpless, desexualized, and broken by old age and a lifetime of walking Delaney's "narrow path." It is a male equivalent of the "auntie" role that has been discussed for women of African descent. Though there have been some exceptional cases of collective hysteria over a "homeless killer" or a "homeless rapist," the homeless man is the ultimate version of what some of my informants used to call, the "Driving Miss Daisy nigger." However, there were moments when much rested on the success of being "ugly" in the right proportion and most of my informants were willing to put on the role when it was necessary.

The most common and feared performance was the transitional housing interview. Transitional housing programs, which depended on public funding, engaged in a practice called "creaming," in which they attempted to screen out candidates who might reduce the success rates of their programs. For those who faced the grueling admissions process there were conflicting demands that they appear presentable and functional enough to live with others and participate in day programs, yet disaffiliated, passive, and dysfunctional enough not to cause trouble by trying to take control of their lives. If they arrived at a transitional housing facility and started looking for a job, it would reduce the importance of their work in the psychosocial programs that were the reason for the facility to exist. If they found a job, it would endanger their right to receive the government support that guaranteed their rent and paid for these programs. If they found affective kinship by establishing a love relationship with someone, it would raise a number of questions related to space, privacy, and commitment to other pursuits outside their "rehabilitation." In short, they had to be perfect inmates and perfectly homeless.

This was a tall order and required much practice. To prepare for these interviews, the men often spent weeks practicing and being coached by social workers at the shelter on how to beat the interview process.[3] For many of my informants, this was proof that the entire homeless support industry was a race-specific ritual of humiliation. I heard frequent comments suggesting that the only appreciated black man is one who has been castrated. As one man who got housing but was forced to leave because he was "too independent" said about the process, "it's like the opposite of a job interview, they want to know what you can't do."

Once inside a transitional housing facility, some of my informants were required to take psychiatric medications in order to keep their housing. They constantly complained that this impaired their sexual performance and prevented them from having sex. There was a widespread belief that this was no incidental side effect, but rather the conscious work of white doctors who wanted to guarantee that their black patients were impotent. I often heard informants make comparisons with ante-bellum castration of male slaves who had acted inappropriately around white women and there were frequent discussions about whether or not blacks were being given larger doses of medication than Latinos in the mental health unit of the shelter.

One man summed up this fear by saying, "They all afraid of black people. The whites, the Spanish, the Chinese. We bigger, stronger and we a whole lot angrier than these little Hispanics. They see a big black man who's been shit on all his life and they know it's gonna be trouble unless they get a needle into his ass." For my informants the price of housing was often taking a passive, desexualized, and "ugly" role that made them hate who they were.

The ugly and passive aspects of this role were only a little easier than the desexualization. For many of my informants who had grown up in black communities where a neat and attractive appearance was valued at least as much as among whites, there was a constant battle with social workers over clothing. As part of granting them housing and services for the homeless, they were supposed to be helping to rehabilitate and resocialize these men. Part of the process of teaching them new values was to get them to throw out their materialist obsession with fashion. They were to be taught that there are more important things in life than the latest sneakers or a fancy winter coat. It was hard to receive any help, services, or consideration if a man dressed like a "bad nigger," a "good nigger," or even just a run-of-the-mill New Yorker. To be homeless was to be cast off and "ugly." The clothing was one of the crucial markers that indicated this role. While neatness was certainly valued by the social service workers, the sense of style, fashion, and identity that they had been raised with as ordinary Americans going to school, watching television, and so on was seen as part of these men's pathology.

I met many people over the course of my fieldwork who lived in a stereotypically "homeless" way and were so deeply disoriented and mentally ill that they were the embodiment of the role of "the ugly." Some others were conscious of what role they were playing and could identify every aspect of the role, while others, though fairly lucid, had internalized the problem, or as Franklin would have said, had been too long without "a prophet to remind them of who they are." However, for most of the people who lived in shelters, abandoned buildings, or other semipublic spaces and had received public services designated for the homeless, the role of "the ugly" was one that they could not successfully play while remaining human in their own eyes.

Though many of my informants feared and hated interviews for housing programs and the requirements once inside, because they knew that they would be expected to be "ugly" under the scrutiny of individuals who had tremendous power over them, they were particularly harsh with the bigger public performances that they felt further enshrined this social role on them and those around them. Politics was not a common topic of discussion and there was little interest in homeless policy. However, there were moments when the social performance of homelessness appeared on the political map, and some of my informants responded with political views about the relationship between themselves, homelessness, and public policy.

Among the most spectacular public homeless performances was the 1989 David Dinkins mayoral campaign, which employed a strategy that came to be known as "mobilizing the homeless." Dinkins had positioned himself as the key homeless advocate as early as 1986, when he coauthored a contribution to the journal *Social Policy* with Nancy Wackstein entitled "Addressing Homelessness." When Dinkins finally challenged then sitting mayor Ed Koch for the Democratic Party nomination, he hammered him on the issue of care for the homeless. In the autumn election against Republican candidate Rudolph Giuliani he filled the streets and highways of New York City with scabrous looking black men carrying Dinkins signs and distributing literature.

Some of my informants in the shelter had been offered work on the Dinkins campaign, but had refused, because of a combination of low pay and the requirement that they dress up as what one informant called "dirty-ass niggers." Another informant told me that he had refused because he did not want to "put on a show for the Jews," who he said were Dinkins's real constituency. Despite not meeting any men who had actually participated in the "mobilization of the homeless" I remembered being harassed in my car at traffic lights by black men who looked homeless, carrying signs for Dinkins and shoving flyers into my car window. They were saying to everyone, "the homeless are for Dinkins." At the time I was taking a research methods course in graduate school and my professor was describing them as a "poor people's movement" much like the one described in Piven and Cloward's book of the same title.

Several years later, when I was beginning my write-up, I interviewed a Dinkins campaign worker who had also studied at CUNY. He told me about how the mobilization of the homeless was conceived. As he put it, "It was not a poor people's movement, it was political theater, where the directors were 'clean' (Dinkins administration internal slang for Euro-American), but the actors were black and dirty." He directly confirmed what my informants from the shelter had told me: homeless people living in shelters or on the streets who were white and ragged looking were excluded. Those who were black and continued to dress well were described as looking like Farrakhan men[4] and no thought at all was given to using the many homeless white youth who lived in and around the abandoned buildings of the East Village. Despite the fact that many of these young people worked for the Dinkins campaign of their own accord, the campaign officially sought to distance itself from these apparently undeserving poor and strove to shield their participation from newspapers, television and other media publicity. Though all the above-mentioned groups shared many of the same challenges in their housing and employment lives, they did not properly display the desired performance of homelessness: ugly, disheveled, poor, helpless, black, and victimized by the Reagan revolution and the Republican Party.

Roughly a year later, when *New York Daily News* truck drivers went on strike against the *Chicago Tribune*, owners of the *Daily News*, the homeless performance was once again front page news. After truck drivers convinced most news dealers to remove the *New York Daily News* from the shelves of their stores, management used "homeless streetcorner salesmen." Again the most scabrous African-American men were selected for political theater and expected to play homeless. The Chicago Tribune Corporation argued that unions should be broken because they were mostly composed of white men protecting high-paid union jobs. They claimed that the organization of strikebreaking newspaper salesmen was an antiracist act of integration. "Homeless" newspaper sellers feared that the union might become violent and oppose this politically charged form of integration. The management of the *Daily News* informed them that they would be safe, because truckers would not attack defenseless homeless people and risk race riots. Once again being homeless had everything to do with casting and very little to do with housing.

For those who sold newspapers for the Chicago Tribune Corporation it was a particularly taxing performance in a high-stress situation. They were forced to stay in character and humiliate themselves, but also function at a high level in public, selling papers, accounting for stock, protecting earnings and dodging striking workers and student solidarity activists, who stole bundles of papers. I met one man who had spent a few days selling papers and claimed to be proud to have helped the *Chicago Tribune* break a racist union; most of my informants hated playing the victim too much to have participated in strikebreaking activities. Delaney, who probably could have played the part but had refused work as a scab paper seller during the strike, expressed the general feeling among my informants when he said, "you spend all day working and selling newspapers, but ya gotta look like something the cat dragged in, because they didn't want them drivers to beat you up. Couldn't pay me enough to do that." Many of my informants, when talking about the *Daily News* strike repeatedly referred to the fact that all jobs have uniforms and this supposedly "antiracist" newspaper had decided that "the black man's uniform is rags." One informant called it "wearing tar and feathers."

Despite the general hatred for being stereotyped and the special animus reserved for the role of homeless and ugly, living by stereotypes was sometimes the only thing separating life and death as Franklin pointed out to me one day while telling me about role switching in prison. He had been arrested for crack dealing and decided he should play the homeless card by calling his social worker at the shelter to get someone to mediate between him, legal aid and the courts. When he first arrived in prison he became a crackhead again to avoid being victimized, then made the difficult switch back to homeless while still in prison because he owed money to someone there. He said, "I'd rather be a homeless crazy person than be that nigger's bitch." He later managed to be transferred to a mental health unit which often housed imprisoned homeless men.

Most of my informants hated playing the role of homeless in any situation, because it violated virtually every U.S. norm of adulthood and masculinity. The homeless person appeared passive, pathetic, dependent, uneducated, unskilled, mentally ill, desexualized, ugly, and disgusting. However, as Franklin had once pointed out to me about being homeless, "it's no worse than anything else the system makes you do. It ain't like you gonna get any pussy at the supermarket when you give her those coupons (food stamps)."

Notes

1. Handkerchief head refers to the head coverings that "house slaves" were expected to wear in the ante-bellum south. These domestic servants were often privileged over field workers and common lore has it that because of their greater privileges, they were also more loyal. A large literature has generated around this assumption that there was less anti-slavery consciousness among more educated and resourced domestic slaves.
2. Several years later, when I became involved in research and work in the criminal justice field, I came in contact with policemen from that very precinct who confirmed Franklin's assertions about patrolmen being more ready to stop Latinos and African immigrants than African-Americans. Some of the police I talked to used almost exactly the same words to describe the way they were ready to engage in a variety of everyday policing with Latinos that they would never do with African-Americans. The reason given is something like blacks are unpredictable, violent, and don't give a damn.
3. The social workers at the shelter were under severe pressure to up their rates of placement and worked very hard to help their clients beat the interview process.
4. This is a reference to the Nation of Islam, whose followers dress in suits and bow ties.

— *Chapter 3* —

NEW YORK CITY AND
THE HISTORIOGRAPHY OF HOMELESSNESS

The First Homeless Book

The publication of *Private Lives/Public Spaces* by Ellen Baxter and Kim Hopper in 1981 marks the beginning of the homeless crisis and its study in social science, in the United States. Though there had been a brief flurry of articles in national news magazines showing "homeless families living in cars in the Midwest" during the 1979 to 1980 national election period, very little in the way of public policy or debate came from these articles. Similarly, there have been important studies of housing loss, urban and rural American nomads, and semipublic living over the last hundred years. Alice Sollenberger published a 1911 study called "One Thousand Homeless Men: a study of original records." In the same sociological vein, Nels Anderson published a 1923 study called "The Hobo: the sociology of the homeless man." The term homeless has been used in both popular and scholarly discourse in sporadic ways ever since. However, it never emerged as a unified concept, a body of literature, or a major public issue until Baxter and Hopper published their book.

When *Private Lives/Public Spaces* was first published, it was generally seen to be part of the literature on "skid row" populations or what later came to be defined as "the old homelessness" (Hoch 1989; Sheldon and Walsh 1994). Geographically defined, isolated from residential areas, and populated primarily by older white men as well as homosexuals, transvestites, prostitutes, and other social outlaws, skid row was rarely mentioned in opinion polls about social problems, campaign speeches by politicians, or even the literature of organizations devoted to charitable causes. These urban neighborhoods were home to red light districts, drug buying areas, pre-Stonewall gay bars and "men's hotels" that catered to the gay or transvestite clientele, ex-psychiatric patients living independently, and the studios of artists and other marginal bohemian types. Skid rows and the "bums" and "skells" who inhabited them were seen as a dangerous but colorful underworld to be heavily regulated by police vice-squads, social workers, and other public functionaries of social control, and avoided by "upstanding citizens," with the exception of the occasional journalist doing a story and Salvation Army volunteers.

This was particularly true during the post–World War II boom years from the early 1950s to the late 1970s, when the vast growth of public housing programs and public financing for private housing was steadily driving down relative housing costs for nearly all of the American population (Freeman 2000; U.S. Census Bureau 2004). In such an environment of plentiful housing and economic prosperity, very little significant discourse emerged on housing problems even within skid row. Even the discussions and debates on slum clearance in the 1960s and policies to upgrade or replace older housing stock yielded little literature on people defined by lack of housing.

This lack of concern for those without proper housing began to change in the 1970s when many mentally ill adults were deinstitutionalized. Throughout the urban United States the mentally ill who lived in traditional skid rows and other marginal neighborhoods wandered the streets of center cities and traditionally respectable neighborhoods talking to themselves or otherwise acting inappropriately in public. The discussion of "shopping bag ladies" and their less socially visible male counterparts emerged as a public discourse, but remained largely within the realm of public health and psychiatry.

In 1979, when President Jimmy Carter and Federal Reserve Bank chair Paul Volker implemented fiscal policies designed to halt inflation the United States was plunged into a recession. This was when national publications began to talk about "homeless families" living in their cars in the Midwestern United States. How much of this actually occurred and how much was trumpeted by the Republican Party to position its candidates for the 1980 national elections is not certain. However, the image of "white middle class" families living in cars proved to have little resonance for most Americans and quickly disappeared. But there were many changes occurring in the U.S. economy and political culture that would provide fertile ground for a different kind of homeless crisis, promoted by a different set of political forces.

For several years, there had been clear signs of changes in the urban environment. The fiscal crisis of 1975 that caused New York City to default on its loans became a national cause celebre in which then-president Gerald Ford told national television audiences that he would "veto any bill that has as its purpose a Federal bailout of New York City to prevent default." The next day the *New York Daily News* printed its famous bold type all caps headline "FORD TO CITY: DROP DEAD." This headline was recounted to me by informants (most of whom believed that these were actually the words of former president Gerald Ford) nearly twenty years later, as being the beginning of their lifetime in poverty. This political flirtation with "municipal death" became the excuse for radically reorganizing the structure of city government. In exchange for the right to issue bonds to pay off New York City's municipal debt, the government was put under the fiscal discipline of the Municipal Assistance Corporation, a consortium of bankers and businessmen charged with the duty of making the city financially solvent.

Their version of making the city financially solvent involved the beginnings of a larger ideological project that would sweep the United States, the United Kingdom, and much of the world during the 1980s. The New York City welfare state that provided free tertiary education, a comprehensive public health system, a version of "the dole," and many other social programs that had brought New York City derogatory nicknames such as Moscow on the Hudson and the Soviet Republic of New York City would be no more. As the U.S. Secretary of Treasury, William Simon, testified in October of 1975 about the federal aid program that had been offered to New York City to address its fiscal crisis, it should be "so punitive, the overall experience made so painful, that no city, no political subdivision would ever be tempted to go down the same road" (Freeman 2000: 259). Tens of thousands of layoffs, scores of thousands of jobs eliminated through "attrition" in the public sector, often disastrous reductions in health, firefighting, policing, education, and social services, and a tremendous breakdown in public morale followed.

The next summer policemen handed out fliers at New York's Kennedy Airport warning arriving tourists not to stay, because they could not guarantee their safety as garbage piled up on the streets and major avenues in poor neighborhoods became impassable due to lack of maintenance to the roads. City officials and businessmen feared urban unrest and public protest as unions targeted some of the banks that were implicated in what came to be called "planned shrinkage." There is hardly a New Yorker who lived in the city at this time who does not have some memory of a family member thrown out of work, a favorite teacher in high school saying goodbye to his or her class, or some kind of deterioration of city living.

The "white flight" that had been occurring since the end of WWII sped up, as the city dipped under seven million people for the first time in half a century and Roger Starr, the New York City Housing and Development administrator, published a notorious piece in the *New York Times* that argued that "Our urban system is based on the theory of taking the peasant and turning him into an industrial worker. Now there are no industrial jobs. Why not keep him a peasant" (Freeman 2000: 277). Many such statements appeared during this period of "reorganization" that suggested a racially biased attack on the special relationship between New York City and Puerto Rico, and an attempt to end the policy of free education at the City University of New York.

These changes hit poorer and more marginally working-class neighborhoods such as Harlem, The South Bronx, and The Lower East Side much harder and sooner than more affluent neighborhoods in which employment was more secure and fewer families depended as directly on the public sector. With the dramatic collapse in real estate values many landlords abandoned buildings, leaving them without heat, hot water, or basic services such as rodent extermination. Many landlords burned down their own buildings for insurance money, leaving the burned out shells of buildings that my informants in the Lower East Side had referred to as "bomb craters," while others went bankrupt due to uncollected rents and high operating costs (Barrett & Newfield 1988). Many people moved out of these neighborhoods during this period, often finding themselves in equally bad situations in other marginal neighborhoods. Those who stayed behind described the late 1970s as a time of imploding communities, rising drug violence, prostitutes openly working out of storefronts of abandoned buildings, and general "urban blight." The phrase "the Bronx is burning" became popular parlance as national television networks made documentaries about the South Bronx, Hollywood made movies with titles like *Fort Apache, The Bronx,* European tourists visited to relive memories of post–World War II Germany, and Fidel Castro even offered to send foreign aid and technicians to help rebuild New York.

As large sections of New York City were allowed to become uninhabitable and made fallow, tax and real estate laws were made more landlord friendly, the city government greatly reduced its contribution to health care, education, and other public services; and new investment began to trickle in, improving or replacing decaying substandard center city zones. A quiet reorganization of the New York economy was occurring, as it became what has come to be called a "banking, service and information" economy. This new economy depended for its survival on a combination of low wage, low skill service jobs and high wage, high cultural capital banking, financial, entertainment, and telecommunications jobs (Fitch 1991, Moody 1988, Nash 1989, Nash & Fernandez-Kelly 1983, Susser 1982). New York City was transformed from a working class industrial city, famous for its highly skilled and class-conscious blue-collar workforce to an international banking, service, and information economy (Freeman 2000).

It was in this period, during the early 1980s, that the terms "gentrification" and "yuppie" first appeared. The urban tax base returned, private investment grew, and older substandard housing stock was renovated alongside new construction. Demand for housing returned and the number of people who could afford higher rents dramatically increased. Older abandoned factories were redesigned, renovated and converted into new white-collar commercial uses and high-priced residential housing, and the post–World War II American credo of home ownership was transplanted from the suburbs to the city, with mass conversions of rental units into owner-occupied condominiums and coops, dramatically increasing land prices and fuelling speculation.[1] These changes that were occurring during the last years of the 1970s and the first years of the 1980s were already being discussed in 1979 by Geographer Neil Smith who was developing a broad view of the way in which global changes in the patterns of capital accumulation were changing urban environments nationally and internationally (Smith 1979, 1982, 1996).

As private investment in residential center city real estate grew there were significant changes in the way that poverty and dislocation were viewed and managed. Sensing that something was happening that would dramatically change the living arrangements and spatial distribution of poverty, Barret Lee published an essay in *Urban Affairs Quarterly* in 1980 entitled "The Disappearance of Skid Row: Some Ecological Evidence." This visionary piece prepared the way for a new paradigm that described the spectacle of "street people" being spit out of skid rows and other marginal urban areas and turning up in neighborhoods that had never before seen them in significant numbers: the homeless, as articulated by Hopper and Baxter in *Private Lives/Public Spaces* (1981). For the first time since the pre–World War II literature on "tramps" and "hobos," a population that was defined by a lack of adequate and permanent housing was studied as part of a broader literature on American poverty and urban affairs.

Though Hopper and Baxter had discarded the geographic boundaries of skid row studies, *Private Lives/Public Spaces* was a cautious work that could be fit as easily into the earlier literature on skid row and deinstitutionalization as the later literature on homelessness. However, within a few years the term homeless would generate a national discourse that would become so naturalized, self-referential, and unreflective that nearly all connection with the past would be lost. This discourse would generate a new welfare system category that could be defined in any way that anybody with a connection to low-income transient housing and a social work staff wanted.

Study after study suggested that this new group suffered from the same combinations of personal and professional failures such as alcoholism, drug addiction, mental illness, depression, unemployment, bad luck, and social isolation that had plagued skid row denizens. Despite these continuities, the promoters of the homeless crisis charged that there were significant demographic differences that made the homeless entirely new. Among the changes pointed to were larger numbers of African Americans, Latinos, women, children, and families that were without proper housing, higher per square foot costs of housing, and more peripatetic urban nomadic populations. They called this "the new homelessness" and the short message was that they were ordinary people whose problems were not the traditional skid row problems, but a new conjunction of generalized poverty, retreating welfare programs, and some of the more traditional skid row problems (Hopper and Hamberg 1984; Rossi 1989; Barak 1991).

The idea that the general population had many of the same problems and concerns as those defined as homeless was very much in the air at the time. One of the slogans that homeless activists often used was "we are all only two paychecks away from homelessness" and there were frequent discussions in academic literature about the "working poor" and an occasional observation of the continuities between the old and new homelessness. However, for most researchers and policy advocates the break was so complete that the previous literature and social interventions no longer existed. This break was facilitated by the rapid disappearance of skid rows and the emergence of gentrification in the central city areas of many major American cities. This pattern was particularly pronounced and precocious in New York City, with its famous 1970s collapse and the spectacular entrance of international capital in the early 1980s.

Though these two literatures seem to have so much in common, the break between them is so complete that many important works on homelessness entirely exclude discussions of skid row. A prominent example of this is Ida Susser's 1996 *Annual Review of Anthropology* article entitled "The Construction of Poverty and Homelessness in US Cities" which excludes both discussion and bibliographic citation of skid row. At the level of policy making this break was as complete, with the influential New York City Commission on the Homeless's February 1992 report, entitled "The Way Home" (often known as the Cuomo Commission report after Andrew Cuomo, the chairman) citing only one skid row book in its bibliography and ignoring questions of change and continuity in underhoused populations.

It was this remarkable discontinuity with the past that enabled scholars, politicians, social workers, and ordinary people who were concerned with the emergence of so much visible poverty in the 1980s to define as homeless everyone from Vietnam veterans and people on government disability who were suddenly forced to find extra income selling things on the streets and poorly dressed loners living in single room occupancy hotels on the Upper West Side of New York City to mentally ill people sleeping on steam gratings in winter and families living in shelters. It was this discontinuity that gave birth to the vast cavernous municipal shelters where I did my research and the mass conflation of traditional skid row problems and social presentation with the problems and challenges of social housing policy.

Kim Hopper's Mystery

If there is no mystery about the sympathetic attention paid to the problem of homelessness in America over the past decade, there certainly *is* a mystery concerning why comparable attention and sympathy were not extended to the homeless in the past. Homelessness has waxed and waned throughout our history, but America has always had a goodly complement of homeless people. Nevertheless, compared with the scale of contemporary popular concern, throughout most of our history the homeless have been regarded at least with indifference and often with contempt, fear, and loathing.

– Kim Hopper, 1987

The quotation above is from Kim Hopper's 1987 essay, "The Public Response to Homelessness in New York City: The Last 100 Years." In this essay he presents the history of mass housing loss over the past hundred years, tracing housing loss from the post–Civil War rise of industrialization and growth of cities through the world economic crisis of the 1930s to the homeless crisis of the 1980s. Despite many observations about the different ways in which people have been without housing and the many social policies that have been designed to confront this recurring problem, one thing remained a mystery to Hopper: the question why here and why now.

At the time, Hopper's mystery did not seem that important. Everyone was worried about homelessness and it seemed to be one of the major problems facing cities in the United States. However, after 1993 when news coverage on homelessness dropped to almost nothing, politicians showed little concern for the issue, and many charities reduced their interest in supporting the homeless, it vanished from public view and "waned" as a social concern. Some writers have explained this disappearance in terms of changes in the spatialization of poverty, changes in policing, and new urban geographies of capitalism (Mitchell 1997, 2001; Davis 1990; Harvey 1990). However, the ability to "unmake a crisis" through the management of space or the administration of people makes the questions how, why, and when the homeless crisis was made all the more important.

My fellow researchers, many of whom were debating various issues that had been first raised by Kim Hopper in the early and mid 1980s, each had his or her own answer to why there was so much housing loss, begging on the streets and the other visible outward manifestations of the homeless crisis. However, there was little interest in why it was suddenly of so much political importance in the 1980s. Most saw it in terms of the more visible and mass character of the new homelessness. The general view was that people were shocked by the new homelessness since Reagan had taken office in 1981 and that this had raised interest in the issue.

There were some, such as Joel Blau (1992), who attempted to find a longer historical dimension to the problem. He defined five major periods of homelessness going back to what he described as the "absolute shortage of shelter" (p. 9) that characterized the preindustrial period, moving to the early industrial period in Europe in the late eighteenth and early nineteenth centuries when many people went through a period of homelessness upon arriving in cities; then the mass internal migrations of urbanization in the less developed world, to "mature industrialization" in the United States from 1870 to the 1970s and finally the postindustrial period defined by the new homelessness that was the basis of the 1980s and '90s homeless crisis. As Blau points out (p. 10), what was remarkable was that contemporary homelessness was growing during an economic recovery. Suddenly ordinary people were witnessing poverty and ordinary people were experiencing it, in what were comparatively speaking, good times (Blau 1992). However, most researchers had little interest in pre-1981 homelessness. The "new homelessness" was typically attributed to the fact that Ronald Reagan had cut budgets and forced vast numbers of poor people into public to a greater degree than at any time since the Great Depression threw millions of people into poverty (Barak 1991, Dehavenon 1995, Rossi 1989; Susser 1996).

These attempts to periodize homelessness and explain it in terms of changes in the structure of poverty and U.S. housing policies solved neither the concerns that I opened this book with nor Hopper's mystery since poverty had been a bigger concern during the 1960s and '70s when the economy was booming, the "affluent society" was in full bloom, and poor people were far less visible. It is true that during the 1960s poverty and rising real estate prices were not driving people out of their houses and into the streets of center cities and residential neighborhoods, but, as Hopper pointed out, mass housing loss is a phenomenon that has waxed and waned throughout American history, but rarely been as central to political discourse. This mystery became far more difficult to resolve through empirical data on poverty and housing as the economic boom of the 1990s raged, real estate prices in New York City continued to rise and hundreds of thousands continued to be underhoused, often living largely unnoticed in the public and private interstices of New York City. The passage of the post–cold war economic boom, in late 2000 made Hopper's mystery even more difficult to explain outside such deus en machinae as "people just got tired of hearing about it."

My African American informants, like my friends, neighbors and fellow researchers were not really sure when and where the category of homeless had been developed and Hopper's mystery was of little interest to most of them. They tended to put most of the blame on the then-mayor David Dinkins. This had far more to do with the disappointment that they felt with Dinkins for being an African American mayor who seemed to care only about white people, than it did with Dinkins's actual policies and writings about the homeless. His unprecedented expansion of the police force by roughly seven thousand men was well known and seen as a betrayal, as was his concern with the state of Israel, which was widely regarded as a sign that he was under the political control of powerful Jews in New York City politics. Fundamentally, they, like most of the writers and scholars who have looked at the homeless, were concerned with the lack of affordable housing and not with why homelessness was suddenly important.

Many of my informants traced the origins of homelessness to the New York City fiscal crisis of 1975. They were from families that had depended on the vast New York City welfare state for everything from education and housing to jobs, summer recreation programs, and health care. Even informants who had been young children during the dark days of 1975 could remember adults around them panicking as mass layoffs and budget cuts changed their lives and forced them to scale back their expectations. I had informants who had grown up in New York City who remembered their first experiences of housing loss after a parent was laid off in 1975. They talked about going from being "middle class black folk" to being poor. For most of them it meant a brief period in a welfare hotel followed by a move to a poorer, more marginal neighborhood. Sometimes it merely meant moving to a smaller apartment and sharing a bedroom with younger siblings.

For these informants who were raised in New York City the fiscal crisis was a watershed, but not one that was ever seen in political terms. It was seen as a kind of unavoidable natural disaster that had transformed the environment they lived in and forced them to interact with people who were ruder, rougher, and lower down the socioeconomic ladder. Some remembered that the president had told New York to drop dead and assumed that it was because of the fact that it was such a black and Hispanic city. However, they generally attributed the experience of housing loss and the development of the category of homeless to an almost inevitable decline from a golden age of good old days to an age of decline. The typical folk narration of the historiography of homelessness was something like, "New York has been going to hell ever since the bankruptcy thing in 1975."

Unlike my colleagues and friends, these informants did not see a dividing line between 1981 and the past. They were sure that the dividing line between the brave new world and the gentler past was 1975, when they remembered that the whole country was against them. Like friends, relatives, and colleagues they were sure that the answer to Hopper's mystery lay in the relationship between housing costs and economic resources. Like Hopper, I wasn't so sure. I had a feeling that the answer to this mystery lay somewhere in the history of social housing and methodologies of the poverty studies industry that have represented and crafted policy in the United States during the twentieth century.

When Delaney had urged me in 1993 to look at the social workers to find out about homelessness, he was not pushing me hard enough. It is impossible to really understand the social origins and structure of a concentration camp by studying the guards or the commander; you must look at the entire society. The Germans running the camp were a small group of people caught in the vast web of significance that made up German society. Beyond their little world of the camps lay local and national political leaders, intellectuals, military men, and ordinary people, all struggling to pursue their interests and ideals within the world of German National Socialism. Similarly with the homeless crisis, there were far too many players in the drama to find answers by solely focusing on my informants and the social workers whose job it was to take care of them. In order to solve Kim Hopper's mystery, it would be necessary to interrogate the great web of significance within which everybody was struggling: the social science of poverty and the government policy apparatus that managed America's "reluctant welfare state."

Social Housing in the Twentieth Century

The problem of defining adequate housing for the underhoused and adequate employment for the underemployed has been highly political throughout the twentieth century. In the popular imagination, there have been three major moments in the last hundred years of U.S. history in which the issue of people without housing has been important: the wanderings and dislocations of the great depression of the 1930s, the housing shortages in the wake of World War II, and the homeless crisis of the 1980s. All three of these crises occurred due to the inability of significant segments of the U.S. population to afford what was defined, at the time, as adequate housing. However, each was socially constructed in a different way, reflecting different historical circumstances and political forces, with different economic, social and political goals. A look at the way other crises of semipublic living were viewed gives some context to the formulation of homelessness as a national discourse in the 1980s.

The Great Depression

Much of the literature on underhoused populations in the 1930s originates with sociological literature on "tramps" and "hobos" that discusses housing loss and nomads in terms of psychocultural pathologies and sociocultural difference (Anderson 1923; Minehan 1934). Tramps and hobos were generally seen as social outlaws and lumped together with the poor and the underemployed into a world described in terms of faulty values and individual dysfunction. The recognition after October 1929 that the United States economy was crippled by a world economic crisis that would last for over a decade did not stop much of the academic, journalistic, and political discourse of the time from presenting this individualized vision of the deviant behavior of the poor (Sutherland & Locke 1936).

The "bonus army" conflict of 1932 provides a dramatic example of the power of this traditional discourse on poverty. Largely without real housing to call their own, the World War I veterans and their families who camped out on the mall in Washington, D.C. demanded an early payment of the bonus that was supposed to be paid them in 1945 for military service rendered some fifteen years earlier. They were generally vilified in major newspapers and magazines and portrayed as a plague on the capital. When the U.S. army led by Douglas MacArthur, George Patton and Dwight Eisenhower drove the "bonus army" out of the streets killing civilians, destroying personal property, and injuring dozens, the official discourse on the incident portrayed the veterans as troublemaking vagrants and communist provocateurs who had no right to claim anything from their government. Few would have imagined that this group of people living in tents in front of the Capitol were people who had risked their lives in foreign service for their country. Red Cross records from the charity stations set up near the city of tents indicated that nearly all of the families present were veterans' families (Zinn 1995).

Despite the power of this traditional discourse that blames the individual whose poverty has become visible, the scope of the economic crisis in the 1930s was too great to convincingly argue that millions of people had all at once become lazy, spendthrift, and intemperate. With armies of immigrants leaving the Midwestern states to look for work in California and eighteen million unemployed in 1938 the problems of those who no longer had fixed housing were rarely defined in terms of where they were sleeping.

Similarly, it was difficult even for Chicago School sociologists who had been trained in geographical paradigms involving questions of placement, housing stock, and community of experience and values to argue that the problems of these multitudes of displaced persons were based on their housing status or geographical placement. The decline in housing starts, continually rising social expectations, and widespread substandard housing stock that was little changed from the nineteenth century meant that what was coming to be the basic residential standard for American housing was in short supply in many parts of the United States. If the U.S. economy had been strong during the 1930s rather than depressed there might have been a national housing crisis due to the presence of too little modern housing. However, even within political and social circles that promoted large slum clearance programs like those of New York City mayor Fiorello La-Guardia, who oversaw the building of the first federal housing projects on 3rd Street and Avenue A on the Lower East Side, there was little public discourse that tied the problems of poverty directly to housing concerns.

The popular radical discourse that emerged around this crisis put little stress on the lack of proper housing. Though there were many positive portrayals of yeggs, tramps, hobos, and vagabonds that emerged from this crisis, such as the Charlie Chaplin character in *City Lights* and some of the early "talkie" road movies and traveling stories of the 1930s, the dominant image was one of people who had been thrown out of work by a system that put profits ahead of people. John Steinbeck's *The Grapes of Wrath* is probably the classic of this genre that has best survived the test of time. However, there were numerous other examples of popular movies, books and songs on this theme. The Preston Sturges movie *Sullivan's Travels* and the late silent comedy by Chaplin *Modern Times* are excellent examples of the way semi-nomadic unemployed Americans were portrayed in this period.

The Communist Party USA was one of the key organizations giving voice to these sentiments. It had a membership that may have been as much as one hundred thousand[2] but its influence within American society and popular culture was broader than its numbers. Drawing prestige from the October Revolution, which was still popular in much of the world, and its connection to the Soviet Union, the only major country not affected by the world economic crisis, the Communist Party helped to pose the massive loss of housing in militant class terms: unemployment and substandard living conditions were blamed on capitalism. One of the most important movements connected to the Communist Party was its "Unemployed Councils," which became famous for illegally reversing evictions and restoring gas and electricity. Along with radical organizations like the Congress of Industrial Organizations and the Socialist Workers' Party, the Communist Party vied with a left-leaning president for the right to narrate this crisis in specifically class terms.

During this period the Roosevelt administration initiated a variety of important forms of legislation, such as the National Housing Act, the Homeowners Loan Act, and the charter for the Resettlement Administration that would eventually change the way Americans think about housing. Most of these programs were not viewed as crucial parts of the New Deal and did not create dramatic changes in American life until the affluent postwar period, when the economy was booming, living standards were rising, and the 1930s housing shortages were finally resolved through government intervention. This may, in part, be due to the fact that Roosevelt, along with a majority of Americans, understood that the thousands of displaced Midwesterners massing on the California border hoping to be allowed in for low wage agricultural and service sector jobs had much bigger problems than a lack of housing.

Today the dominant contemporary cinematic image of depression-era economic problems is a sign reading "foreclosed" in front of a family farm or house, referencing the famous bank foreclosures of the 1930s and ensuing California migrations. However, this represents something of a historical anachronism, since the majority of Americans did not own their own houses at the time. The concern that ordinary Americans were losing their family house or farm was a significant part of depression-era social concerns, but certainly not the dominant one of the time. This rearranging of the past may resonate with the economic fears of contemporary Americans who now actually own houses in large numbers.

Dislocations of the Early Postwar Period

In the late 1940s the continued existence of massive numbers of people without proper housing came to be defined in a different way than it had been in the class militant, communist influenced 1930s. Large numbers of urban families lived in crowded or substandard housing and many rural Americans still lived in unrenovated nineteenth-century housing. Stories abounded of industrial refrigerators sold as homes and families sleeping in army tents, Quonset huts, shacks, abandoned buildings, and doubled up in parents' houses. The combination of record birth rates, returning soldiers, reduced housing starts, and the decay of existing housing due to twelve years of depression and nearly five years of World War II rationing and austerity led to a severe shortage of affordable housing for the lower paid segments of the American population.

Though the housing shortage of the late 1940s was probably worse than any since the arrival of settlers from England, this crisis is generally remembered in patriotic national terms rather than in terms of poverty and social inequality. The standard historical description in textbooks, newspaper articles, and other secondary sources is that "there was not enough housing for returning soldiers." There is no mention in the literature on the late 1940s housing crisis of hobos, homeless, vagrants, tramps, or other categories that are defined by the dislocations, forced geographic movement, and residential instability that millions of the poorest Americans experienced. The discourse on 1940s housing shortages has always been phrased in purely demographic terms focusing on returning soldiers, despite the fact that clearly fewer soldiers had returned than had gone to fight. However, their years in combat had given them a sense of entitlement and a social weight that put their interests and concerns at the center of the problem and enabled them to influence the way the problem was framed. Much had changed since the bonus army had marched on Washington in 1932.

As the period of war capitalism and direct government management of industrial relations came to an end, domestic conflicts, which had been building during the war years, became manifest. In the United States, this was most apparent in the form of the World War II no strike pledge passing into history, and conversion of war industries to civilian applications. Though the United States economy had posted record growth rates of over 10 percent per year and U.S. business had amassed unprecedented profits during the war, the no strike pledges and war patriotism had reduced industrial conflict during the war to sporadic wildcat strikes and isolated griping. When the war ended in 1945, the nation was plunged into its most widespread industrial conflict since 1877. Subsequently, 1946 saw the biggest wave of industrial strikes in U.S. history with over 100 million work days lost to strikes. Though the U.S. trade union movement never regained its militancy of the 1930s nor recouped lost wartime wages it created a terrible shock for American industry.

The United States was the only major capitalist country to emerge from World War II wealthier and stronger than it had been before the war.[3] With much of Europe in ashes, Japan under U.S. military occupation, and some of the most important industrial sites in Germany under the direct control of the East German Communist Party, the United States was perfectly positioned to expand its economic dominance in the capitalist world. The United States economy could produce nearly everything better, faster, and cheaper than its economic rivals. The defeat of all its rivals coupled with the United Kingdom's crippling debt from two world wars and the increasing cost of colonial possessions left the United States with an economic "open field." In such an environment of economic dominance every workday lost to industrial conflict or housing problems was a guaranteed loss of profits. National industry was united in its search for industrial peace. One of the forms that this took was the vast expansion of government subsidies for low-cost housing.

The period 1946–1966 saw an incredible expansion of permanent housing options, driven by increasing demand for affordable housing (Jackson 1985; Tabb and Sawyers 1984). The stringent rent control laws in some of the older center cities, a tremendous expansion of Roosevelt's experiments with public housing, the construction of major roads to newly developing suburbs, and low-interest loans for new construction created a drop in the relative cost of housing for nearly all Americans, helped to underwrite the postwar "affluent society."

Despite this vast expansion of suburban development, public housing, and other low-income housing initiatives, there were whole neighborhoods in older center cities where the housing stock was still little improved from the turn of the century. Though housing became far less problematic during the twenty years after the war, "cold water flats" remained a common feature of the poorest neighborhoods in the many deteriorating center cities of postwar America. With bathtubs in kitchens, shared toilets in hallways, one fifteen-amp electric line for a whole floor, and little heat, hot water, or insulation, these "relics" remained a dramatic symbol of the decline of the cities in face of suburban development, until the gentrifications of the 1980s (Jencks 1994).

The Late Postwar Period

In the mid 1970s a variety of economic factors that scholars are still debating occasioned the end of the golden age of postwar economic prosperity. Tensions between national profitability and the American standard of living had been present for a long while. However, the combination of stagnation in stock prices with declining values for the dollar against crude oil, domestic consumer goods, and international hard currencies became a national concern that was commonly referred to as inflation. Republican President Richard Nixon, a seasoned federal politician and big government Keynesian, responded to this synergy of economic tensions during the early 1970s with classic welfare state measures designed to regulate supply and demand (Joan Hoff 1994). The most dramatic of these were wage and price freezes, expansion of Social Security and public health benefits, and increased public expenditures. It is not clear the degree to which these measures would have worked had Nixon finished his term, but the combination of political scandal and partisan conflict forced Nixon to resign and signaled the end of the expanding welfare state.

It is probably no accident that the word "homeless," which came to signify the intersection of housing problems with dependence on the welfare system, first appeared briefly during the presidency of Democrat Jimmy Carter. A tightfisted, self-proclaimed "outsider" to Washington politics, Carter was a religious southern businessman/politician who oversaw the reversal of the welfare state of the Eisenhower, Kennedy, Johnson, and Nixon years. Carter's presidency, like that of his successor fellow "outsider" and ex-governor Ronald Reagan, was characterized by the use of market responses to national economic problems. His attempts to reduce government spending across the board were largely unsuccessful. However, the runaway inflation that characterized the first three years of his presidency augmented his fiscal restraint and the mild reductions in welfare benefits to create a market-based correction in the American standard of living.

The welfare system was under siege, but in a still mostly indirect way. The confluence of inflation, sluggish wages, and frozen benefits prepared the way for the cycle of urban destruction and renovation that would impoverish millions, reconfigure center cities throughout the United States, and empty skid rows and marginal neighborhoods or their most socially vulnerable residents. These changes put the type of people who came to be known as "the homeless" into public view for the first time since the 1930s. The arrival of Reaganomics and full-scale "supply side" neoliberal economics would put the entire public sector,[4] particularly the highly controversial and perpetually unpopular welfare system, in jeopardy and force many of the most economically marginal into public view. The Reagan Revolution put the New Deal/Great Society Welfare State and all those who benefited from it under siege. It was in this nexus between the endangered apparatus of the welfare state, the opposition Democratic Party, and the academic poverty studies industry that the representation of housing loss, underemployment, and human services cutbacks came to be a homeless crisis.

Notes

1. Joshua Freeman (2000) reports that in 1950 fewer than two out of ten New York City households owned their own home and by 1993 the number had risen to 30 percent, though this number is still far lower than on the mainland United States.
2. Estimating the number of members of the CPUSA remains a difficult task, due to definitions, political agendas, the tendency of the party to inflate numbers, problems with counting the youth section, and the high turnover during the turbulent 1930s. However, Fraser Ottanelli (1991) reports that in 1938 there were seventy-five thousand members of the CPUSA, twenty thousand members of the youth section, The Young Communist League, and a yearly recruitment of thirty thousand members.
3. Australia also emerged from World War II wealthier and stronger, as did several of the Latin American countries that were able to profitably export products developed under import substitution programs.
4. The already heavily private sector military-industrial-complex was the one exception to Reagan's attack on the public spending.

— *Chapter 4* —

THE POVERTY OF POVERTY STUDIES

It was not the shockingly large numbers of people sleeping on steam gratings and in shantytowns in parks and under bridges, nor residents of single room occupancy hotels spending their days selling discarded clothing and magazines that created the homeless crisis. They were only the raw materials. Neither was it the creation of Kim Hopper, Ellen Baxter, or later homelessologists such as Joel Blau, Segal and Specht, Ida and Ezra Susser, or Peter Rossi. Public poverty is nothing new and Hopper and Baxter were writing at the tail end of a long tradition of social science/social policy poverty studies. It was in the confluence between academic social science, public policy, and political partisanship that the publicly impoverished people wandering the streets and parks of the United States in the 1980s became the homeless.

In the quotation from Kim Hopper's 1987 article "The Public Response to Homelessness in New York City: The Last Hundred Years" cited in the previous chapter, Hopper tells us that "there is no mystery about the sympathetic attention paid to the problem of homelessness in America over the past decade" and wonders why "comparable attention and sympathy were not extended to the homeless in the past." In questioning the absence of such concern in the past, Hopper and other homelessness scholars were assuming exactly what needed to be explained: the sympathetic attention here and now. The sudden and overwhelming concern for the weak abstraction that was "the homeless" is a far greater mystery than why Americans have, at most times, been able to largely ignore the small percentage of the country that has been inadequately housed.

In order to find an answer to Hopper's mystery, it is necessary to look at much more than either the empirical reality or the "public response." It is necessary to look at the political and theoretical assumptions of those who have provided the descriptive categories that framed the key issues surrounding poverty for which there have been "public responses."

As with the studies of contemporary homelessness, the historical home-lessology that Hopper was trying to create assumed that there was an objective category of homelessness with a historically coherent continuity through time and place. The cursory history of mass housing problems in the twentieth century provided in the previous chapter should suggest some of the problems with studying a hundred years of history for a category that has existed only for ten to twenty years. Instead of looking at the public response to homelessness over the last hundred years, Hopper and others who wondered about the history of the homeless might better have turned more attention to the intellectual history of the urban question and poverty amelioration studies and projects, than the one specific entitlement category, homeless.

Poverty Studies: The Early Years

With the development of the steam engine, machinofacture, and the increased division of labor, the newly industrialized economy of the nineteenth century often grew more during one person's work years than it had in the previous five hundred years. New inequalities and social problems developed as more money circulated. Industrial barons who controlled vast holdings and inestimable wealth arose almost overnight, along with vagabonds, whose tie to place and community disappeared. Workers in the factories of Europe watched their labor make employers fabulously wealthy, while their own families lived in poverty. Thus began the urban question.

As it became clear that a fundamental divide had been crossed, many people questioned the new world. Among those who publicly questioned this darker side of industrial progress and "modernism" in the nineteenth century were those who lived in urban hells, generals whose conscripts were too short and vitamin D starved to serve in the army, and threatened older elites who found themselves accosted on the streets and boulevards by the urban poor who had been broken from the traditional rules of European social hierarchy.

In this newly empowered industrial North Atlantic, where anything seemed possible through the rational application of science, political economists and other fledgling social scientists attempted to apply their ideas to answer the questions and solve the problems of human society. Though many different forms of explanation and social intervention emerged, the issue of increasing inequality yielded two principal progressivist paradigms: Social Darwinism and Marxism.

For Social Darwinists, who most directly represented the interests of the emergent capitalist class, "what ever was, was right." Human progress was their explanation for the tremendous inequalities and dislocations. Life was a continual war of every man against all in the survival of the fittest, with the winners on top and the losers disappearing from the face of the earth. In the end, this sorting of the wheat from the chaff would make humanity stronger and wealthier. This progressive explanation for the urban problem yielded a variety of proposals based on the notion of laissez-faire economics, in which the market was seen as a natural determinant of "fitness." The Social Darwinist vision held that the poverty, dislocation, and misery of the cities was an unfortunate, but necessary, by-product of the Apollonian struggle to improve human life and move forward toward strength, wealth, advanced technology, and social fitness.

Marxists, who claimed to represent the emergent industrial proletariat and a strange congeries of threatened, devalued, or excluded older elites, were also committed to the idea of human progress, but believed that ceaseless competition was not the progress that had been promised by the tremendous growth of the industrial revolution. They believed that capitalist competition was an impediment to progress. They believed that progress should be defined in terms of the fulfillment of the human potential of individuals as part of a society, rather than a competition for dominance. They claimed a direct relationship between the wealth of one person and the poverty of many, based on the labor theory of value, elaborated by British economist David Ricardo.

Rather than viewing industrial triumphs as the genius of the fittest, they viewed them as a form of theft based on the organization of the class of wealth takers against the class of wealth makers. Rather than accepting the vision of a war of every individual against all, they identified the ways in which the state and economy were constructed to benefit the capitalist class at the expense of the proletariat. They viewed society under capitalism as a ceaseless war of one organized class, the bourgeoisie, against another less organized class, the proletariat (Marx 1954).

They claimed that the competition that Social Darwinists held to be the basis of evolution was retrogressive rather than progressive and saw the reduplication of production and the overproduction of commodities in a competitive market as a waste of human labor that could otherwise be redirected to further development. They rejected the "law of the jungle" for the law of rational human planning, arguing that the allocation of resources to protect the haves from the have-nots was wasteful and counterproductive to the goal of human progress. Marxism proposed a society based on cooperative forms of property ownership, in which there was no surplus taking class and eventually, when the capitalist class had been vanquished on a world wide basis, no state.

These two explanations for and solutions to the problem of dissatisfaction over social inequality stood as dominant for most of the latter part of the nineteenth century. Through much of the twentieth century, Social Darwinism and Marxism would continue to provide an unrelenting conflict based vision of life under capitalism for some scholars, writers, and politicians in the United States,[1] but for the vast majority of the twentieth century, political liberalism dominated the intellectual environment.

First identified in the United States in the twentieth century as "progressivism," political liberalism proposed a "third way" between the socially corrosive and highly conflictual visions and political projects of Marxists and Social Darwinists. It mixed a commitment to capitalist property forms, a capitalist state, and an economy based on competition, with many of the ideological commitments of Marxism. Softening the Social Darwinist phrases "survival of the fittest" and "law of the jungle" to "reward excellence" and "meritocracy," liberals grafted the Marxist ideals of social cooperation, work for the collective good, and the struggle against extreme inequalities onto the competitive and ultimately individualist structure of capitalism. Like Marxists, they believed that ceaseless social conflict was wasteful and endangered rather than spurred excellence, or what they called "merit." However, unlike Marxists, they assumed that a competitive economy was not only inevitable, but also universal. They saw their practical role as waging a ceaseless voluntary struggle to educate, inculcate, and bear witness to the ideas of community service, collective good, and citizenship into a population that was rudely driven by the competitive and imperfect nature of human life.

Though liberals accepted the idea that a competitive economy was inevitable, they were not principally concerned with human progress like Marxists and Social Darwinists. Their principal concern was social equilibrium and harmony. This usually meant various attempts to actually slow down the competitive forces of the market, reduce economic growth, and divert direct confrontations between capital and labor. Their social project was one of peace and community building as social conflict was to be avoided at all costs.

A natural voice for managers and bureaucrats, liberals posed human social life as a corporate structure or community in which moderation, equilibrium, and "play nice" are the main social goals. Those who do not play nice and exceed the bounds of generally established social etiquette and those who cannot, for whatever reason, meet the minimum standard for economic fitness are seen as deviant in their values, and when outside these limits of community for long enough, deviant in their culture. They are then defined as something separate and apart from the functional main currents of society and must be shamed, resocialized, or otherwise brought back into the functional "mainstream."

Because liberals rejected the Marxist and Social Darwinist analyses that held differentiation to be the fundamental process in capitalist society, social problems like poverty had to be externalized. This required the invention and imagining of distinct social categories like "homeless" and "poor" that could be defined as culturally, socially, geographically, or emotionally separate in order to mark off the rest of society as still functional.

Among the many nineteenth- and early twentieth-century theorists who laid the intellectual foundations for this liberalism were the two early giants of sociology, Emile Durkheim and Max Weber. They described a social balance, consensus, or pendulum based on rationality and humanism that swings from equilibrium to disequilibrium and determines the health or morbidity of society. For Weber, the focus of social health was the proper creation and dissemination of positive meanings and values to the mass elements in society. A strong and integrative state was necessary to insure that people were prevented from drifting into anarchy that might prevent the best meaning makers from creating and sharing the proper values. Society and therefore the state were functions of a competitive interplay of meaning construction that Weber saw as the basis of politics.

Unlike Weber, who saw the construction of meaning and political order as first principles upon which social structure was built, Durkheim primarily focused on the division of labor and its effect on social integration, social solidarity, and social cooperation. Durkheim viewed society as a giant machine in which the division of labor determined everybody's function and position. With each major change in the division of labor a new set of cultural institutions and social solidarities had to be developed to keep the machine from falling out of tune into disequilibrium.

In these liberal views of society history is not the war between classes or individuals, but rather a set of social solidarities involving some unsaid contract, consensus, or rational order. The existence of truly abhorrent suffering suggests that there is something that is not functioning correctly causing society to go out of balance. This lack of balance may represent the shortsighted vision of government leaders who have not provided enough padding for the less successful. It may represent too much social solidarity on the part of some successful group, such as White Anglo Saxon Protestants who have sometimes been accused of excluding minorities from higher education, or venal industrial elites who are too greedy. Conversely, it may represent some popular flaw such as the dysfunctional cultural patterns of the poor. Both the Weberian view of poverty as a problem in "the mind of society" and the Durkheimian focus on a changing division of labor that requires new social engineering share the liberal assumptions that poverty and suffering are not acceptable or expected parts of a progressive quest for the future, but places where an otherwise healthy society is failing to function properly.

Origins of the Welfare System

After the Civil War, the United States went through its most intense period of industrialization. With the arrival of millions of immigrants and the dramatic rise in urbanization, traditional forms of managing poverty and inequality became obsolete. Though poverty has been widespread throughout the history of the United States, the contradiction between the massive wealth that was being produced and the increasing numbers of people who wanted for the basics came to be seen as a national social crisis (Katz 1990). The United States saw a steady growth in the labor movement and the importation of what are often described as foreign ideologies such as socialism, communism, and anarchism. Rising social tensions found their expression in massive strikes such as the Homestead Strike of 1892, the Pullman Strike of 1894, the movement for the eight-hour day, and the ill-fated 1914 Ludlow coal miners' strike, which ended in a massacre (Brecher 1997; Zinn 1995).

Liberal social reformers who came to be called progressives wrote books, magazine articles, and newspaper columns with titles like *Poverty and Progress* (George 1879), *How the Other Half Lives* (Riis 1890), *Shame of the Cities* (Steffens 1904), *Poverty* (Hunter 1904), and *The Jungle* (Sinclair 1906). It was in this time of turmoil and change that U.S. culture developed many of the basic understandings of poverty and inequality that would shape the 1960s/'70s culture of poverty debate and then the 1980s homeless crisis, nearly a century later (Gordon 1994; Katz 1996).[2] It was during this "progressive era" that the state came to be seen as the principal institution for managing poverty and extreme inequality. Progressive era reformers made many changes in American life, limiting the power of corporations to control the national economy and creating laws governing workplace safety, the length of the workday, the age of the workforce, and minimum standards for housing. The work of progressives was particularly important to the more visible urban poor.

There has been much debate about the degree to which progressivism represented a new class of forward thinking technocrats (Hays 1957), older threatened elites (Hofstadter 1955), a new middle class (Wiebe 1962, 1967), socialists and social workers (Weinstein 1968), a rising labor movement (Gutman 1987), or radical journalists (Weinberg 1961). Though none of these interpretations agree on who the key players were, they all agree that the key players were liberal Americans who feared that society was becoming overly competitive, corrosive, and dysfunctional. They all shared a remarkable degree of faith in social work, social research, and state planning to restore equilibrium.

An important part of restoring equilibrium rested in differentiating between the poor and paupers. A poor person was held to be poor through bad luck or mistaken choices. This social definition carried no stigma and was generally described as "deserving poor." The poor person works, struggles, gets nowhere, and suffers in silence, asking nothing, and remains morally pure. The pauper, on the other hand, refers to the person who lives in poverty and is seen as somehow having brought the poverty upon him or herself, through bad values, poor personality traits, laziness, and so on. By definition, paupers comprised the vast majority of the poor who became publicly visible by accepting relief (Katz 1990).

Liberal reformers, such as Florence Kelley, Jane Addams, and Lincoln Steffens, used the image of paupers as the dangerous seed of social chaos to shame the affluent into supporting programs of relief and resocialization to prevent the poor from becoming paupers. Even left progressives influenced by the labor movement and socialism like Robert Hunter, who wrote the book *Poverty* in 1904, strongly distinguished between those poor who were poor through viciousness and sin and those who were poor through bad luck. These fledgling progressive era attempts to mediate between categories of badly socialized "vicious" poor people and badly socialized "robber barons" and "new rich," were the basis for later poverty programs of the New Deal and Great Society, debates over the "culture of poverty," and reified entitlement categories like homeless and underclass.

From Square Deal to New Deal: Poverty in Black and White

Though self-identified progressives would reemerge onto the national political stage from time to time in the years between the first and second World Wars,[3] World War I represented the end of the progressive era, as millions were drawn into the war effort and the U.S. government clamped down on internal criticism and dissent. Despite the excitement generated internationally by the Bolsheviks and the October Revolution of 1917, the few voices of opposition left after the war were largely cowed by a fierce period of repression and reaction. The red summer of 1919, the defeat of fragile attempts to integrate the labor movement, the Palmer raids, the Johnson-Reed Act of 1924 which restricted overseas immigration, and the growing world dominance of the U.S. economy, combined to create a social climate of triumph for big business in the 1920s that had little room for progressive reform. Though there was widespread rural poverty in the 1920s, particularly among African Americans, and a continuing urban crisis, concern for "the poor" faded from public policy circles. Without threats and inputs from below, the social reformers and progressives, who had a generation earlier relied on the specter of socialism and urban chaos to gain support for their programs, were in retreat.

It was during this period of reaction and retreat for social movements that the study of poverty became academicized. In research institutions such as the University of Minnesota and the University of Chicago, studies of poverty, paupers, and urban problems flourished. It was during this period that the most static and rigid typologies developed. Devoid of any notion of history, change or politics, the studies that came out of the Midwestern social science of poverty generally posited geography as destiny and saw physical distance as the crucial factor in keeping paupers from entering the mainstream (Park 1925; Park, Burgess, Mackenzie 1967; Shaw 1929, 1938). The famous University of Chicago concentric urban geography model is only one among many geographic models that appeared during this time. Much of the literature on tramps and other rural poor also based its social categories on physical isolation of varying degrees for urban centers of culture (Anderson 1923; Minehan 1934).

Despite the fact that the geographical paradigms were important throughout the 1930s, there was little focus on paupers and far more focus on unemployment. The great depression and the Roosevelt administration's New Deal directly confronted unemployment and the labor uprisings of 1934–35 and 1936–37. This led to public programs such as the Federal Housing Act, the Social Security Act, the Works Progress Act, the National Labor Relations Board, and the National Recovery Act (Fraser & Gerstle 1989; Leuchtenberg 1963; Tomlins 1985). The concern with the demands of an explosive labor movement took most of the focus away from paupers and put it on unemployed workers, cutting the bottom out of poverty studies and permanently weakening geographically bounded approaches.

Most of Roosevelt's programs floundered due to a mixture of lack of funds, opposition by Republicans, and Roosevelt's concern for a balanced federal budget. However, the lasting legacy of the New Deal was the rise of a national bureaucracy to manage social inequality, smooth labor relations, and regulate everyday life for the majority of Americans. The New Deal is where the origins of those who were to become the homeless can be found, as well as those who would provide the services to them. Though not a racist personally (Weiss 1983), Roosevelt excluded African Americans from most of the benefits of the New Deal (Fraser & Gerstle 1989; Katz 1990; Weir, Orloff, and Skocpol 1988). As the standard-bearer for the Democratic Party, one of the central pillars of his electoral support came from the "Dixiecrats" who controlled the Southern wing of the party. The Dixiecrats were the legacy of the 1870s defeat of Reconstruction, the return of the Southern plantocracy, and the rise of Jim Crow.

In creating the powerful Democratic Party electoral alliance that would dominate American politics for fifty years, Roosevelt practiced a political triage in which he addressed the concerns of immiserated white Americans, while sacrificing blacks. Major problems facing white workers such as housing, retirement income, minimum wage standards, and the right to strike were addressed in sectoral ways that largely excluded blacks, who were still underrepresented in trade unions, rarely received standardized wages, and were often trapped in the confines of paternalistic post–Civil War sharecropping arrangements.

Roosevelt's New Deal gave little to black Americans, while increasing the power of Dixiecrats who had yet to fully recover from the Republican dominated post–Civil War period. This alliance of the federal bureaucracy with Southern white leadership favored white workers and provided the legislative context for addressing African-American working class concerns in a language of exception and difference rather than national citizenship, social class, and equality. The New Deal bureaucracy would eventually become the caretaker of those who were not part of the world of permanent employment, trade union protection, weekly Social Security contributions, and public higher education. Black Americans were overrepresented in this group and would come to form the social and symbolic core of the 1960s golden age of poverty studies and policy that sought to address the problems of African Americans who had been excluded from the New Deal and left out of the postwar boom. (Kirby 1980; Sitkoff 1978; Weiss 1983; Wolters 1970).

Civil Rights and the Other America

It is said that John F. Kennedy was moved to tears upon reading Catholic activist and Yale law school graduate Michael Harrington's 1962 book *The Other America*. Though Kennedy was moved by Harrington's account of poverty in America, it was not until the outbreak of the 1964–71 ghetto uprisings that Lyndon Johnson began the famous war on poverty that was one of the key themes of his Great Society. In 1965 Johnson appointed Harrington to his antipoverty task force as part of the vast expansion of the welfare system and the growing connection between liberal scholarship and the welfare state.

In his book Harrington repeated what he had written many times, while editor of *The Catholic Worker:* it was feelings like shame and compassion that should "stir us to action" against economic injustices. The nonviolent combination of shame and political-economic pressure that Martin Luther King had so successfully used to further civil rights for Negroes in the Southern United States still provided little for the impoverished black ghettos of the north that had been excluded from the "affluent society." The right to vote, drink from the same water fountain, and sit with whites at lunch counters and on buses had never been officially taken away from northern blacks as it had in the South after the reversal of Reconstruction. The blacks of the urban North remained as they had in the 1920s, '30s and '40s, primarily concerned with economic equality and work site integration.

As blacks in the South began to reach the limits of the 1950s civil rights movement there was a growing frustration in both the Negro South and the black ghettos of the north. The spread of anticolonial African revolutions and the ideology of pan-Africanism along with the arrival of the charismatic and explicitly antiracist revolutionary leader Fidel Castro in central Harlem in 1962 helped create a feverish optimism for equality among youth throughout the Americas and ignited the frustrations of economically marginal black ghettos. It was neither shame nor tears that would stir a president to act against poverty; it was fear. In 1964–65 black ghettos from Rochester to Los Angeles exploded in mass violence, as calmer voices such as the Mississippi Freedom Democratic Party found their paths blocked by liberal Democrats.

As the war on poverty grew in importance with each ghetto uprising a golden age of poverty studies developed that would give ordinary academic researchers the chance to influence policies of the state and change the way people lived. In such heady times, when there were potential huge economic and professional rewards and recognition for academic work in poverty studies there was very little interest in questioning the basic paradigm that had been established by Harrington and the other early father of poverty studies, ex-communist anthropologist Oscar Lewis.[4] For three decades after the publication of *The Other America* Harrington's work provided the primary vocabulary of debate within poverty studies.

Two Nations, Two Assumptions

In the final chapter of *The Other America,* Harrington asserts, "... the United States contains an underdeveloped nation, a culture of poverty.... They are beyond history, beyond progress, sunk in a paralyzing, maiming routine"[5] (p. 158). He concludes his book by saying that "until these facts shame us, until they stir us to action, the other America will continue to exist, a monstrous example of needless suffering in the most advanced society in the world" (p. 191). In this last chapter, Harrington makes two assumptions that were crucial to nearly all subsequent literature on poverty: the poor are different and separate from the rest of the United States, and social shame is the means for ending suffering in America.

The first of these assumptions is the one that most directly created the methodology for subsequent poverty studies and has confused attempts to understand the nature of poverty. Harrington's functionalist typology divides society into two groups, or as he calls it, "two nations" (p. 158). The first nation is a cross-class group in which the system functions. The second nation, which he calls "the other America," is a place that he describes as underdeveloped, where nothing functions. Like Jacob Riis's nineteenth-century classic on urban poverty, *How the Other Half Lives,* Harrington inscribes his liberal methodology in the title of the book, assuming an "other America" and an implied "same America," neither of which he defines or delimits. Though Harrington never denies that "the other America" is populated by people who are spit out of the "same America," his dismissal of the possibility that a minimum wage store clerk, a welfare mother, a $75,000 a year truck driver, and a well paid doctor working for an HMO may represent different parts of the same category of people who share an interest in social housing, public health and education, and a national labor market militates toward a cultural model of difference expressed perfectly by the objectifying adjective "other."

Harrington actually does use the term culture, claiming that the "other America" has a separate way of life, but never explaining how the cultural traditions and social expectations of the "other America" are different from those of the same America. He neglects to suggest how these groups could be defined. He provides no defensible objective criteria for establishing his two nations. He never explains what he means by "culture" and never gives a hint at where we might find signs of a collective consciousness, self-identification, or sense of belonging for either of these two groups. Without answers to these questions the poor becomes an imagined group, reified and bounded by the fantasies of the researcher, who only needs to find a new catchphrase and population to study that is "different from you and me."

Harrington's primary category for analysis, "the other America," became the basis for subsequent research in the anthropology of poverty and inequality. Over the roughly four decades since the publication of *The Other America,* debates on poverty in America have focused on a variety of versions of this imagined category, cobbled together with often arbitrary empirical criteria. With no subjective consciousness, self-identity, or organic social organization defining "the other America" and no two researchers able to agree on a theoretical or scientifically replicable objective definition, research on poverty in America has typically used a unit of analysis defined by the poor people who are most easily seen (Katz 1996; Marcus 2003; Marcus 2005; Mitchell 1997).

This has given anthropologists, who have a strong tradition of empiricism, direct engagement with research subjects, and a tendency to imagine coherence, community, and identity, where they may not fully exist, comparative advantage over other social scientists in studying multiple "other Americas." However, it has left much of the theoretical debate on poverty in America focused on arguments over who the poor actually are and where they came from (Harrington 1984; Katz 1993; Maxwell 1993; Sawhill 1988; Wilson 1987), rather than the politics of social inequality in America.

For Harrington and later poverty scholars the political practice of poverty studies involved a second liberal assumption that guided most future research and advocacy. They believed, like their progressive era forebears, that the problems of poverty and social inequality could be solved through the use of normative values like compassion, shame, and guilt. With the proper application of these normative practices a social consensus could be reached that included everyone in a more balanced community of shared values. It would henceforth be the task of the scholar to be the conscience of society, shining the light of research on the suffering of the poor and advocating for a rebalancing of society.

With their social harmony model of life in a competitive economy and a level of advancement that clearly provided for more than enough resources for everyone, poverty scholars had to find some person or group of people to blame for having deviated from the social imperative of order. In the case of Harrington it was the shameless. Though he never precisely defines who this group is, we may take him to mean politicians, the smug, the self-satisfied, the wealthy, and the greedy of all classes. Harrington also identified the social, cultural, and educational isolation of many of America's poorest (particularly those in rural areas) as a key challenge for eliminating poverty, thus creating a second category of dysfunctional or deviant Americans. It remained for later scholars to wage public debates in journals and at conferences over who was most dysfunctional and responsible for the poverty, the wealthy or the poor.

The scholars, politicians, and advocates who followed the approach of liberal Weberian Harvard professor and advisor to president Richard Nixon Daniel Patrick Moynihan in his assertion that there was a culture of poverty suggest policies intended to shame the poor back into the mainstream. Though these policies often involved the expansion of programs for the poor, particularly educational projects such as Head Start that were designed to resocialize them, the overall approach was to try to wean people off public assistance. It was probably also this approach that promoted the many ritual humiliations involved in the growing welfare system. The most famous and specific of these humiliations is the use of separate currency known as United States Department of Agriculture Food Stamps, for basic nutrition for the poor. Never before had programs for housing, food, education, and health care used such complex, specific and bureaucratized method's for distinguishing many different levels and types of paupers from poor.

Within this vast bureaucracy represented by politicians, civil servants, social workers, and academics, new categories regularly emerged to describe the groups of visible poor who continued to haunt American cities and inspire a combination of fear, disgust, and compassion. Some of the most popular and famous categories of paupers and pauper-geography that came to be discussed and debated within this literature were the underclass, the underprivileged, the truly disadvantaged, the ghetto superpredator, the inner-city, the career criminal, the slum dweller, and finally the homeless. For most of these categories, the name itself implied the disease and the cure.

On the other side of the culture of poverty debates were a group of liberals who believed that they were closer to the spirit of Harrington's work in suggesting that the most dysfunctional perpetuators of the problem were those at the top of society. Rejecting the notion that the poor were poor because of faulty values, they stressed what later came to be called "macrostructures"[6] or the shamelessness of the system as a whole. Their work generally focused on the way poor people managed, through cleverness and good values, to adapt to the meager environment in which they were placed. The most celebrated of these works was Carol B. Stack's *narodnik* criticism of Oscar Lewis in the book *All Our Kin*. Set in a black ghetto which she refers to as "the Flats," her vision of poverty is a world of female solidarity and community cooperation to make up for the economic inadequacies of welfare. Implicit in her work is the idea that the poor actually have better liberal values than the mainstream, rather than worse ones.

These scholars working in the Durkheimian tradition of privileging the division of labor put particular focus on shaming and blaming those on top, whom they held to be more responsible for social policy. Early in this debate adjectives like greedy, uncompassionate, and beholden to "corporate America" were used to describe those who exacerbated the problem or impeded relief. This literature openly called for sacrificing American profitability to a more just society and clearly identified those who benefited from the continued pauperization of large numbers of Americans. As the political climate in America became more staid and conservative in the 1970s and 1980s this direct terminology for protecting the honor of victims of poverty and criticizing the perceived victimizers yielded to increasingly vague and ill-defined terms borrowed from 1970s academic Marxism such as deindustrialization, postfordism, and globalization (see for example Hopper, Susser, and Conover 1986).

The underlying assumption of this intellectual tendency was that people would stay on welfare and therefore needed more socially generous policies that did not create such torment at the bottom.[7] Their social recommendations generally involved economic expansion of the welfare system. They argued for more social workers, bigger benefits, more child care programs, more food stamps, vocational programs, and other ways of making life on welfare better able to provide for the social expectations of families.

As the welfare state continued to shrink through the late 1970s and early 1980s, these advocates for more support at the bottom became increasingly specific about who needed social intervention. It was in this climate of retreat from the big goals of the 1960s Great Society liberalism that a final category of pauper came into the political lexicon. It was an individual who was not defined by the lack of the basics of life in America such as a proper environment to raise children, a social safety net for tough times, an overall class background or way of life, or even a location like the ghetto. This individual became defined solely in terms of a lack of location: homeless. The concern that had once been directed toward "urban renewal," "the culture of poverty," and "the dark ghetto" was suddenly focused on the homeless and the name presaged the treatment: building shelters and addressing the problems that people encountered inside them.

Notes

1. It may prove to be important that at the turn of the twenty-first century, when Marxism is finally disappearing as an intellectual paradigm, Social Darwinism is reemerging.
2. For a look at the prehistory of the homeless crisis, see Alice Sollenberger (1911) for a progressive era study of "homeless" men and social work in pre-WWI Chicago.
3. The most spectacular re-emergence was the 1924 presidential election in which Progressive Party candidate Robert La Follette took 4.8 million popular votes, and 13 Electoral College votes. At roughly 17 percent of the popular vote, this is the third highest total for a third-party candidate in the twentieth century, after Theodore Roosevelt's anti-Debs/ anti-Tariffs Bull Moose run of 1912 and Ross Perot's 19 percent (Perot failed to win a single electoral vote) in 1992.
4. Lewis's work, which preceded Harrington's, was somewhat atypical of later work on poverty due to his insistence that self-emancipation through social organization was the principal road to economic equality for those who had missed the "affluent society." However, he and Harrington shared many of the same liberal assumptions, which had helped define the welfare academic complex.
5. That Harrington uses the word underdeveloped is worth noting for the suggestion of an active force from somewhere else that has underdeveloped it. This dynamic view of the creation and maintenance of poverty generally disappeared from later works.
6. Though the term macrostructures has the sound of 1970s Althusarian Marxism, those who used this approach were far closer to Harrington's class-blind assertion that there was a poor America and a non-poor America and that it was the lack of concern, knowledge, or compassion of the non-poor America that was to blame.
7. There was a branch of this literature that argued that only through an expansion of the welfare system and an expansion of the benefits could people have enough comfort and security to make the difficult transition from welfare to steady employment.

Chapter 5

SHELTERIZATION:
IN THE LAND OF THE HOMELESS

"Shelterization can be described as a process of acculturation endemic to shelter living…. The adaptation to shelter life includes the development of a shelter vocabulary, the assimilation of shelter themes, the acceptance of shelter ideals and beliefs, and an eroding will."

Jeffrey Grunberg and Paula Eagle (1990: 522–524)

Like the *Star Wars* trilogy that appeared during this same period, the homeless crisis became an important national drama, despite its stereotyped characters, hackneyed moral and thin plot. This was because the homeless drama presented a strongly directed seamless and archetypal vision of familiar themes, characters, and moral dilemmas regarding race, poverty and social inequality that was resonant for many Americans. One of the crucial factors that made it possible to realize a new national drama involving so many of the same old actors and story lines was what film theorists call the mise-en-scène, or what is seen in the frame.

Among the most compelling aspects of this mise-en-scène were the spectacular and evocative sets, costumes, and locations that made up the land of the homeless. Life for most of my informants who were living in the shelter was often a mundane struggle to get a long enough extension cord for a steam iron or figure out how to get phone messages from a certain pay phone in a shelter. However, the distance between audience and performer was more than enough to conjure up Dantean visions of urban nightmare infernos.

Like movies that use day for night filming, where murky backlit scenes and silhouettes establish night while gradual increases in light and continuity errors like automobiles without headlights burning fail to reveal that all the action is being filmed in bright daylight, the homeless crisis created a largely convincing image of utter darkness.

As ragged beggars drifted into formerly respectable residential neighborhoods and news reports and public service announcements showed men huddling for warmth around fires in metal garbage cans images were presented of women and men who it was said could be grandparents, parents, or siblings pushing shopping carts containing all their worldly possessions. "We are all only two paychecks away from homelessness" asserted one of the key political slogans connected to the public discussion of homelessness.

Such dramatic day for night settings were more than enough to convince most ordinary Americans that there was a homeless crisis. In fact large numbers of people in many cities were without proper housing and were becoming more socially visible by the day. Rising center city rents, the elimination of skid rows through physical renewal and increased property values, the decline of public housing subsidies, stagnant welfare and Social Security benefits, and the elimination of vast quantities of substandard or unprofitable prewar housing stock was driving some people to pay higher rent and others out onto the streets. Nearly everybody who rented housing in New York City came to realize how precious their domicile was and identified in some way with the homeless.

It was in this climate of concern for those who had been spit out of their domiciles that the New York City municipal shelter system grew from one small shelter at 8 East 3rd Street in Manhattan to twenty-five massive warehouse-like facilities, housing an average of nine thousand adults per night in 1988 (Fantasia and Isserman 1994). This tremendous expansion had started with the landmark court case known as *Callahan v. Carey*. In this case, a civil rights attorney named Robert Hayes brought a law suit against the city and state of New York in 1979 on behalf of a short-order cook named Robert Callahan. Callahan had been without work for four years and had been evicted from his apartment. He had attempted to find shelter at the East 3rd Street municipal facility which was, at the time, the only public shelter in New York City. The case was based on both legal precedent and customary conduct. Hayes argued that the New York State's constitution of 1938 provided the right to shelter and that the practice of New York City providing shelter for the indigent had been customary since the nineteenth century.

The New York Supreme Court granted an immediate preliminary injunction requiring the city to provide "shelter (including bedding, wholesome food and adequate security and supervision) to any person who applies for shelter at the Men's Shelter." Then-mayor Edward I. Koch responded by opening a temporary shelter on Wards Island in the middle of the East River, which was rapidly filled. When the case was finally settled in 1981, the City of New York agreed to provide shelter and food to any man (later applied to women too) in need of home relief or temporary shelter. This led to the vast expansion of the homeless shelter system in New York City and the social science research that accompanied it.

There were probably thousands of isolated individuals living in the interstitial semipublic spaces of New York City and passing days as public nuisances begging for quarters and far more people employed in low-wage temporary work that kept their housing status perpetually uncertain and forced them to live in bad situations in crowded apartments, where any night might be the last one. It was, however, as Kim Hopper observed in *Private Lives/Public Spaces*, difficult to define, locate, or help these individuals in the places where their problems had developed. The social science of the underhoused or homelessology could not become an academic growth area until there was a real physical environment in which to study and engage this exotic group of New York's most underemployed and underhoused. The shelters provided the perfect location and the *Callahan v. Carey* settlement provided the perfect guarantee that this was an issue that would be important for years to come.

Though it had been initiated as an ad hoc emergency response to cold winters and public spaces crowded with bodies, the municipal shelter system went far beyond the everyday mise-en-scène of homeless advocacy. Drawing thousands of non-white New Yorkers, with a variety of long-term or immediate housing problems, the municipal shelter system became a vast multi-site interactive poverty theme park for researchers, poor non-white New Yorkers, and caregivers in a new version of the "Other America."

Shelterization and Its Discontents

In 1987, United States President Ronald Reagan signed into law the Stewart B. McKinney Act on Homeless Relief, apportioning one billion dollars in federal aid to homeless research and relief. Though homelessness had been an important issue in both the social sciences and popular culture since the early 1980s, the passage of this key piece of federal legislation created an unprecedented boom in homeless services, research, and advocacy. Much of this money was directed toward work in the shelters. In 1990 Jeffrey Grunberg and Paula Eagle launched the debate over shelterization[1] with their controversial article entitled "Shelterization: How the Homeless Adapt to Shelter Living" (see epigraph for this chapter). In it they raised concerns over the long-term behavioral and psychological effects of shelters on the individuals who resided in them.[2] Describing New York City municipal shelters as hellish places where deviant behavior such as public sex, homosexual rape, drug addiction, money lending, organized violence, and lack of personal grooming had become naturalized into a set of norms and behavioral patterns, they raised fundamental concerns about the value of public shelters and questioned whether New York City homeless policy was "doing no harm." Furthermore, their assertion that shelter residents became acculturated to a "shelter subculture," which

they described as "physically similar to the early life surroundings of homeless people who have emerged from ghetto dwellings" (Grunberg and Eagle
1990: 521, 522), suggested yet another new version of the culture of poverty theory that had sparked so much controversy in the 1960s and '70s.

Though much of the applied research on homelessness at the time focused on such psychosocial problems connected to the experience of
being homeless, most commentators did recognize that the underlying
problem was underemployment and a shortage of permanent low-cost
housing (Blau 1992; Gerstel et al. 1996; Hopper 1990; Hopper, Susser,
Conover 1986; Rochefort and Cobb 1992; Susser 1996). However, this was
generally viewed as a structural environmental problem, requiring solutions that were beyond the immediate power of local governments and
the social scientists advising them. Instead, much of the research and re-
sulting literature focused on questions of institutional reform for the
emergency and transitional housing system and counting, recruiting, and
providing psychosocial and social service remediation for the homeless
(Dehavenon 1995; Dinkins and Cuomo 1992; Hopper 1992, 1995; Lovell,
Barrow, Streuning 1992; Stark 1994; Susser et al. 1997; Susser 1993; Susser
and Gonzalez 1992).

This focus was greatly strengthened by the funding environment of the
late 1980s. Drastic cuts in funding for social services and social research
during the "Reagan Revolution" of the 1980s gave particularly great weight
to the $589 million over two years that the McKinney Act initially commit-
ted to programs tied to "supportive housing,"[3] "service-intensive shelters,"
and demonstration projects that brought together issues of sheltering and
psychosocial training (Bogard et al. 1999; U.S. Congress 1987; Gerstel et al.
1996; Toro and Warren 1991).[4] In this context, the dramatic representations
of shelter behavior as a self-perpetuating pathology offered by Grunberg
and Eagle, a clinical psychologist and a psychiatrist, captured the spirit of
the moment and did much to steer debate about homelessness and shelter life further in the direction of psychosocial rather than socioeconomic
explanations.

Most researchers were deeply skeptical of Grunberg and Eagle's sensa-
tional accounts of shelter life, use of the culture concept to explain shelter
behavior, and faith in psychiatry as a panacea for curing the shelterized.
Kim Hopper, in his December 1990 letter to *Hospital and Community Psychiatry* went as far as to describe Grunberg and Eagle as presenting a view that
"borders on recklessness." Even those who embraced the term shelterization were dubious about describing it as a culture, subculture, or alternative
form of socialization (DeOllos 1997; Gounis 1990, 1992; Stark 1994; Susser
and Gounis 1990). They generally rejected Grunberg and Eagle's concepts
of adaptation, acculturation, and mastery and instead opted for a more
cautious model of shelter life that identified a provisional and often an-
tagonistic tension between the institutional environment and behavior.

At the core of the criticism of Grunberg and Eagle, was an argument
over the proper approach to institutional studies. Grunberg and Eagle like

most other researchers who took up the question of shelter behavior, presented an underlying belief that shelters represented, to a greater or lesser degree, what Erving Goffman had called a total institution. Goffman had defined the total institution as "a place of residence and work where a large number of like-situated individuals, cut off from the wider society for an appreciable period of time, together lead an enclosed, formally administered round of life" (Goffman 1961: xiii). He included prisons, mental hospitals, boarding schools, and work camps in his catalogue of "total institutions" and identified two categories of people, inmates and staff, who were affected in different ways and to different degrees by being part of a total institution.

Recognizing that even the most "enclosed" institution was highly permeable and dependent on the outside world, Goffman explicitly rejected the idea of an institutional culture, insisting that "total institutions do not substitute their own unique culture for something already formed; we deal with something more restricted than acculturation or assimilation" (Goffman 1961: 13). Grunberg and Eagle held shelters to be far more "total" than the prisons, boarding schools, military forces, and other institutions discussed by Goffman. However, their work both explicitly (Grunberg and Eagle 1990: 523) and implicitly engaged the "total institution" model and provided the basis for a discussion of how influential, how permeable, and how "total" was the institutional life of the New York City municipal shelters (Gounis 1993; Stark 1994; Timmer 1994).

Such an approach abstracted shelter life from the surrounding city, overemphasized the shelter's impact on the behavior of residents, and often explained the persistence of homelessness through reference to the psychocultural effects of shelter norms. Whether interpreting shelters as largely impermeable institutions that resocialize inmates as did Grunberg and Eagle or semipermeable "total institutions" that force temporary adaptations as did their critics (DeOllos 1997; Gounis 1992; Stark 1994; Susser and Gounis 1990), the use of the total institution paradigm had the effect of suggesting that the shelter environment was far more important in residents' lives than it usually was. This chapter will expand on the approach advocated by researchers who argued that shelters imposed a variety of physical constraints and social impediments on residents, some of them quite significant, but no systematic changes in socialization or culture (Bogard et al. 1999; Gerstel et al. 1996; Hopper 1990; Snow et al. 1994) and that shelter stays were generally too short to conform to the shelterization model (Culhane et al. 1998; Link et al. 1994; Phelan and Link 1999). New York City municipal men's shelters were neither cultural spaces that redefined the self, nor "total institutions" that radically reorganized behavioral patterns. They generally constituted little more than places to sleep that underhoused individuals drifted in and out of over the course of days, months and years.

The use of the metaphor of the "total institution" led to weak explanation and problematic policy that was based on the assumption that there was an enclosed community sharing homeless-specific problems that could be treated with homeless specific interventions. It will be argued that the focus on "total institutions" and behavioral problems connected to them derived from a combination of a number of factors: the power of the McKinney Act to define and delimit the unit of analysis of research as "homeless"; the difficulty of studying peripatetic individuals in parks, subways, basements, friends' living rooms, and the like; and the shared experience of like situated (Goffman 1961) researchers projecting and generalizing on their own McKinney Act driven experience of working in shelters for months or years. In short, if there were shelterized individuals experiencing something approaching a "total institution" it was researchers who sometimes never met their informants outside the shelters.

The Fort: Total Research Institution

Of all the research settings for studying the homeless, a public shelter is the one that could most easily be a set for a movie about hell. The Fort Washington Men's Shelter was in a huge old city armory that filled the equivalent of a city block at the corner of 168th Street and Fort Washington Avenue in upper Manhattan. An aging gray stone edifice, built to control unruly turn-of-the-century immigrant mobs, the three-story structure had a vast size which seemed even more impressive when compared to the tiny barred windows and diminutive entrance on the side of the building. Past metal detectors and guards who frisked everyone at the gate, the sun and sky disappeared at the narrow entrance to the ancient foot-worn stairs up to the shelter living areas.

The low-ceilinged donut-shaped first-floor corridor that ran the length of the block was crowded with African American and Latino men in every state of dress and undress. Inner city Goliaths wore sleeveless white cotton singlets that revealed massive "cut" prison yard bodybuilding physiques, while six-foot-plus long-legged black she-males with fully grown breasts from hormone injections wandered amid improvised barbershops and beauty salons made from folding metal chairs and white towels. In the distance rats scurried under ancient standing metal radiators in the empty Eastern end of the long hallway.

A dark room off the hall revealed dozens of men dozing under the faint blue light radiating from an aging nineteen-inch color television mounted high up in a corner. Past the TV room, the hallway curved around to the other side of the building where ropes marked off the cafeteria line and its conflicts over stale bologna sandwiches and mealy apples. Even the air was different in "the Fort." Industrial disinfectant mingled with the smell of human sweat, cafeteria food and residual radiator moisture. Not unbearable, the smell was unpleasant and just nauseating enough to put one a little on edge.

A guard sat at a card table by the huge white tiled bathroom dispensing pieces of toilet paper and soap chips, while a tall ragged, probably mentally ill African American man with a wandering eye and dozens of rubber bands embedded in his forehead talked to himself and waited for his self-created exercise in ritual scarification to be complete. I was studying the "exotic other" in a field site made as distant as the deepest recesses of the Amazon by the distinctions of the American system of caste and social class. Uptown, I was "upriver."[5]

Ascending the broad open staircase at the end of the first floor corridor, the third-world bazaar of used small electronics, hair cutting, drug deals, and other petty commerce gave way to the vast drill floor where nearly seven hundred beds stretched out in long rows spaced two feet apart. The wooden floor was larger than a football field, and was enclosed high above by a cavernous sloping, domed ceiling. This main room was like something between an indoor sports arena and one of the orphans' workhouses in *Oliver Twist*. Residents were forbidden to go up into the bleachers that ringed the room about twenty-five feet above the floor, where the director of the shelter had his office.

At one end of the drill floor was a giant steel shutter door that was raised electronically every morning, including in winter, "in order to air this smelly place out," as shelter workers put it. This was also seen as a way of getting residents out of bed and making it too cold to comfortably stay there during the day. The director of the shelter and a few of his assistants parked their cars at the end by the steel gate, displacing beds to create space for the cars to be parked and washed with hoses and sponges by shelter residents in return for a few dollars.

The men near the center of the drill floor, who continued to sleep through the noise, cold air, and movement of a late winter mid-morning, lay on metal cots with spindly iron legs stuck into tennis shoes, oxfords, boots, and all variety of other footwear. For those who had no permanent home, had little spending money, and constantly risked a night on the streets, footwear was one of the keys to survival and was a prime target of theft. Despite the common precaution of putting the legs of one's bed into shoes and tying the shoes to bed frames with tight knots, some shelter residents told me that they had actually lost shoes to thieves who lifted up their bed while they slept.

At the far northeastern corner of the drill floor a few beds had been pushed together and lashed in place with tightly coiled belts. Most were empty due to the proximity to the open gate and the cars being washed, but one or two still held sleeping couples composed of the large muscled "husbands" and fully breasted she male "wives" that I had heard made up "shelter marriages."

The Sexual Mythology of the Shelter

The shelter marriage was at the heart of the sexual mythology of shelterization. To new observers and recent arrivals the "shelter marriages" between macho prison yard bodybuilders and feminine transvestites constituted the most dramatic example of imagined difference, exotic "otherness," and the perversion of ordinary social standards. However, this view assumed exactly what needed to be proven: that such activity would not have occurred without the shelter to facilitate it.

During the 1980s many of New York's shelters housed transvestites, whose economic marginality was exacerbated by a tightening New York area job market, reductions in public assistance, and rising rents for the group apartments they often shared, leading to intolerable housing densities. Many returned to natal families only to move out onto the streets or into shelters as they found it impossible to "go home again." Among the public shelters in New York City, "the Fort" was known as a meeting place for transvestites and was often referred to as "fag house." The many transvestites and prison bodybuilders who were sexually involved led many shelter workers, researchers, and residents to conclude that "the Fort" was a place where gay men were dominant.

For most of my colleagues and informants, even those who were not homophobic, this was a sign of a different set of social norms than existed outside the shelter. The notion that "the Fort" was a place where such open violations of ordinary social rules occurred was generally understood as a sign of the breakdown of social norms and their replacement by codes of conduct that could not possibly help shelter residents get their lives back on track.

This assumption that gay men had established same-sex contact as the norm was so widespread that during a government site visit to inspect our research project, a site inspector asked me if it was true what he had heard in Washington, "that in the Fort gangs of gay men hold power through violence and intimidation." He went on to ask if the straight men living in the shelter felt threatened by this "gay space." During the daylong site visit many presentations reinforced the belief that the shelter was dominated by a gay Mafia that dealt drugs, loan-sharked, and used violence to control shelter resources.

This perspective was strongly contradicted by the experiences of all my informants who consciously identified as gay. They all felt that gay life in the shelter was a lot like gay life outside the shelter. As an African American gay informant of mine used to say, "the only thing worse than being homeless is being gay and homeless." I had another informant who spent occasional nights in the shelter with his boyfriend but kept their relationship secret out of fear of being attacked. He explained how he saw the situation:

> These big gorillas get out of prison come live here and figure they can own everything. They got the food line, they got the showers, they got every damn thing in here including the girls (transvestites). Hell, most of the guys probably have wives or girlfriends outside. You watch sometime, they act as if they don't know those shelter girls the minute they get out on the streets. No hand holding, no kissing, no nothing. Those are straight men that want somebody warm to sleep with and somebody to stick it in at night. Men will stick it anywhere.

They stick it in a fag don't mean they fags. They stick it in sheep don't mean they're farm animals. It's the gay men that's afraid to touch their boyfriends.

Another African American man who had struggled unsuccessfully for years to get his family to accept his homosexuality put the problem of confusion over life inside and outside in the clearest terms:

Those guys ain't gay. There ain't one of them that had to tell his mama that he likes to do it with men. There ain't one of them that had trouble finding work cuz he's gay. There ain't one of them that fell asleep on the piers after a trick. [a reference to the famous gay cruising spot at Christopher Street and the Hudson River] There sure as hell ain't one of them that ever wished they were Donna Summer. They're just a bunch of horny prison hoods that want to put their dick in something warm. None of them was ever chased home by a gang of teenagers yelling kill the fag. I been a fag all my life and this shelter is just another place where you have to spend your time hiding yourself.

The researchers, journalists, and government officials who were swapping cowboy stories and describing an upside-down upriver world where the patterns of everyday life were inverted were not taking into account traditional patterns of behavior by straight men who are deprived of women[6] and were defining homosexuality solely in terms of their temporary sexual encounters rather than a fundamental change in sexual identity (D'Emilio 1988). The myth that men having sex with transvestites in the dark made the Fort Washington Men's Shelter a "gay space" was premised on a model which held that the shelter was a separate and different environment from the outside world and that it had its own culture which transformed people into something other than what they were when they had entered.

Inside and Outside the Fort

A more important reason that my colleagues and our informants were mistaking this very negative environment for gay men for a "gay space" was a problematic understanding of the overall nature of the shelter and its role in neighborhood and city life. They were using Goffman's model of the total institution and creating a typological isolate in which people were defined solely by their behavior in the shelter, thus ignoring the majority of their days. The surprise I felt upon seeing a huge bodybuilder from the eastern end of the shelter politely holding a stack of boxes while waiting for me to enter an auto parts store a few blocks from the shelter where he sometimes worked reminded me of the shock that children often have when they see their teachers outside the classroom and realize that they have an existence, independent of their teaching duties.

This relationship between the inside and outside of the shelter became even clearer when a Cuban shelter resident I knew took a job as bookkeeper at a local store that often hired day laborers from the shelter to do heavy lifting. In this little grocery store, my skinny middle-aged Cuban informant at times acted as the de facto boss to men of the sort that he generally feared in the shelter. Though he had no real power to hire and fire the men who unloaded trucks for the shop, he was clearly far more important to the shop owner than the interchangeable hired muscle.

The bookkeeper and hired laborers kept a relatively polite distance in the shop and acknowledged each other's presence in the shelter. The law of the jungle that commentators believed was operative in the shelter was clearly subordinate to the experience these men had working in the outside world. Since all parties involved were more committed to and dependent on their work than the shelter, the division of mental and manual labor that existed outside the shelter gave my Cuban informant more overall social power. He earned enough to eat his meals at the bar and Chinese restaurant across from the shelter, while the people who worked with him fought it out over stale baloney sandwiches in the shelter cafeteria. In a prison or other "total institution" where people are not free to stay or leave as they choose, the tough guys at the Eastern end of the shelter might have stood second to the staff in a hierarchy of power. However, amidst the crowds of New York, the merchants on Broadway hoping to sell their products and services, and the police with their monopoly on the use of violence, they were far less imposing.

"The Fort" was neither a site of social contagion that threatened to turn ordinary Americans into dysfunctional shelterized savages nor a miraculous oasis from "heterosexism" where community building "muscle queen" gay men had triumphed over the vast anonymity of heterosexuality. "The Fort" was a very sad place that provided a small part of the housing strategy for poor New Yorkers. The tough guys at the eastern end of the shelter were probably heterosexual men whose poverty and sociopolitical weakness had damned them to being under the spotlight of observation while engaging in a variety of socially proscribed, but not unusual behaviors.

Bed, Bath and Beyond

Those social scientists who did not succumb to Grunberg and Eagle's descriptions of exotic shelter subcultures generally counterposed sensationalist "upriver" data with proof of the persistence of normal life in the shelter. They matched signs of social breakdown with signs of mutual aid and showed the ways in which ordinary New Yorkers struggled to survive and even make a decent life for themselves despite the dangers and substandard conditions in the shelter. In short, they argued that the excesses of the shelters were an exception to what were, for the most part, ordinary people trying to maintain the patterns of their lives. Though they did not deny the deviant behavior that existed in the shelter, they argued that approaches that focused solely on such behavior confused attempts to resolve the social problem of homelessness by falsely demonizing and stereotyping many ordinary people who were forced to live in the shelter (DeHavenon 1995; Shinn 1992; Snow, Anderson, Koegel 1994).

These approaches to studying shelter life that avoided "blaming the victim" and stressed the persistence of ordinary values present a far more accurate description of the complexity of shelter life. However, their attempts to match the deviant with the ordinary do not fully disprove the claim that acculturation to a set of distinct and deviant norms is a powerful force shaping shelter life. They merely suggest that at any given time there are shelter residents who have not been acculturated. This may be due either to extenuating circumstances or to the duration of time required to become fully acculturated to the shelter.

What most researchers on both sides of this debate failed to recognize was that the description of the drill floor as bedroom to nearly seven hundred men (Gounis 1993) was more than a metaphor, it was a fact. The interpretation of abuse, violence, revenge, strange sexual practices, drug use, and compulsive or obsessive behavior as shelterization was based on the premise that shelter residents were acting abnormally in public and that such behaviors do not occur among normal unshelterized people. However, the shelter was neither the public space that most researchers imagined nor the private space that most residents dreamed of. In many ways the shelter was like a giant apartment share or roommate situation. As one of my informants told me when I asked about how it is possible to sleep surrounded by total strangers, "you'll never get any sleep if you don't get comfortable, but you always have to remember there's six hundred guys who also want to get comfortable."

The shelter was, in fact, a giant room that was somewhere between a subway car and a private bedroom in an empty locked apartment. The idea that a space is either public or private misses the fact that the level of deviance and the social power of the deviant determine the amount of privacy and secrecy necessary to avoid notice and trouble. Heterosexual couples are allowed far more freedom to express their sexuality in public displays and risk far less notice and weaker sanctions if caught. Privacy is determined by more than merely doors, walls, locks, and other physical barriers. It is also determined by who is made aware of an act. This is why "love motels" have individual locked garages for the cars of heterosexual couples who are "cheating" and need to hide their automobiles as much as they need to hide their bodies.

If there was a distinct characteristic that defined shelter living, it was the blurring of the public and private that was forced by sharing a bedroom with over six hundred men. Most of my informants were very conscious of this blurring of public and private, seeing the outside world as the place where they would be judged to be appropriate or inappropriate and the shelter as a semiprivate space, where they made every attempt to be as private as possible, but inevitably needed an outlet for their "private lives" despite the "public spaces." It was not, in fact, the unified, coherent, and sedentary culture of the shelter that created so much deviant behavior. To the contrary, it was the transitory anonymity that allowed some illusion of privacy and the possibility to "get comfortable enough to sleep."

With such a large, varied, and ever-changing population, the shelter was a site of tremendous amounts of socially proscribed behavior, as commentators advocating the shelterization hypothesis argued, as well as a site of relatively normal activity by people battling to get by, as critics of the shelterization hypothesis argued. Most of the deviant behavior my informants engaged in derived from patterns and needs that they brought with them to the shelter and not from shelter-induced acculturation. What made life inside the shelter appear different from life outside the shelter was that the deviant behavior and strange acting out that is usually reserved for the home, the bedroom, or the family was visible to social scientists, like myself, who were paid to surreptitiously watch people in their beds, showers, and television rooms.

In the way that long-hidden, usually tolerated, and sometimes even appreciated family deviance becomes fully public in nasty divorces, lawsuits, and the gossip of loose-lipped psychoanalysts, social scientists studying the shelter had a privileged view into the inner recesses of thousands of people's personal lives. In an unusual twist of fate, they were able to see a broader vision of the inability to fully fit square humans into the round hole of social norms and public life. The man who doesn't feel like getting up on a Sunday morning and urinates into a glass by the bed and the one who likes to be slapped while having sex lived side by side in the shelter. Morning people had to share space with night owls and people who cannot sleep without masturbating first. The macho heterosexual man who wears women's underwear and the straight conservative family man who uses the services of young male street hustlers after work coexisted with all variety of angry fathers and forgotten middle children in this giant bedroom. There were people who urinated in the shower and those who were disgusted by such behavior, bodybuilders, people who were intimidated by bodybuilders, and those who could only resolve conflict through yelling.

My informants were as sure as my research colleagues that the deviant behaviors that occurred in the shelter were ones that would be better hidden. They accepted that there was something crazy about somebody who acted on private needs in a space that was as public as the shelter drill floor. However, they also recognized that the demands of public presentation are difficult, if not impossible, to sustain forever, without "going crazy." Despite being forced to witness fetishes that were different from their own and acts that they regarded as objectionable, there was a fair amount of forgiveness and flexibility among residents, who understood that "you'll never get any sleep if you don't get comfortable."

This sense of the contradictions inherent in the blurring of public and private engendered on the shelter drill floor was often missed by literature on shelterization. Instead of taking the opportunity to violate the privacy of thousands of people and discover our own world through more than divorce proceedings, Ken Starr reports, and hidden video cameras in local motels, homeless life was externalized, made exotic, and put into cultural terms. Neither side of the debate over shelterization considered that people do a lot of peculiar things in their beds, baths, and surrounding environs that do not explain their successes, failures, and ability to get and keep housing.

Side by Side But Not Together: A Partial Institution

It is stating the obvious to say that environment affects the behavior and perspective of individuals; therefore that shelters are of some importance in determining action and results. However, "total institutions" are total because they narrow individuals into one environment with one set of customary behaviors, one set of social places and one primary authority. Homeless shelters were just one environment among many that my informants engaged with in their daily lives. The acculturation concept represents something yet more totalizing than a total institution. It represents a collective regime of environment and behavior that is conscious, is self-perpetuating, and depends on individuals internalizing the norms and ideas of that regime.

Homeless shelters did not follow either the acculturation or the total institution model. They were not enclosed, conscious communities, and there was little in the way of collective institutional life and very few residents who could be described as cut off from the outside world and without access to other environments. Though the shelter was a large-scale institution and a built environment where people slept when they felt they had no other choice, it did not structure men's lives the way prisons, mental hospitals, and the armed forces do. In such totalizing environments as these leaving is difficult or impossible and people have a tremendous stake in finding a social place, because, for better or worse, they are home.

The lack of a comfortable, secure place to call home can have a devastating effect on a person's self-image and personality, and the quality of the place where a person sleeps can be the difference between life and death. However, the notion that public shelters could create a culture, a personality type, or a set of customary responses (positive or negative) on the part of transitory residents is methodologically unsustainable. The freedom that residents had to come and go and the relative anonymity that they retained while living in the shelter prevented the development of a set of behavioral complexes that could be seen as totalizing.

There were men who spent weekends at girlfriends' houses and the week at the shelter and some who ate meals at a relative's house, but slept at the shelter. Others used shelters as poverty motels, where they went for a night or two to escape a crowded multiple roommate situation, and some only resided in a shelter for a few nights when they needed help with applications for government social programs. Regardless of what brought them into the shelter and how much choice they had over where to sleep, there were always other environments, institutions, and influences that they were forced to contend with every day. The power of the outside world was never fully hidden by the stone walls and musty humid air of the shelter.

The notion of shelters as a site of social contagion that recast the character and sense of self, restructured residents' behavior, prevented the development of healthy habits in dysfunctional people, or threatened to infect functional people with dysfunctional values imputed too much importance to the physical space and extrapolated a culture, collective consciousness, or group design onto what was little more than a huge bedroom and some public space. Shelter residents entered the shelters carrying with them the prejudices, aspirations, kinship patterns, ideal social norms and individual deviations from those norms that are ubiquitous in the United States. They left with most of the same ideas and behaviors with which they entered. Like most New York City apartment buildings, office buildings, and other locations where large numbers of people come and go every day, the shelter was a space of relative anonymity and alienation. More like a beach on a crowded day than a unified institution, community, or small town, the human networks within the shelter mirrored the dispersed and atomized surrounding city.

Conclusion: Whose Total Institution Is It Anyway?

The problem of selecting, using, and defending a given unit of analysis is one of the critical decisions that scientists must make in developing any conclusions from primary data. This is as true for an anthropologist studying the Nuer, the Bushmen, or the Trobriand Islanders as for a physicist who must decide what factors to exclude from discussions of the nature and behavior of subatomic particles, or an historian who must decide what period to study.

During the homeless crisis of the 1980s and early 1990s there were tens of thousands of isolated individuals and families living in the interstitial semipublic spaces of New York City and passing days as public nuisances begging for quarters. There were hundreds of thousands of people facing rising housing costs while employed in low-wage or temporary work, making their housing status perpetually uncertain and forcing them to live in bad situations and crowded apartments, where their housing situation was in constant jeopardy. As Baxter and Hopper had observed in 1981, it was very difficult to define, locate, count, or help these individuals in the places where their problems had developed (Baxter and Hopper 1981; Hopper 1992, 1995). Social science and social remediation that focused on housing loss required a real physical environment in which to study and engage the target population. The shelters provided the perfect location for such studies. However, some researchers ended up studying the shelters rather than their occupants.

Like many of my colleagues researching homelessness in the municipal shelters and other institutions set aside for emergency housing, it took me only a few minutes on fieldwork to believe that I was in an exotic differ-ent world apart from the New York City in which I lived and had grown up. The otherness of the physical location led me to see another culture rather than the revealed darker side of the everyday life of my own cul-ture. The minute I left the shelter at the end of the day, it seemed I was in a different world where there was far less deviance. It was easy to believe that the shelters were composed of "like situated individuals together" (Goffman 1961) and that there was something about the environment that made people deviant.

What I and many of my fellow researchers and the social service pro-viders often did not realize at the time was that McKinney Act funding that created many opportunities for homeless research at a time when the Reagan Revolution was reducing so many other funding sources made us "like-situated individuals ... together lead[ing] an enclosed, formally ad-ministered round of life." As researchers, we were literally tracked into studying the homeless in the shelters where they were plentiful and easy to study in a way that enabled us to fulfill our obligations to the govern-ment agencies that funded our research.

In such a situation in which the field site and the social typologies are overdetermined by external parameters such as funding guidelines and the pressure for research that produces policy recommendations, the meta-phor of the "total institution" proved dangerous. Many researchers who focused on shelter life had relatively limited contact with their subjects outside shelters and therefore had difficulty contextualizing their data and conclusions. This was particularly problematic for those whose research design focused specifically on a shelter.

The transience of shelter residents and the lack of supervision from the director's office made the shelter, at best, superficially similar to the total institutions described by Goffman, where inmates "live, work, and play." A small percentage of those who slept in the shelter might have been de-scribed as living there, virtually none of them worked there, and play al-ways involved going out. If there was any validity to the total institution model, it applied to the researchers who had to work there. It was they who were required to be there for large parts of their waking lives. It was they who became dependent on the behavioral norms that are part and parcel of surviving life on fieldwork, it was they who expected to be col-leagues for life and it was they who were seeking a professional transfor-mation from their experience in the shelter.

Notes

1. There is some controversy over who is responsible for launching the term "shelteriza-tion." Kim Hopper (Hopper 1990) has argued that Edwin Sutherland and Harvey

Locke coined the term in their 1936 study of homeless men in Chicago and notes in the same piece that Steven Segal and Harry Specht (1983) resurrected it many years later. Anthropologist Kostas Gounis (Gounis 1990) claims that he and his colleagues brought the term into current usage in 1987. The issue reappears with each period of mass usage of emergency temporary shelter.

2. Grunberg and Eagle used the gender neutral terms "residents" and "homeless persons" throughout their 1990 article, despite the fact that the shelter they were discussing was all male and most of the literature they cited referred to the experiences of homeless men. It has been recognized by many writers that the experiences of homeless women, particularly mothers with children, are often quite different. Ellen Bassuk and Lynn Rosenberg (1988) and Ida Susser (1993) both point to some of the problems with the approach of taking homeless men's experiences as a universal model. However, since this chapter is primarily about the experiences of homeless men, I will refer to the literature on homeless women and the shelterization concept only as far as it illuminates dynamics affecting the homeless men that I studied.

3. Bogard et al., 1999 argue that the term "supportive housing" was introduced by the McKinney Act.

4. None of this should suggest that all McKinney Act funded projects were based in shelters or used an explanatory model based in psychiatry.

5. "Upriver" is an allusion to Joseph Conrad's novel *Heart of Darkness*.

6. In fact heterosexual men who are not deprived of women are also likely to have had some same-sex sexual experiences. Long before the gay liberation movement made such activity more acceptable, Alfred Kinsey noted that 37 percent of men had at least one sexual experience with a man that had led to orgasm (Kinsey 1948).

— Chapter 6 —

DOIN' IT IN THE SYSTEM

"You want privacy? Move. This ain't the Hotel California."

An overheard conversation between a worker and a resident at the
RCCA community residence

"Everybody in New York City is looking for a job, an apartment, and a
lover. If they already have one of them they are looking for a better one."

A popular saying in New York City in the 1980s

A New Direction in Social Policy

By the early 1990s the municipal shelter system was in terrible disrepute.
Perhaps most discredited among all the shelters was Fort Washington, which
had such a terrible reputation for violence, drugs, and sexual perversion
that a major Hollywood motion picture starring Matt Dillon and Danny
Glover named *The Saint of Fort Washington* had used the shelter as its setting. In 1991 then mayor of New York David Dinkins commissioned a report on homeless policy in New York City that addressed what was viewed
by many as a nearly intolerable problem. This committee was chaired by
then Governor Mario Cuomo's son Andrew and came to be called the
Cuomo Commission, issuing a document that would direct homeless policy for the next decade. Entitled *The Way Home: A New Direction in Social
Policy*, the Cuomo Commission report featured a call for the city of New
York to phase out the municipal shelter system in favor of small not-for-
profit community residences. As they put it on page 13 of their report:

> "the commission recommends 'not-for-profitization.' The transitional housing
> system should be turned over to private not-for-profit operators wherever pos-
> sible ... Privatization does not diminish the government's role, but instead en-
> hances it by allowing the government to focus its efforts on setting policy."

Although lower costs and more efficient use of resources were one of the key benefits mentioned in the report, the demand for community residences was based mostly on humanitarian concerns for the homeless. The small not-for-profits were seen as more personal, more comfortable, more homelike, and more able to provide for the individual needs of homeless people than a shelter. In fact, they were presented as so far superior to the shelters that it was necessary to pass through the series of interviews, programs, and tests to gain admission mentioned in chapter 1. During my first weeks at the shelter I heard nothing but good things from the social workers who had visited these "spanking new" residences that were being built by not-for-profit corporations with names like "The Manhattan Bowery Corporation" and "Services for the Underserved."

The new facilities were defined as total treatment communities and divided by the level of support and structure of the programs. The small not-for-profit movement began in the late 1980s and included everything from lightly supported "single room occupancy" residences that could be directed toward specific demographics such as age or gender to the "intensive supportive community residences" that were mini–psychiatric hospitals for the mentally ill and drug or alcohol dependent. Dinkins, Cuomo, and other homeless policy makers argued that a small community residence with a very specific level of treatment and structure could best match the differing needs of different "homeless" who had been poorly served or lost by the vast bureaucratic municipal shelters.

The report spoke of the potential to demand results from private operators, allow a bidding process to keep costs low, and put the issue of results at the center of homeless policy. The transitional housing that the city had provided until that point was described by Dinkins and Cuomo as "process oriented." This was seen as a weakness and was posed as the opposite of "results oriented." Not-for-profitization was seen as a way of demanding results from a residence. Exactly what the results were was never clearly specified beyond vague statements about resolving the homeless crisis. However, all parties agreed that what was most important was to reduce the duration of residence and avoid more bouts of homelessness.

My first trip to a community residence did little to dissuade me of the obvious power of Andrew Cuomo and David Dinkins's observations about the superiority of a small community residence over a huge municipal shelter. It was a lovely sunny spring afternoon in 1991 and there was a grand opening party for the R.C.C.A., an intensive supportive community residence on 48th Street and 10th Avenue in Manhattan. The residence had only been open for a few weeks, but had generated a lot of excitement among social workers and clients who wanted to get in on the ground floor of what promised to be the end of the shelter system. It was a gloriously new double-tenement-size six-story building on West 48th Street. New red brick and clean glass, its cheap, slightly institutional fixtures outshone the other buildings around it.

Inside, there was a crowd of officials and administrators dressed in high heels, ties and casual office clothes. They were scattered around the grounds talking to each other. Interspersed were residents, drifting around in clean, but poorly matched sweat suits, polo shirts, and other casual loose-fitting clothing. The residents seemed to be doing a lot less talking to each other than the administrators and officials and I assumed that it was due to the fact that they were all newly arrived and did not know each other well. Most of them sat at picnic tables eating hot dogs, hamburgers, and macaroni salad or congregated around the barbecue. There were plastic barrels of fruit punch with little spigots and plastic drink cups. Everybody seemed to be having a good time and the sun was streaming in little side windows and casting long shadows in the backyard, which I could see through big sliding doors at the back. It was a dramatic contrast to the nineteenth century workhouse nightmare of "the Fort."

It was still early in my fieldwork and this was a big event with lots of potential data to be gathered and many coworkers from the shelter who were still wondering what an anthropologist does. I felt pressure to obtain some data and demonstrate my worth and the worth of my field. I was sitting alone in a field situation not sure how to talk to the woman next to me. I turned to her and introduced myself.

"Hi, I'm Anthony Marcus," I said in the most positive and outgoing voice I could muster.

"I'm Ola," said the woman, looking up from her macaroni salad and giving me a quite warm smile. I counted the smile my first victory and my mind raced to think of something more engaging to talk about than my name.

"It's a beautiful afternoon for a party, huh," I said, as I continued to try to figure out how to engage her, while collecting data. "Movie makers and photographers call this late afternoon time 'the perfect hour,' because of how beautiful the light gets."

"Perfect, huh," she said in a flat way that did not betray much emotion. Was I losing her with my film school rambling about cinema? "So how long have you lived here?" I asked.

"One week. What are you doing here? You don't work here and you ain't no VIP."

It was time to out myself and try to explain anthropology.

"I'm an anthropologist studying how the homeless live, up at the Fort Washington Men's Shelter."

"What's an anthropologist?"

"It's someone who spends time talking and living with people in order to find out how they live and what their culture is. Then we write up their stories and explain their lives to people who might never meet them or understand why they do the things they do. Sort of like a journalist, but more in depth."

"How do you make money doing that?"

"I work for a professor and a lawyer who have a government grant. Then I hope to get a job at a university."

"What are you doing down here, if you're studying Fort Washington?"

"I know people who were placed here, but haven't moved in yet."

She was silent for a pregnant second and then she blurted out to me, "My name is Ola, I'm 32 years old, and I got no money. Anything else you want to know?" She turned away from me and went back to playing with her food. I was a bit flabbergasted. Somehow what had started with a warm smile, had ended with a hostile brush-off. I wasn't sure what to do next and like everyone who has ever been at a party and wants to move on to somewhere else, I asked her if I could get her a drink while I was up. She muttered something about fruit punch and I wandered away to find my colleague Alfredo, with whom I was doing the fieldwork.

I went to share my failure with him and he reassured me that it was a success. He had prior experience working on the anthropology of homelessness and he informed me that our supervisors would be thrilled by this perfect bit of vocal proof that poor people were human beings. If a grossly overweight black woman living on public assistance could produce irony, sarcasm, and above all conscious-self-consciousness by vigorously brushing off an anthropologist, everybody else in the room was probably even more human. He proved to be correct and this became something of a legendary piece of data.

Over the course of the next weeks I watched as two shelter residents entered the R.C.C.A. and several others found placements in other small not-for-profit community residences. There was a sense of optimism among the social work staff as they saw their workshops, interview coaching, and overall caregiving efforts begin to pay off for the men at Community Support Services (CSS). The principal investigators of the project that employed me began to lose the look of panic that they had had for several months as they watched their proposed research agenda become retarded by bureaucracy, failed placements, and programs in other shelters "beating them to the beds." Even the clients at CSS began to look more cheerful, imagining that their housing nightmare might finally be ending.

There had been dozens of placements and we were suddenly swamped with appointments in far-flung parts of the city. Since there were all manner of community placements and a huge variety of different types of people we were interviewing, Alfredo and I decided that we would accompany each other to the first community interview for each informant. This would give both of us a big picture of all the different types of placements, give both of us a working knowledge of all the men in the study and their new homes, and insure that neither of us was walking into a dangerous situation without support. As we pursued our interviews over the course of this first summer, we found that the people we met who had been placed in "the community" were often all too human in their self-consciousness, their sarcasm, and their ability to express a range of negative human emotions. The transitional housing system that was being set up, with its attempt to avoid "one size fits all" blanket solutions, was, in fact, fitting nobody. The airy optimism of the R.C.C.A. disappeared quickly into a summer of disappointment, as each cure for the problems of the shelter revealed itself to be as bad as the disease.

Employment in "the Community"

One of our first trips that summer was to the R.C.C.A. to interview Alfredo's informant, Roger M. Roger was an African-American man in his mid 30s. Unlike some of our other informants who seemed to have been diagnosed as mentally ill, largely to enable them to get extra government money or be part of the study, Roger M. seemed to have some very serious personality disorders. He had been diagnosed as schizophrenic and for this reason he was placed in the R.C.C.A., because it was an "intensive supportive community residence," the highest level of support available in "transitional housing." Because neither Alfredo nor I had known who was going to get Roger as an informant, we had both spent some time with him before the placement.

All our previous meetings with him had been at CSS where, despite his regular intramuscular injections of such drugs as Haldol and Prolixin, he had shared an enthusiastic optimism with us. He had been at the shelter for almost a year and had been without his own housing for a year before that. He had lost his tiny studio apartment in Midtown when the landlord raised the rent on him. After that, he passed a year living on friends' floors, imposing on relations, and even committing a minor crime "so I could take some time off in jail," he told us. He had learned about the shelter while he was in jail. Another prisoner in the mental health ward had told him about the Fort and he headed straight for it when they finally released him. When he first moved into the shelter it had seemed wonderful to him. It had all the security of jail, but you could go out anytime you wanted. However, he eventually decided to go to the CSS program, because he got tired of living in public and wanted to "do something with my life." He informed us that "they promised me housing and to help me make something of myself." His dream was to get Section 8, government-subsidized housing; find a job; and find a girlfriend. He had enthused about his new start when we had talked with him just before he moved. He knew the R.C.C.A. was a very structured housing facility, but he had seen the backyard and the new common areas and as he put it, "it's the best thing out there, because it's not in some Bronx ghetto, where you gotta travel forty minutes just to get anywhere. I'm going to find some part-time work and there's no better place for finding work than midtown."

From the first day he was unhappy. When we returned to the R.C.C.A. in light of day there was no barbecue, no people sipping fruit punch on the patio, and none of the airy optimism that we had seen at the party. The residence was like a newer version of a state psychiatric hospital, but too small for Roger to find a comfortable routine outside the view of the staff. We had to go through a variety of procedures to get in the front door and once inside we had to wait as they brought Roger to meet us. There was a program going on in the eating area that looked out onto the empty patio and they gave us three seats by a table near the door. When Roger arrived and came to sit with us, he looked ashen and unhappy. He sat down at the table and we greeted him. He was agitated and edgy. He was clearly nervous about the staff hearing what he was saying and Alfredo gave me a look as if to say, "Is this paranoia or is there something to be afraid of?" I picked up his meaning and suggested that we go outside, figuring that it did not matter what the reality of his fears were, it was a bad ethnographic situation lacking the safety, security, and privacy necessary. "It's not allowed," Roger replied. "Is there anyplace we can go that is private?" Alfredo asked. Roger wasn't sure. "Maybe we should go out to a diner or something," I suggested. Roger said that it was possible, but that the staff became very suspicious when anybody went outside. They regarded it as a kind of noncompliance with treatment. He did not want to make them any more touchy about his movements than they already were. We resolved to continue the interview where we were.

He told us in hushed tones that he hated the highly structured environment and wanted to strike out on his own. He had to share a room with someone with whom he had nothing in common except that they both had been diagnosed mentally ill. He complained that there were too many rules and he did not like being required to take antipsychotic drugs, which he claimed impaired his ability to work and to function sexually. They kept records of when he came and went and humiliated him at the door, with tests and inspections for drug use. The finances enraged him. Like in most intensive supportive community residences, all but $100 of the roughly $850 in SSI that the government paid was eaten up with room, board, supervision, and the drugs that he disliked. The $100 that was left over each month was doled out in small sums as spending money. He knew that he would never be able to save up enough money to get his own apartment. In addition, if he left the residence, his SSI would automatically drop to $508 per month, hardly sufficient to even cover rent. "I'm going to be stuck in here forever," he whined.

He knew he needed a job. However, a person who received SSI was not allowed to earn more than $74 per week. Roger broached the subject of getting a job with the residence staff and found them extremely hostile to the idea. They rightly reasoned that with his diagnosis and lack of skills, and the weakness of the employment market, any job he could get would be very insecure and low paying. If he lost that job it would be hard to find another one. Even minimum wage could get him thrown off the SSI rolls. His workers predicted that he would be back in the shelter in less than a month if he found a job. In spite of all these perils, Roger continued to look for work, insisting that "I gotta make something of myself."

The mere act of looking for work endangered his housing, as Roger was labeled uncooperative and hostile. His relationship with the people who ran the facility in which he lived became very tense. He was severely punished for his first conflict with staff—pushing a guard who refused to leave his bedroom when asked—and he was sent back to the shelter for several days. Though he was not sure which he disliked more—the prison-like community residence or the shelter—he rightly reasoned that it would be a lot easier to find a job from a real residence, with an address and telephone. Since he was a member of the experimental group, the CSS staff intervened strongly on his behalf and he was allowed back into the residence.

Once back, he continued searching for a job, much to the consternation of the residence staff and his CTI social worker. The one job that seemed relatively flexible and easy to get was bicycle messenger. It could pay a livable wage if one made enough deliveries in a day, and there was no need for much formal education or strong interpersonal skills. Roger spent several months saving his money to buy a bicycle, a messenger bag, and a license. Squirreling his money away, instead of putting it into normal consumption items like cigarettes, soft drinks, and recorded music further alienated him from the social environment in which he lived, but he persisted. He had shopped around to find a messenger service that promised to hire him in advance, before investing in these necessary items. There was one just down the block from the residence that agreed to give him a chance.

The further he moved with his project, the more the staff regarded it with suspicion. This attitude alienated him further from his living situation and made him feel less supported by his workers. When Roger finally started working he discovered that messenger work was very difficult and as he put it, "I'm not in shape anymore." The drugs he was required to take as part of retaining housing were not conducive to the physical stresses of riding a bicycle around Manhattan all day long, and Roger found himself unable to continue with the job. He worked a few days, only managing to make $30 on his best day, and gave his bicycle to his cousin.

When I last saw him he was trying to find a less structured community residence and had not found any employment. Roger's attempts to take control of his life suggest only one aspect of the intense conflicts that developed between client and worker around issues of personal autonomy. Because the system was arranged to deny government support to anybody who was earning more than $74 per week, workers were forced to oppose his attempts to get a job. However, he continued his efforts in the face of opposition, only to be stopped by the lack of an appropriate permanent job for someone with his limited job skills.

Despite often having little or no work history outside the informal sector, informants frequently expressed the need to find rewarding careers. One informant wished to be an architect and had taken mechanical drawing classes at City College and another was working toward being a housing policeman. Many informants took classes in computers, literature and even history, and philosophy (as mentioned earlier). They were all adamant that they took these courses in order to improve career chances.

Attempting to fulfill such ambitions from inside transitional housing is in some ways even harder than from the shelter. Because of the strict rules against holding a full-time job while collecting SSI, my informants who followed the programs laid out for them by the workers at their residences languished in make-work programs, dead-end jobs, and piecework provided by voluntary agencies at significantly less than minimum wage.

There were employment programs at the shelter that paid pennies per hour, but most of my informants avoided such low-paid and humiliating work in favor of day labor as a security guard. However, I had two close informants who were involved in a similar program at a Salvation Army residence. Eugene, an African American man in his 30s, had chosen the Salvation Army over several other facilities due to its work socialization program. He had heard about the importance of employment training to their program and told me that he would, "rather be getting some real work experience than sitting with a bunch of mental patients learning how to make friends or practice proper hygiene." Although their facilities were older and less pleasant than the newly renovated "small not-for-profits," as he put it, "if I put in six months working in one of their stores, I ought to be able to get a real job somewhere and move out pretty quick."

My first visit to interview Gene was about three weeks after his placement. They had not yet given him a job, but they were paying him 17 cents an hour to mop floors in the residence and had promised him that within the month they would find him a real job working in one of the thrift stores. He was not very happy with the housing, which was a rodent and bug-infested aging flophouse on the Bowery that the Salvation Army had converted into a transitional housing facility, but he was optimistic and believed that he was on the way up.

The second visit, a month later, found him still mopping floors and becoming increasingly discouraged at how little his life was improving. As he put it, "I'm not saving any money at 17 cents an hour, I still don't have a job, and I can't even afford to go see a movie after work. The shelter was a much better deal." When they finally moved him to the thrift store after several months, he was not given an actual job, but remained part of their work rehabilitation program and therefore had neither a job description, a job title, nor a minimum wage salary. As he put it, "I'm not a cashier. I'm not an assistant manager. I'm not a sales person. I'm not even an assistant to the assistant janitor. I'm a nigger that pushes a mop and unloads trucks for a couple of dollars a day. I must be some kind of idiot." He went on to point out that "with my SSI, I am actually paying these crooks $900 a month to give me a seventeen cent an hour job."

At my next monthly interview, he informed me that he had a new plan for moving out. He was saving money by stealing from the Salvation Army. As he put it, "it's always a half price sale when I'm around. Why don't you come and visit while I'm still there." I did.

It was a Saturday afternoon and I brought my companion along to the vast cavernous thrift store where Gene worked. He had warned me that we should walk in and browse as if we did not know him. The way he worked it was to approach customers who were browsing and ask them if they wanted to take advantage of "a special half-price sale." "Just let the clothes you want drop to the floor under the rack and I'll put them in the cart and meet you out front. Half price every day," he would say to customers. We wandered around looking at the endless shelves of used clothes. Though they had little that interested me, it wasn't long before my companion had surreptitiously dropped enough clothes to fill the big cloth bin on wheels that Gene was pushing around behind her. We met him outside, where he arrived with plastic grocery bags filled with the clothing she had selected. We paid him the $18 he claimed we owed and he handed the bags to us and said, "Thank you, please come again." I told him I'd be in touch about next month's interview and we walked off.

My companion was overjoyed with her purchases and had plans to return every couple of weeks. However, it wasn't long before Gene was back with his mop at the residence. Caught selling half price merchandise to a young woman in front of the Salvation Army, he understood that they would never let him near merchandise again. He believed that there was no way into the formal economy for an uneducated and somewhat disreputable looking African American man with a criminal record and few of the social or job skills necessary for success. He used his psychiatric diagnosis to get out of the work training program and began to secretly disappear from the residence for freelance work. The residence was supposed to be as "supportive" and restrictive as the R.C.C.A., but there was virtually no paid staff to enforce the rules of the treatment programs. My other informant at this facility had recruited him to unload trucks on the street behind the residence for a Chinese store owner. The $5 an hour off the books wage was far superior to the work training program's 17 cents an hour, but it was a situation that would never enable him to get his own housing.

Even the smallest, most carefully tailored employment programs ran up against the rules of the SSI system and the conflicting expectations of workers and clients. One of Alfredo's informants, Paco, was employed by the project that we worked for and therefore was briefly both an informant and a coworker. This put us in a questionable position regarding the ethics of research. We raised this point with the project director, who derided our concern as abstract and ridiculous. As he put it, "Paco is not a coworker, he's a homeless person." It was this perspective that enabled him to be easily incorporated into the work environment, but it was the same perspective that ultimately damned his efforts to improve his life through the paths prescribed by "the system."

Paco had come to the United States from the Dominican Republic as a teenager in the 1970s. He went to high school in New York City and graduated with an excellent academic record. He then went to Hunter College with dreams of professional success. Halfway through his sophomore year, Paco was forced to drop out due to the first symptoms of mental illness, and he was later diagnosed bipolar. He held a variety of jobs during the next ten years but found advancement difficult, possibly due to his mental illness.

When I met him he was a client of the CSS program at the Fort Washington Men's Shelter where he had come after his last hospitalization. He was placed in a supportive SRO and "rewarded" with a $74-a-week part-time job cleaning the CSS/CTI offices and running errands for the director. He confided to me that he did not like this arrangement and found it demeaning. Not only was the work boring and menial, but the combination of having no clear job description, no security, and almost no salary made him feel humiliated every time he came to work. The job did not pay anywhere near enough to enable him to move out of the supervised housing that he abhorred, and he had no chance for advancement. As he pointed out, the previous three people who had run around for the director had not been given any placement assistance when they left, and there was nothing about the job that could be put on a resume. He was in the experimental group and told us that he thought that the job was a handout, designed to help boost the numbers for the study by tying him to the project. After two unsuccessful attempts to quit, he sent the keys back with his resignation. He said, "I'd rather be going to school or be a volunteer helping disabled senior citizens. At least then I'd be able to put it on a resume."

Because he was one of the highest functioning and better educated clients at his program, Paco was singled out for a job that was considered to be a reward for his success. The workers at the program couldn't understand why he wasn't happy with the job. They regarded the job as a clinical reward for someone with no resources and few options. They felt he should be grateful to have such an opportunity. For Paco, who had not given up his dreams of a "real job," an apartment to call his own, and a life, such a handout meant very little. While he had scaled down the aspirations of his youth, he believed that a job with a title that might lead to something else was the least that he should expect. In a different way than Jeffrey, the informant who had been taking a philosophy class at City College and working in an employment training program, Paco was running up against the limitations of programs that seemed to expect the participant to fail before it was revealed that the program could not deliver.

Transitional Housing: Sex in the System

The problem of finding and maintaining sexually based kinship and affective relationships was even greater in community residences than in the shelter or on the streets. Popular images of isolated homeless old men always competed with images of two people sleeping together under a pile of cardboard boxes. Though the number of couples that shared a steam grating or the interstices of a construction site was always far lower than the number of disassociated individuals dragging themselves through a solitary life in the public spaces of the city, there was certainly a place for such people in both the popular imagination and the reality of life on the streets. No such trope existed for those in "transitional housing." The policy of the City of New York and of homeless facilities throughout the United States was, for the most part, to break up families and opposite sex couples and lovers into separate same sex residences (Bogard et al. 1999; Susser 1993). Through random room checks, denial of privacy, rules against visitors, and heavy pressure to be committed to a totalizing treatment regime in lieu of kinship, same sex couples were as strongly discouraged in transitional housing as opposite sex ones.

Though there was very little space for publicly declared sexual relationships, a fair amount of secret sexual activity occurred in the not-for-profits. Since few residents ever had much privacy, workers had pass keys, and there was a high level of surveillance and people reporting on each other to management, sex was generally a quick, dirty, and furtive activity that rarely even involved such premeditation and precaution as using a condom. As one resident told me, "This is worse than living back in my mom's house when I was fourteen. Least back then I could go to the top of the staircase."

As with prohibiting real employment in favor of make-work programs, the prohibitions against forming couples represented a site of explosive tensions between management and residents. As one of my informants, a black male in his 30s, said of the intensive supportive community residence where he lived, "they want you to check your dick at the door." I asked him if he had. "What are you crazy," he answered, but then repented:

> Well to keep my housing, I gotta get those horrible injections. I walk around like a zombie all day, got this terrible dryness in my mouth and feel like a pot o' mashed potatoes. The worst thing is you can't get your dick hard. They know it. The doctors know it, the nurses know it and they love to do it to you. It makes them feel like big men. But for good behavior they reduce your dosage every now and then. I'm gettin' practically nothing these days. Sometimes I fuck the guy across the hall when the medication's wearing off. I'm not a homo, but they don't let me outta here because I'm still getting clean. I gotta stay away from the pipes [crack] and ho's. Besides, they got him so doped up, that he probably don't know what the fuck is happening.

"The guy across the hall" was also an informant of mine and though we never had a direct discussion about sex, I suspected that he was quite aware of the above-quoted informant's sexual attentions.

Even in the least restrictive community residences, unsupported Single Room Occupancy, the desire for love and sex was neither incorporated into the treatment nor accepted as one of the basic needs of residents. The situation of one of our informants, Wilfred, a thirty-eight-year-old Black Crucian (native of the island of St. Croix) who had been an intermittent resident of the shelter for several years, provides an excellent example of how even the most high-functioning resident in the least restrictive residence found his housing imperiled by the basic socially accepted need for companionship.

Wilfred was gay and had maintained many friendships and long-term love relationships over the years. He did not have a drug problem and was so high-functioning and likable that he had been given the same gopher position that Paco had briefly held at the CTI/CSS project office. He had had many of the same reservations about the job as Paco, however, he left it on better terms, convincing everybody that he was sorry to be leaving.

He was prone to occasional bouts of depression, particularly when his relationships ended, and this was his reason for being in the CSS program.[1] However, he found himself losing SRO housing because of his desire to have a satisfying love life. In one instance Wilfred was placed in an unsupervised SRO on 116th Street in Manhattan. This was one of the least restrictive types of housing. Like similar dwellings, this one had rules against visitors. Wilfred, as with the other residents, was forced to sneak in the man he was then dating. He was able to manage this inconvenience until the relationship started to sour. Wilfred, his lover, and their conflicts became more noticeable to managers and neighbors. One day Wilfred's lover wanted to get into Wilfred's room when he wasn't there. Knowing that he couldn't come in through the front door alone, he climbed the fire escape and got in through the window. Neighbors saw him and called the police, who broke into Wilfred's room and found his lover there. In a situation that might have otherwise called for police protection from an abusive ex-lover, Wilfred was evicted for having an unauthorized guest.

After this incident Wilfred came to believe that for a poor man like himself, a long-term relationship may have been a luxury that he could not afford. After having been evicted from the SRO he stayed in the shelter for about a year, where he could pursue his personal life as he pleased, making use of the apartments of friends, lovers, and family members. He was finally placed in a supportive SRO. This was a more restrictive setting, designed for people in need of a higher level of supervision than the initial one. He ended two relationships after realizing that they presented potential threats to his housing. As long as he lived in such managed housing, Wilfred would not be able to even attempt to fulfill his dream of having a "life companion." He decided to prioritize finding a decent paying job, with some security or a regular off-the-books job which would not endanger his monthly checks and would enable him to rent his own apartment.

For another informant, a gentle and relatively compliant gay black man in his late 20s who was living in an intensive supportive community residence, part of the therapy was actually not having sex. There were signs posted throughout the building saying that sex of any kind was prohibited. When I asked this informant about this policy, he said:

"You know it's a rule they can't enforce. There's gotta be people in here who are doing it. That's just the way people are, but they sure keep it a secret. They say the rule's there, because sex is too complicated between two residents who are fighting drugs, but it seems pretty complicated to stop it too."

I asked him if he had ever heard of anyone being thrown out for having sex. He said that he had not, but he had only lived there for a short period. He went on to add that he figured they knew it was going on, but:

"they say that the treatment means giving in and surrendering, like to parents. I think it's to break us down. Lot of us have pretty fucked up lives and need to be broken down."

For those who were in less restrictive environments, there were more options for sexual relationships despite rules against them and the continued imperative of medication which often led to impotency. I found no supportive residences that allowed overnight guests. A manager of one of these residences once explained to me that this was necessary in order to make the treatment environment more important than the environment that caused homelessness, drug addiction, or mental illness. As he put it, "We are fighting a battle for their souls, against all the bad influences and bad examples they have had in their lives." He then proceeded to tell me about his own previous struggle with alcohol and drugs, and how it had been necessary to surrender everything to the treatment. "Like dying and being reborn," he said.

Homeless Services: The Point of Contact

Though the shelters were originally chartered as a vast dormitory facility for New Yorkers who were too poor to afford housing, they quickly became clearinghouses for people who had fallen or dived through the meshing in the social safety net. As long as someone was living with family and subsisting in the margins of the New York City economy, there was little help to be found. Perhaps food stamps and Medicaid could be obtained at a local welfare office, but little else was available to those who lived and suffered in privacy. The minute they entered the shelter, they became a public burden and were entitled to extraordinary forms of assistance that were denied to them while living with family. Besides food, shelter, and the company of others like themselves, residents at a municipal shelter found social workers that could get them approved for benefits that had been lost or never obtained. Their homeless status might enable them to easily qualify for SSI and suddenly bring in several hundred dollars a month.

Shelter workers helped with job searches, provided free subway tokens to get to job interviews, and were seen as the gatekeepers of Section 8 housing. The Section 8 program is a federal program administered by the department of Housing and Urban Development (HUD) that provides rent subsidies for what it refers to as "very low income families." These subsidies, paid directly to landlords, enable poor people to obtain and maintain low-cost permanent housing that they could not have afforded otherwise. Subsidies are usually calculated with the goal of reducing rent payments by families and individuals to about 30 percent of their monthly income, which in the case of my informants who were mostly on SSI, would have been about $180 from their roughly $540 a month.

With the most minimal studios in New York City renting for at least $500 a month, this program stood as the pot of gold at the end of the rainbow for nearly all my informants. With a twenty-year waiting list for public housing, rents rising in poor neighborhoods throughout the city, an increasingly tight low-end job market, and little chance for upward mobility, the section 8 program became a life goal for many shelter residents. In the absence of any hope of making their lives better through work, a career, or starting a business, Section 8 housing stood as the way to finally get one's life together. Shelter residents would jump through the hoops that their social workers set up, endure endless hours of workshops and resocialization programs, and "stick it out" in transitional housing situations all with the goal of making it to Section 8.

The possibility of getting out of the shelter permanently if you were diagnosed mentally ill was quite good, but it required surrendering tremendous amounts of freedom, and was an entirely voluntary decision. As a result, some of the most mentally unbalanced people chose to avoid Community Support Services fearing the stigma of being viewed by fellow residents as "one of the crazies." However, CSS offered many resources and privileges that were not available to shelter residents who were not its clients. Among these was help getting on Supplemental Security Income (SSI), a program run by Social Security to provide for the blind or disabled. Though many shelter residents probably qualified for SSI, few received it. For those who had tried to get on it and had not qualified, participation in the CSS program, which was for the mentally ill, virtually guaranteed one's status as disabled. With two levels of SSI, which depend on the type of housing where one is placed and the severity of the disability, SSI could be anywhere from $200 to $500 a month with a friend, family member, or landlord as the payee, or over $900 per month payable directly to a transitional housing program.

The principal reason that people came to CSS, however, was for housing. Though most of them were certain that employment was the first step to getting their lives together and finding their "American dream," they either had failed to find steady employment or were not really capable of trying. CSS represented the last option for those who had given up on getting out of the shelter on their own. Just to be able to hang on to possessions, have a place to live, and have a telephone to receive and make calls from was a major step toward being able to negotiate the difficult task of finding work.

Furthermore, it was promised that if they followed the program laid out by CSS, real housing eventually would be provided. This typically involved months of receiving injections and medications designed to deal with their diagnosed illness and attending daily programs, workshops, and counseling sessions designed to improve "life skills," ameliorate emotional problems, and prepare them for interviews at transitional housing facilities. Once in these facilities they were expected to prove that they could "succeed" at whatever programs were specific to that facility. Although passing through various forms of transitional housing was usually the first step out of the shelter in the CSS program, the men who went to CSS were encouraged to believe that if they behaved properly and followed the rehabilitation plan that had been set for them, they would eventually be rewarded with Section 8 housing. For many men, whether severely or mildly mentally ill, struggling with alcohol or drugs, or situationally depressed, this promise of housing and a permanent road out of the shelter was very tempting.

There were some clients who had been in and out of CSS and a variety of transitional housing programs over several years who liked to cynically point out to me that nobody ever wound up getting Section 8 housing and that the whole thing was a big scam to keep clients compliant. However, for most of the men I met through CSS, the mere act of coming to CSS and facing the stigma in the shelter of being one of the "crazies" involved a recognition that they were incapable of managing their own affairs. For the most part, these desperate men, who had given up on the possibility of making it on their own, were working very hard to please whoever was supervising their efforts in the hopes that they would be first on the list to get a desirable placement, ahead of people who were difficult, were uncooperative, and still had illusions that they could be independent.

Even for these most pliant and resigned residents of the shelter, there was a competitive individualism that was pervasive. Seeing the process of getting through the CSS program as a competition for limited housing options, these men often expressed highly competitive visions of the struggle to get mentally well and housed. For those who—for either legitimate reasons or reasons related to their illness—were dissatisfied with their treatment or angry at something that they felt was an affront, who believed that they had been treated prejudicially for some reason, or who merely could not fit into some procedure, any conflict or complaints tended to go against them and brand them as troublemakers. The lack of any collective apparatus for client input left these men pursuing a highly scaled down heroic individual struggle to have a place to call their own.

From Shelter to Community

My informants all went through the CSS program and entered residences because they wanted a home, not for medications or personal supervision.

Having recovered some of their dignity in their departure from the homeless shelter, many men resented the high levels of supervision that most residences implemented. The tension between workers who were instructed to supervise residents and residents who increasingly resented supervision triggered intense conflicts.

Although many had been advised about the rules of a particular residence before moving in, it was only when they became residents that they experienced the actual limitations of independence and privacy and the constraints of the rules and supervision as part of their "real lives outside the shelter." Some continued to try to create the kind of home that they dreamed about and this made their stay at the residence problematic and conflictive. Some, who were too sick to articulate their needs in an effective way, accepted the new setting with its rules and supervision in the same way that they once accepted the shelter.

But for most informants there was the desire to be able to come in and go as they pleased without having to explain their activities to anyone. Delaney, the previously mentioned informant, who was a supporter of NOI, was placed in a community residence. He was very unhappy and left after three months, stressing the fact that "a man like me who has worked my whole life should have a home where people aren't always ordering you around." Two men who came to be very close informants were at one time serious musicians. They both constantly resented the cramped, highly supervised residences as they did not allow them to practice. They both kept saying that any place where they couldn't play was not home. For one of them, Henry, the jazz trumpet player mentioned earlier, the chances of ever finding a home to be able to practice in seemed increasingly slim, and this led him to "feel no desire to live, but don't tell the doctor that or he'll up my dose."

Many of my informants expressed tremendous hostility at the constant attempts by social workers to try to restrict their consumption patterns, as part of the resocialization treatment. Though social workers had been concerned when Roger had been saving money to try to get a bicycle messenger bag and refused to participate in commonly accepted patterns of consumption, the problem for social workers was usually getting clients to "learn self-discipline" in the budgeting. This meant imposing a set of treatment-defined standards for what constituted consumption that was appropriate to the lives and income levels of "homeless men." For many of the social workers I talked to, it was simply common sense that my informants were showing dysfunctional behavior by spending their money on "designer" brands of clothing and personal electronics. For my informants it was a sign that part of the treatment was ritual humiliation, social control, and the desire to make them into people who were obviously part of treatment communities. Reference was frequently made to the previously mentioned term "ugly" and proposed racial explanations suggesting that consumer goods were something that only white people were allowed. As one of my informants put it, "only somebody who really was crazy could live the way they want us to live." However, many of the weaker, less articulate, and perhaps less high-functioning residents of these communities did, in fact, struggle to adhere to such guidelines, often seeking out secret pleasures and consumption patterns that they attempted to hide from their social workers.

Finally, there were few people I met who did not want to be able to entertain friends and be able to foster emotional or sexual relationships. Often they felt that having to live in a program with so many mentally ill people was embarrassing. One of my informants who lived in a supervised SRO where he was not allowed to bring any after-curfew guests repeatedly said that he wanted his own apartment "so he could get a real girlfriend, instead of sneaking out and messing with crack whores all the time." Another, who secretly had a girlfriend at a residence that forbade sexual activity, claimed that he needed a real place so he could "start dating women who are not mental patients. Nobody respects you if you're always fucking bad pussy. That's all there is here." Another man complained that "real people don't have to share their bathrooms with strangers."

The desire for independence, privacy, and a life that they could take pride in led some of the men to leave or to be thrown out of supervised housing. The goal of the workers was to aid in the gradual adjustment of the new resident to his housing. However, many of the residents soon felt that they were prepared to take the next step toward independence, and they thus set up the first conflicts with workers who viewed the process more cautiously. The residence support staff viewed the problems of the men as rooted in their mental illness. They connected housing, psychiatric treatment, and drug treatment as a package that could not be separated. The punishment for not taking medications or for using drugs was translated into the loss of housing. Residents were constantly threatened with this possibility and in some cases were sent back to the shelter for a period of time as punishment. The conflicts between residents and those managing the residences embodied the tensions of the different agendas and priorities.

Theorizing the Right to a Job, an Apartment, and a Lover

Employment, or what you do for a living, and kinship, or who cares about you, are the two sites where the American dream is either realized, not realized, or deferred. The underlying view that drove most of the policy that determined the contours of my informants' lives was that the quality of affective kinship established and the quality of housing obtained must in some way derive from economic successes and failures. However, these three principal basic human aspirations are intimately linked, and it is generally thought that without one it may be difficult or impossible to have the others. Although a job, an apartment, and a lover are three things that nearly everybody on this planet wants, the way they are culturally managed varies from society to society.

In the United States there is a common belief that a job is not a right, but a privilege that must be earned through a variety of forms of service testing to prove worth and fitness. Though this is not the case in every country and every culture, under the ruthless discipline of the social lottery known as the American dream, and with a set of government policies that are regularly revamped to maintain that ruthless discipline, 10–20 percent of the population are kept in a state of roughly permanent underemployment in the United States. Black Americans tend to be the leading edge of this population that is denied employment, with official unemployment rates often double those of Euro-Americans and actual unemployment for blacks—many of whom do not report employment status to the government—far higher than that.

For those who lose this social lottery, the penalties can be very great. Similarly, with countries where a job is commonly considered a right, adequate private housing is also considered a right. For those who have not competed effectively enough in the economic arena, it stands to reason by the individualist logic of U.S. culture that a private and safe home is not deserved. As one of my informants always used to say, "If they gave me anything good, why would white folks like you pay your rent?"

Finally, the right to the form of kinship that is tied to sex is clearly a powerful form of social control. Whether one analyzes the family and marriage as control of women; a site of support, care, love, and escape from commodification and the rat race; or simply a neutral unit of social reproduction, denial of full access to this basic institution of all human societies, and the denial of the specific kinship forms that are normative in the United States is a powerful social sanction for failure to beat your neighbor in the economic lottery. Though it might be argued that a job, an apartment, and a lover are all part of the same set of socioeconomic rewards for social power, for my informants, they were connected, but separate. These three goals were the ways in which my informants measured their progress in life and tried to figure out how well they were doing. They are also the three arenas that can bring the greatest feelings of failure and shame. My informants saw them as very real. When these men were reduced to being "the homeless," only one of their problems was being addressed, and poorly at that. When they were reduced by the system to being the "mentally ill," none of these concerns were addressed, reducing almost any treatment or intervention to a failure before it started.

For those who tried to obtain their desires through the system, there was a need to turn off their sense of themselves as individuals, as Americans, as men, and as people with connections in the world. The only way to truly succeed in the system was to take the very ordinary goals of friends of one's own, ordinary consumption patterns, sexual satisfaction, privacy, independence, kinship, employment, respect, love, and personal accomplishment, and check them at the door of whatever residence or program one entered. Usually this meant a renunciation of the desire for sex-kinship in favor of a variety of dangerous, fleeting, and fugitive sexual en-counters, a renunciation of the desire to be employed and pay one's own way, and a lack of concern for the basic housing amenities that they had been raised with as Americans.

If there was any definition of homeless, it was probably those who had given up hope of finding a job, a career, or a business and accepted the homeless career ladder up to Section 8 housing that was offered them by social workers and city officials in the shelters. Though these full-time Section 8 seekers were relatively rare in the shelter, they were often the ones that researchers and social workers contacted the most. The selection for people who had given up trying to make a place for themselves in the work world represents yet another way in which information about the homeless tended to become skewed toward debates over function and dysfunction. After a brief climb up a few rungs into a transitional facility, a single room occupancy, or a resocialization program, most ex–shelter residents found the competition too great, the rewards too small, and the program expectations too far from the life goals which had been the orig-inal attraction. If there was a homeless person who had been shelterized into dysfunction, it was the person who had come to realize too late that he was climbing a ladder to nowhere and that the homeless bureaucracy could not really give him anything that he needed.

Notes

1. Wilfred was very high functioning and seemed to have found his way into CSS and onto SSI, due largely to this fact. Nobody, including the psychiatrist and the social workers seemed to think he was actually mentally ill, though people were generally very happy to include him among the mentally ill because he was so easy and pleasant to deal with and everyone figured that he would eventually become a program success story.

— Chapter 7 —

THE BLACK FAMILY
AND HOMELESSNESS

"Latinos value families more than blacks do. That is why family placements work for the Latinos and not for the blacks. They always find a way to work out their problems, because they value family."

Latino supervisor of a federal homeless relief project

"With all the advantages blacks have over Latinos, they should be the ones running all the businesses on Broadway, not the Dominicans. A Latino family will save money for years to buy a business and the whole family will help out until it's a success. Blacks just don't stick together like that, that's why there's so many homeless."

Latino social worker on same project

The Black Family and Homelessness

The debate over the nature, function, and dysfunction of the black family has been one of the key questions that Americanist scholars in nearly every field from sociology to comparative literature have argued about. Politicians, political activists, and employees standing by the watercooler frequently discuss it, weigh in on it, and use it as an explanation for a variety of social problems and concerns from crime in the cities to continuing inequality. The debate over homelessness in the 1980s and '90s was no exception to this phenomenon. National magazines ran cover stories about why black men were homeless and what was wrong that black kin networks in the cities were not functioning to protect their most vulnerable members. Numerous public discussions of homelessness focused on aspects of the black family, from the traditional discourse about matrifocality and the damage of slavery to discussions of race-specific oedipal pressures and the lack of black male role models.

As the CTI study developed over the three years and no significant difference emerged between the experimental and control groups it came to be very significant to staff that African American family placements were rarely "successful" and Latino ones usually were. The director started writing a grant proposal to study why black families were not as well equipped to respond to poverty as Latino ones. The project psychiatrist was circulating a paper he had written on black family psychopathology since slavery, tentatively titled "Oedipus Begs." And some researchers started a paper on homelessness and the black family that drew on Moynihan's comparison of African American and immigrant families. They all presented Latino families as strong and adaptive and the black family as psychologically damaged by slavery and incapable of "taking care of its own." Discussions about this issue took a contentious tone, with African American staff complaining that this debate misrepresented the black family and "blamed the victim" for racism. Latino staff responded that they too faced racism, while African American staff countered by questioning the intensity of the racism that Latinos face.

At the time, I was influenced by revisionist history suggesting the adaptive strength of the black family and anthropological approaches that highlighted the macrostructural advantages accrued by white ethnics and the disadvantages constraining African Americans. However, none of these approaches were fully satisfactory, as they were unable to resolve the problem of why throughout three years of fieldwork similarly impoverished nonwhite immigrant families were far more willing to reincorporate lost members than were African American ones. It was clear from my field research that there was some different conception of family—its responsibilities and obligations—at work among Latin American immigrants.

In 1997 I returned to the field, studying drug marketing and use in Upper Manhattan. During this research, I intersected with networks of Latin American immigrants engaged in kinship-based formal sector legal and informal sector illegal economic activity. Discourses of success and failure often involved the Moynihan comparison, with Dominican immigrants attributing relative success in small businesses and the drug trading which often subsidized such enterprises to the strength and trust of the Dominican extended family. They frequently compared it to what they saw as a weak, chaotic and fragmented African American family. The few African Americans I met on fieldwork, largely salaried employees and owners of local small businesses, needed little prompting to express utter disdain for "those people" who "use their women and children" for "dirty business." Issues of morality, legality, and "self-representation" aside, the Moynihan comparison was so prevalent and the kinship norms of these two groups so different that I was led back to another look at the strengths and weaknesses of the discredited Moynihan model.

The Continuing Lens of Kinship

Orlando Patterson begins his book *Rituals of Blood: Consequences of Slavery in Two American Centuries* (1998) by saying, "Afro-American gender relations, and consequently their marital and family relations, have always been in crisis.... This crisis is the major internal source of the wider problems of Afro-Americans." Though Patterson has come under fire for "fuelling the blame game," he is not alone in connecting Afro-American kinship and gender relations to broader social challenges. In public policy and social science literature African American gender relations and the black family remains a key question that informs discussions of crime in the cities, low educational attainment, and the crisis of the welfare state (Auletta 1982; Bennett et al. 1989; Gould 1999; Hogan & Kitagawa 1985; Roscigno 2000; Sampson 1987; Wilson 1987; Wilson 1989).

At the popular level conservative politicians continue to focus on such family issues as virginity, teenage motherhood, illegitimacy, divorce, and male role models. African-American churches and community groups promote family strengthening activities. Maya Angelou's "Black Family Pledge" is featured prominently on the National Black Family Empowerment Web site, and the black nationalist organization, the Nation of Islam, holds campaigns directed at bringing the economic benefits of strong family values to African Americans. Their 1995 "Million Man March" was one such example. For many, the problems of African Americans in poverty continue to be viewed through the lens of kinship.

Despite being almost forty years old and largely discredited in academic literature, former U.S. Senator Daniel Patrick Moynihan's model of black family dysfunction continues to be central to popular discussions of African-American success and failure.[1] His famous 1965 report to President Lyndon Johnson, "The Negro Family: The Case for National Action" described the black family as "a tangle of pathology" (Moynihan 1965: 29) and made the comparative observation that "a number of immigrant groups were characterized by unusually strong family bonds; these groups have characteristically progressed more rapidly than others.... By contrast, the family structure of lower class Negroes is highly unstable, and in many urban centers is approaching complete breakdown" (Ibid: 5).

Numerous critics have demonstrated the weakness of Moynihan's causality and the sloppiness of his data, presenting convincing alternate variables that provide better explanations for racial and ethnic stratification.[2] However, the Moynihan model continues to be intellectually compelling to both professional and lay audiences, partly because its underlying methodology has never been fully deconstructed. The central assertion that there is a useful comparison between the mutual aid and small business formation behaviors of immigrant ethnic kinship networks and those of African Americans in poverty remains largely unchallenged. Based on simple comparisons of popular narratives, the model continues to be quietly convincing to many Americans.

However, it is not just "new Americans" and older Euro-Americans who have internalized the Moynihan and Glazer comparison and made it a part of their Americanization narrative. Many African Americans still view the comparison between their own small business networks and immigrant family accumulation as relevant. The question of why immigrants continue to climb up the economic ladder ahead of African Americans has been the source of much urban conflict and soul-searching on the part of African Americans (Abelmann & Lie 1995; Cherry 1990; Kim 2000). Despite the dramatic expansion of the African-American middle class during the last three decades, a significant tradition of mutual aid, community building, and "buy black" campaigns (DuBois 1970; Gregory 1998; Orr 1999; Washington 1907), African Americans still have one of the lowest rates of self-employment of any social category in the United States. In-Jin Yoon reports that in 1990 African-American self-employment stood at about 3.7 percent compared with 24.3 percent for Korean-Americans (Yoon 1997).[3]

This chapter will argue that popular discourses on immigrant extended family economic activity lead to the error of holding immigrant families as a yardstick by which African Americans are measured. It will be my argument that, indeed, African-American families living in poverty are generally less suited to certain types of mutual aid in poverty than are their immigrant counterparts. However, this is not because of a defect in the black family or some failure to live up to American kinship norms. Rather, it is because the cultural templates of the black family, even among the poorest and least integrated into "the mainstream," are fundamentally similar to those of other American families. Nuclear and neo-local in its norms, the African-American family, like its white counterpart, is built around voluntary companionate marriage; the shared values, identity markers, and consumption patterns of its members, and the right to seek individual accomplishment and emotional self-realization. Typically supported on a foundation of legally regulated wage labor, subsidized mortgages, individual savings, public education, state entitlement programs, and socio-legal protections by police and courts, this family type, which I will refer to as the "consumption family," appears dysfunctional in the absence of such state provisioning and when compared to certain immigrant kinship structures, which I will refer to as the "accumulation family."[4]

The accumulation family is built around extended kin networks, intense group sacrifice, delayed or permanently postponed gratification, and large amounts of captive low-wage or unpaid family-based labor, particularly from women, children, new arrivals, and other dependents with less recourse to external labor options and social rights. Accumulation families were the predominant form of kinship before the rise of the modern corporation and wage labor and continue to be common in some agricultural areas and mercantile sectors of the developing world (Chayanov 1986; Smith 1985). They are sometimes reborn in the claustrophobic liminal space of U.S. immigrant enclaves, with a foot in sending countries and a foot in the receiving one. It is in these socioethnic hothouses that the blurring of distinctions between household and commercial work and loans, investments, and extortion can provide the labor and finances necessary for stronger members of a kin network to form capital syndicates and successful small businesses through use of the labor of weaker members. The intense interdependence of such ethnic immigrant environments and the sojourner quality of their members' life narratives often yield short and medium term values and norms that facilitate a variety of mutual aid strategies among the poor that would not be easily accepted or implemented in American families, regardless of ancestry.

A focus on the black family that compares it to these select immigrant kinship forms rather than providing a holistic evaluation situated within broader patterns of American culture impedes the resolution of social problems faced by African Americans living in poverty. The narrative of the poor, weak and dysfunctional black family assumes a solution based on altering values and norms that are actually American rather than black or white. The cultural imperative of these American kinship norms strongly militates against solutions based on reprogramming values and renders such solutions inappropriate, ineffective and counterproductive, even among people who have the least to lose in changing their way of life. Though obviously not characteristic of African-American families in general, the extreme situations faced by my informants and their families allow a privileged view into the way American kinship norms influence some of the coping strategies of African Americans in times of crisis.

Critiques of Moynihan

Like most social theorists who focus on the continuing legacies of slavery, Moynihan started from the evolutionary progressive position that there has been "a declining significance of race" in the twentieth century and asked why African Americans are still unable to benefit from this progress (Ginzberg 1956; Hannerz 1969; Myrdal 1964; Wilson 1978). Drawing his framework from postwar scholarship on ethnicity and immigration, particularly that of Oscar Handlin (Glazer and Moynihan 1963; Handlin 1957; Handlin 1959) and his understanding of the black family from E. Franklin Frazier's classic work *The Negro Family in the United States* (1948),[5] he concluded that slavery had destroyed the black family and denied it the cultural skills that immigrants have used as the building blocks of success in the United States. Privileging cultural resources, values, and norms over political economic factors such as the division of labor and social class, Moynihan called for "a national effort ... directed towards the question of family structure" (Moynihan 1965: 29).

A generation of scholars from nearly every social science discipline contested his views. Numerous scholarly works proposed alternate "macro-

structural" economic, political, and historical variables to explain continued inequalities, and criticized Moynihan for "blaming the victim" (Billingsley 1968; Gans 1967; Leacock 1971; King 1967; Ryan 1967; Valentine
1968). Some scholars identified empirical weaknesses and misinterpreta-
tion of data, highlighting the strengths of the black family (Aschenbrenner 1975; Leacock 1967; McAdoo 1980; Reissman 1967; Stack 1974), while
"revisionist" historians challenged the accuracy of Franklin Frazier's observations about the destruction of families in slavery (Blassingame 1972;
Fogel & Engerman 1974; Furstenburg et al. 1975; Gutman 1976).

More recent approaches have focused on "redlining" or lack of access
to credit, residential segregation and lack of homeownership, educational
inequality, the structure of the welfare system, labor market disadvantages,
stereotyping, inequality in the criminal justice system and racial violence
(Butler 1991; Chen and Cole 1988; Feagin and Imani 1994; Lichter 1988;
Marable 1983; Marcus 2001; Maxwell 1993; McNulty 1999; Oliver and Shapiro 1995; Steinberg 1995; Susser 1993; Tonry 1995). Finally, some scholars
have questioned "the ethnic myth" that underlies Moynihan's comparison. Following Stephen Steinberg (1981) they have argued that the "just
so" moral tales of self-made immigrant success upon which Moynihan's
comparison rests are an illusion that hides "macrostructural" advantages
accessed by certain ethnicities (Kim 2000; diLeonardo 1998; Oliver and
Shapiro 1995; Sanjek 1998).

These approaches have added tremendously to understandings of racism, ethnicity, and the uniquely difficult socioeconomic challenges African
Americans face. However, there has been little work that directly addresses
the methodological issues embedded in the comparison central to Moynihan's work. This may be because the Moynihan model has usually been
discussed as part of the literature on race, ethnicity and social stratification, rather than as part of a broader anthropological discussion of American culture and kinship. As an example of this, Michael Peletz's *Annual
Review of Anthropology* essay "Kinship Studies in Late 20th Century Anthropology" (1995) does not cite a single publication on African-American kinship that is less than ten years old. Katherine Newman, a leading urban
ethnographer, does not mention the word "kinship," much less raise the
question of how it is related to economic outcomes in her review essay on
urban poverty, published in the *Annual Review of Sociology* (Small and
Newman 2001). Instead she limits her discussion to a brief section titled
"family structure," containing a largely empirical review of literature on
out-of-wedlock births, teenage pregnancy, and "the marriageable-male-
pool-hypothesis."

Regardless of the side taken in this debate, most writers, like my informants and coworkers at the CTI project, passively or actively, accepted
Moynihan's two fundamental assumptions. The first is that there is a dis-
tinctive black family that is different from American families generally,
and the second is that immigrant families can be viewed as a norm against
which African-American families may be judged. In the following pages

I will interrogate these unproblematized assumptions about American kinship patterns and their application to studies of African-American kinship in poverty through an examination of my informants' narratives, the actions of their kin networks in poverty, and public policy approaches.

U.S. Consumption Family Norms

One of the most common complaints from my African-American informants about the black family was that African-American women are not loyal in face of economic necessity. They frequently made the same negative comparisons between their families and immigrant families that I heard from social workers and small business owners. One informant, a divorced African-American male in his 30s who made money off the books selling clocks and other merchandise on streets for a Korean importer, expressed a common sentiment to me one afternoon while I talked with him in a diner in Upper Manhattan over coffee and donuts:

> Look at the Koreans. Their women work twenty-four seven in the fruit stands until they're rich. Then everybody sits back and enjoys the money. You don't find no black women doing that for their men. They want what they want and they want it now. Hell, I know Africans [recent immigrants from Africa] who got mothers, sisters, daughters, wives, shit, two wives working in their goddamn stores. Don't take no pay. The black woman don't do nothing to help us get ahead. Just sit on her ass wanting to be treated like a queen.

The classic accumulation family evident in this informant's narrative is built around petty entrepreneurship and family based labor. The invidious comparison between this immigrant family form and the black family led him to criticize African-American women for having inappropriately high expectations and not supporting their men:

> Black women are the most demanding 'ho's you'd ever want to meet. You gotta be good looking, dress like some rich guy, spend all kinds of money on them, and be ready to do anything just to please them.

African-American informants who were not as bitter expressed a more positive view of kinship that is tied to consumption rather than petty accumulation. One afternoon I was hanging out at the shelter with Franklin and some other informants while they were talking about women. One of the favorite topics of my heterosexual informants was to compare white and black sexual mores and practices. I asked them about the accusation that African-American women are materialistic and Franklin gave me an answer that revealed a similar view of relationships between men and women that prioritized romantic conventions and desires for self-realizing identity:

The black women, they got something deep inside them. I don't know whether it's in their hearts, or in their heads. But it's there, they just love a poet, a preacher, a prophet and that is what I am. See that social worker over there? [Points to a black woman in her late 20s who is working with another client] She knows I'm crazy. She knows I'm a drug addict. She knows I already spent about half my life in prison. Shit, I'm a homeless guy and it's her job to help me, not to like me. That woman wouldn't be nowhere near my ass for all the money in the world. But you know what, when I get my shit going and I'm writing my poetry and telling her stories about Africa and all the things here and now and all the times past and what's coming in the future, I can touch that little spot in her soul, the one that says I gotta have a piece a you Franklin.

While many informants were resentful and bitter about perceived demands and lack of support from the women in their lives, Franklin's somewhat sympathetic view of African-American women was not atypical either. Regardless of the representation, they all describe a woman who expects to build sexually based adult kinship on the individual goals of voluntary shared consumption, identity creation, and emotional satisfaction. Franklin dreamed of becoming a published author, a husband, and a father when he was finished living between prison, the shelter and the streets and he wanted a woman who could share his intellectual passions. His ideal family was built around complementary identities linked to a set of shared values and consumption patterns.

As with any group of men, praise and criticism of the women often took on mythical proportions and rarely managed to properly reflect real-life gender relations. It is thus perhaps not surprising that my African-American informants believed that Korean, Jamaican, Italian, and other immigrant women acted as slaves to their husbands, fathers, and brothers. What was surprising was that they typically expected African-American women, who had been raised in the same kinship system as they had, to have emerged into adulthood with the expectations and behavioral patterns of recent immigrants. One of the appeals of the Nation of Islam was its claim that they were putting African-American men at the head of families and pulling together kin resources in the manner that had brought success to other ethnic groups. This sentiment was reflected in the comments of Delaney, an informant who claimed, "the Nation of Islam is about us learning to work together the way Jews do."

Consumption Families Under Siege: Family Placement

Though there was much talk among my African-American informants about immigrant families and their successful small businesses, of far more immediate importance was the problem of residence in a domestic unit. African-American informants believed that a return to their natal family was the ultimate indicator of failure to create an adult life and an adult family. It represented passivity and a loss of manhood and standing among peers. Almost universally, my African-American informants dreaded being burdens to their families and believed that moving back with parents or even siblings was shameful. Some of them were in frequent contact with natal families, sometimes joining them for dinner, while others were completely estranged, but most still regarded a municipal shelter, with its dangers, discomforts and inconveniences, as preferable to moving "back home."

Despite these widely held feelings, project social workers persisted in attempting family placements. A family placement was seen as a success because it removed people from "the system." With regular Social Security checks, growing savings in "money management accounts" supervised by social workers, memories of good times past, and an outside authority mediating and sanctioning the return, many natal families were susceptible to the pressure to accommodate an adult relative. Some of my African-American informants found themselves pushed, pressured, and cajoled to "give it a try." Social workers would often dangle the possibility of highly coveted government subsidized Section 8 housing for those who "made a go of it" with parents or siblings.

Franklin was one of those African American men who had agreed to a family placement. Project social workers helped him get monthly government disability payments, enabling them to convince his sister that with the additional income she could build a more secure household. His placement with his sister was considered to be one of the few successful African-American family placements. However, project social workers frequently had to intervene and he often used the shelter for a few days at a time as a "cooling off" spot when the conflicts with his sister or her boyfriend became too intense.

One afternoon, we sat on our favorite benches above the Harlem River and he talked to me about life with his sister:

> Well, it's like this. Life's pretty tough for black women. I don't hate them for who they are. Lots o' times I'm ready to kill them for who they are, but I don't hate them. They really ain't got much besides a lot a dead beat men who can't take care of themselves. They gotta protect themselves and be out for what they can get, 'cuz they can't get much. But shit, this sister of mine, what a pain she gives me all the time. I tell her save that shit for your boyfriend. He the one you gotta be gettin' some shit from. I'm just your no good mentally ill brother.' Say to me Franklin you fuckin crazy, get out a the house before somebody kills you. I stay out of that woman's way.

Franklin's description of the tensions between him and his grown sister reflect nuclear, neo-local, and consumption oriented kinship norms. He is contrasting an ideal relationship between his sister and a husband or lover in which sex and shared finances are intertwined, with his own problematic relationship to his sister. His comments suggest an attitude that the ideal relationship between brother, sister, and extended family involves distancing, economic independence, and "staying out of the way" when such ideals are breached. Franklin did not draw the kind of invidious comparisons between women in immigrant ethnic groups and African-American women that some of my other informants did. His inclination was to blame his own personal failings: bad choices, drug use, and so on. However, he did feel that there was something wrong with contemporary African-American kinship.

Kelvin, an African-American man in his late 20s, was placed with two sisters and their four small children who shared a three bedroom apartment in a public housing project in Queens. Kelvin had serious mental illness, but social workers had argued that the two sisters living together meant there was strong family cohesion, which would help Kelvin. The sisters resisted taking Kelvin in, knowing how difficult he was, but one of the sisters was unemployed and the other was saving to move to her own place. They both needed the money and were convinced by the assurances of project workers that they would guarantee rent from Kelvin's Social Security and see that he received regular injections to keep him "manageable." Kelvin was given a sofa to sleep on in the living room and pressed into babysitting duties. He claimed that his sisters were preventing him from "living his own life" and tried to avoid them by sometimes sleeping on the roof of the building.

When winter came, Kelvin spent more nights at the apartment and the situation deteriorated. The sisters were not getting along and Kelvin had fought with the employed sister's boyfriend, who stayed over frequently. The employed sister and her children moved to their own apartment early, citing concern for her school-age child. When she moved, Kelvin received her bedroom. However, he was no happier: "now she thinks I owe her something" he said about the remaining sister. He felt that his contribution to her rent from his Social Security checks was more than enough. "She don't understand that I want to live my own life," he complained. Though it was difficult to imagine how someone as low-functioning as Kelvin could live his "own life," he believed that continued residence with his sister insured that this would not happen. For her part, Kelvin's sister continued to believe that, despite the contribution to rent, her brother's presence was a terrible imposition.

Early in the study I interviewed an African-American informant in a family placement that had been described as "promising." Alvin, a large and gentle man in his mid twenties, was the son of a storefront Christian minister whom the project director described as a solid family man who would provide moral guidance for Alvin. At the time, there were no available transitional housing community placements and Alvin had been promised support if he made a success of it with his parents. From his first moments back in his parents' house their hugely different social identities came into conflict. His parents were judgmental of his lifestyle and tried to force him to go to church and repent his "sinful ways." He was bisexual and had never sustained a serious relationship. His view was, "when you smokin' the pipe [crack] it don't matter if it's men or women, it's just somethin' you do." He lasted less than two weeks with his parents, then went to stay at a shelter in Brooklyn, where, he hoped, "there ain't nobody around tryin' to get me back with my dad."

Though most of my African-American informants were "dead sure" that they did not want a family placement, and typically responded to the suggestion that they "try to make a go of it back home" with angry invectives about not having taken on the stigma of coming to CSS, the mental health unit, "to have some white psychiatrist trying to put me back in with my family," there were a few who had "self-placed" with family. This had always involved moving in with siblings or extended family for a brief period, and living far away from New York City. At the time of the study, it had not registered for me, my fellow CTI colleagues, or any of the CSS social workers handling such cases that these were "family placements." These men had essentially abandoned the entire social environment in which they were living, disappeared to distant locales like Galveston, Texas and Honolulu, Hawaii and moved in with extended family.

This had removed them from the context in which their treatment was occurring and the study was being done, making their housing outcomes somewhat unimportant and their physical beings non-existent. In fact, the very notion that a "homeless person" who had been diagnosed as mentally ill could do something as active and agential as migrating to a distant new place appeared somewhat absurd and impossible to social workers. It may have also been this distance, change, and derangement of context that enabled these few men to imagine a family placement as desirable. An instructive case, in this regard, was that of Charlton, a mentally ill African American man in his late twenties who went to Honolulu to live with his brother.

Charlton was diagnosed schizophrenic and had never been able to hold a job for more than a brief period. He was placed in an old private shelter in the Bronx that had been converted into not-for-profit transitional housing in order to benefit from the expanding government programs. It was one of the least pleasant placements offered to clients at CSS. Much like the Salvation Army, this residence had many of the infringements on personal autonomy of an intensive supportive residence, with little of the spanking new infrastructure. Housing men in a giant room on the third floor of the old shelter, bedrooms were invented with clever use of room dividers, giant pieces of fabric and large book cases.

Charlton was miserable and uncooperative from his first day there. I went to visit him for the first time since his placement and found him hostile and grim through the whole interview. He was extremely unresponsive and somewhat delusional. I listened patiently as he discussed his fear that enemies were sending their thoughts into his food. We discussed the need to eat in private and secret so this wouldn't happen. It was a gray cold winter day in the South Bronx and he quickly started to get on my nerves. I had a late afternoon appointment coming up at a locked psychiatric ward farther north in the Bronx, with an informant, who I genuinely liked and the experience of dealing with Charlton was making me feel tired, angry and frustrated that I was not enjoying homesickness in some exotic anthropological fieldwork locale.

When I finished the interview, I hurried to leave, telling him that I would call him a week before coming the next month. "Don't need to" he said, "I'm going to Hawaii. I've had enough of this cold weather." It was terrible outside. There was snow on the ground and the endless dead of winter in the post-industrial South Bronx seemed to make his objection to the cold weather and his desire to escape his squalid indoor surroundings the sanest thing he had said yet. "Sure," I said, "we'll do the interview on the beach with Piña Coladas." He suddenly seemed lucid and connected to the rest of the world for the first time and said, "Ok, if you can make it, I'll be waiting." I went off to find the director to say goodbye.

The director asked me what I thought about Charlton, since they were having trouble with him. He informed me that Charlton was uncooperative, disassociated, non-compliant with medication, avoiding other residents, and refusing to participate in any group activities. I told him that I had seen nothing positive, except when he mentioned his fantasy about a trip to Hawaii. "Yes," the director laughed, "he has deluded himself into believing that he is going to Hawaii to visit his brother." "I know plenty of guys with much worse delusions than that," I responded. He laughed and I told him, "I gotta go to another interview up at the Bronx Psychiatric Center, but I'll see you next month, unless Charlton goes to Hawaii." We both chuckled and I left.

I thought nothing of the whole discussion until I called the residence about three weeks later and asked to speak to Charlton. "He's gone to Hawaii," I was told by whoever answered the phone. I asked to speak to the director who assured me that he had seen the plane ticket. I was shocked. I immediately went through all the old files on Charlton and found a next of kin address in Brooklyn. I called it and spoke with a woman who said she was Charlton's aunt. She gave me a phone number in Hawaii for his brother. I called his brother in Hawaii and found that Charlton was already without shelter. "I said I'd help him get a job" said the brother, "not let him take over my home. You know I got children. I can't have him living with me." I asked him how I could contact him and he told me that he had found his brother a job at the junkyard where he worked, but his brother had quit after a few days and was sleeping in a local park.

I informed the people I was working for that, through his brother, I had located him in a park in Honolulu and that I would try to collect information by telephone. Once before, I had done a few monthly interviews over the telephone with Delaney in Galveston, Texas, when he had briefly tried to escape the depressing confluence of poverty and winter in New York City. His migration had also shocked workers and researchers, who had laughed at his mention of going south for a break from the winter. However, Delaney was a very lucid man, with whom I had developed some kind of a relationship and he had been glad for the chance to talk to someone back home in New York and get sent money for doing it. I could accomplish none of this with Charlton, who I barely knew and who would not make the collect phone call. His brother had little interest in helping me and the CTI director refused to send me to Hawaii. I was unable to honor my pledge to interview Charlton over Piña Coladas.

Though there were at least two other "self-placements" with family, by African-American men, none of them were with parents, none of them lasted for more than a few weeks, and they all involved long trips to very different places. As with Charlton's trip to Hawaii, all of these attempts to escape the difficulties of poverty and lack of housing in New York City had put migration and change into the foreground and family issues and dependencies into the background, making it possible to imagine residence with family, albeit briefly, in a way that probably would not have been possible in New York City.

The preference that African-American men had for transience over life among natal families mirrored the expressions and decisions I had observed among white men and women in their 20s in my prior fieldwork on housing, displacement and transient residence among Euro-Americans in the gentrifying Lower East Side. Many of these young Euro-Americans without permanent housing had parents who owned homes in the New York City area. However, they nearly always preferred to sleep on friends' floors, in converted walk-in closets and pantries, in squalid East Village squats, and occasionally in Grand Central Station, if they were male, to returning to natal homes where they could not escape intergenerational conflicts, huge differences over social identity, and their failure to create successful adult lives.

Latino Immigrants and the Accumulation Family

The type of intergenerational conflicts that Alvin faced are difficult for anybody. Latino informants often found themselves in similarly difficult living situations involving heated conflicts with family members and rooms shared with adolescent siblings or young children. Though they were not happy with the conditions, they usually stuck it out, saying, "they're impossible, but they're still family." Alex, a gay Dominican who had struggled with depression and briefly stayed at the shelter after a fight with his brother, was typical in expressing this view, "It's not like we want to be crowded in, but you never know what somebody can do for you ... If you don't have somebody to share your place it makes it tough to go back to the island [the Dominican Republic]."

He did not feel comfortable being gay, using drugs, and living with his highly traditional and religious family, who put pressure on him to go to church. There had been huge conflicts over his sexuality, but after his stay at the shelter his family had agreed to a "don't ask, don't tell" policy and the living situation stabilized. Though he was unhappy and dreamed of moving out and living "like the gringos do, in their own houses," he saw living with his parents as more of a burden and an irritation than something to be ashamed of. He often heaped scorn on U.S. born gay men he knew (mostly white and Puerto Rican) who he felt would rather ruin their lives in deplorable circumstances than accommodate their parents, who he believed were far more accepting of homosexuality than his traditional rural Dominican family.

The fact that so many of the homeless men whom I met were Latin American immigrants suggests the degree to which many of the problems of poverty, mental illness, overcrowded housing, and internecine family dynamics were identical to those facing African Americans. However, the kind of explosive tensions that built around expectations of autonomy, freedom, and identity were far less in immigrant families than in American families. Ultimately, the primary difference seemed to rest on expectations. No matter how abusive an extended immigrant family was, its members typically spoke in a discourse of obligation and believed that they had little choice and that there might even be some protection from the hostile alien society that lay beyond the front door.

For African Americans I met on fieldwork, like the white Americans I had met previously, the right to make your own household was seen as something approaching a "human right." For these men who were raised as entitled citizens, with consumption family kinship norms, no matter how good an extended family was and no matter how successful the living situation was, they usually preferred transitional accommodations, municipal shelters, and straining the hospitality of friends or lovers to moving back home. There was less of a discourse of obligation and returning was seen as a mutual imposition and a sign of failure to create the autonomous independent life of an adult male.

Latino immigrants, even those who had made serious breaks with family, often found that once they had government disability payments, food stamps, and the help of an authority to patch a break in the fabric of family life, "going home" was an acceptable outcome. They used family as a source of informal employment such as sweeping hallways in exchange for food and a place to sleep and felt that their tie to extended kin remained strong, regardless of the poverty they faced. Starting one's own household was seen by poor Latinos not only as less important than it was by African Americans, but often less desirable, as large and flexible households were necessary to retaining the below market rent stabilized leases and highly desirable public housing tenures that do so much to structure domestic units in New York City. Such flexible domestic units enabled members of a family to make extended visits to their home country, change jobs, change boroughs, and take up a variety of short term opportunities.

Becoming American: Immigrants and U.S. Kinship

Despite some successes, Latino family placements did not always work. Most of my Latino informants had been in the United States for several years and some had attended high school in the U.S. Though they viewed themselves as immigrants, their expectations and kinship ideals were often at odds with those of their parents. Even their relatives "back home" were sometimes at odds with the traditional values of immigrant families. Some family members in sending countries had moved to cities and, with the help of remittances, U.S. education, and other benefits of "transnationalism," developed more consumption oriented kinship units. For informants from these transnational families that had spent decades in and out of the United States, kinship was necessarily seen through several different lenses.

They had developed kinship norms and patterns that were closer to those of consumption families than those of traditional agricultural or immigrant accumulation families. They usually viewed these changes as a form of social breakdown, the way African Americans saw their own families as weak, corrupted, and needing "atonement" and white Americans saw their families as "selfish, inflexible, and dysfunctional." However, what they may have been experiencing was a new family form and an increasing sense of embeddedness in U.S. culture that they did not have words to describe, except through invectives against the materialistic values of the United States.

Gabriel, a Dominican man in his early forties who had spent nearly twenty years in the United States, was one of many informants who faced such contradictory kinship norms. He had been married several years before and had two children, but became estranged from his wife and children after losing his job. He was placed by project social workers in a supportive community residence. His dream was to have another family. However, his residence forbade overnight visitors, he shared a room with a stranger, and he was required to take drugs that made him impotent. He soon felt that his situation at the residence was hopeless. He took his SSI checks and moved into a room in the Bronx that was rented out by a Dominican couple who were distant relatives. He lived quite peacefully with them for a few months, doing occasional work "off the books" for his landlady, until he returned to the Dominican Republic to visit his mother. While staying there he ran into an old girlfriend from his teenage years who was the sister of his New York landlady. They talked about old times and she confessed that he had been the only man she ever loved. She had a daughter, but insisted that she was no longer involved with the father. She asked him to consider the possibility of getting back together. Gabriel thought about it and said yes. After a brief courtship they decided to marry.

The arrangements for the wedding were made by her family, who according to Gabriel had some money. They bought him a suit for the occasion and the couple spent a few nights in a hotel for their honeymoon. After the honeymoon, Gabriel returned to New York City while his new wife waited to receive a visa. He returned to the room that was rented by his sister-in-law, happy to be "part of a real Dominican family," instead of the "degraded" type typical in the United States. However, as he talked to people outside his newly found extended family about the marriage he discovered that his bride was in a long-term common law marriage with her daughter's father and that the two of them owned a house together in the Dominican Republic. He also learned that in the recent past his wife had unsuccessfully attempted to sneak into the United States through Mexico, spending a large amount of money in the process.

When Gabriel realized that he had been used to obtain a green card, he stopped looking for a job and decided to remain on SSI, knowing that it is impossible for someone on public assistance to request legal status for a relative. He wanted to turn his back on the whole situation but his sister-in-law continued to demand that he find a job and bring his wife north. She offered him a job at her in-laws' bodega, but he felt humiliated by the whole situation. Fearing the ridicule of his friends and family back in the Dominican Republic, he moved out of her apartment and returned to the shelter.

This relationship was doomed from the start by Gabriel's wife's attempt to exploit him, facilitated in part by his idealization of traditional rural Dominican gender roles. Like African-American men who complained that their families are not supportive enough and their women are too demanding, Gabriel believed that overly demanding and disloyal women were responsible for his lack of success. However, unlike my African-American informants, he did not blame these women or himself. He blamed the United States. He believed the common saying that was circulating among my Dominican informants that "a woman from the island is better" because Dominican women, like his first wife, "are ruined" by the United States. He attributed the failure of both his marriages to the seductive shallow materialism of U.S. culture and the atomized families and "unnatural" gender norms that it encourages.

Love and Marriage: Theorizing Consumption Families

Regardless of ethnicity, gender or caste/color designation, kinship is one of the most problematic areas for Americans living in poverty. As residents of the advanced industrial nation with the weakest welfare state, Americans are forced to rely heavily on the family for the basic needs of social reproduction. Unlike most other advanced industrial nations, where education, health care, housing, and support for the poor, weak and infirm are generally provided directly to end users through national bureaucracies, United States social provisioning is heavily weighted toward direct or indirect tax breaks for "middle class" families and homeowners

(Coontz 1992; Katz 1996; Niemonen 2002; Oliver and Shapiro 1995; Piven 1971; Piven 1997; Unger 1996).

However, despite the extraordinary pressure on American families to provide large amounts of help paying for education, providing down payments for government subsidized mortgages, and obtaining work-based health care, the structure of the American family is fundamentally like that found in the rest of the advanced industrial world. Marriages are exogamous and companionate and families are nuclear and neolocal. This means that Americans believe it is important to marry out of one's kin network, in the process spreading resources thinly; choose a spouse based on compatibility of consumption habits and identity rather than family economics; and form new households in separate residences from natal families. This can place terrible stresses on even the most economically sound American kinship units. However, for many African Americans, who face segregation, racism, and long-standing disadvantages in resource accumulation, the combination of heavy economic demands on nuclear families and lack of resources for sustaining them has made African-American kinship units especially vulnerable to the centrifugal forces that tear families apart.

Conclusion: The Black Family, Class and Kinship

That the success of waves of impoverished immigrant families has been due, at least partially, to family based sacrifice, cooperation, and petty accumulation is not controversial. The small business/extended family accumulation model for success has been as useful to African descended immigrants such as Jamaicans, Barbadians, and Senegalese as for Polish, Italians, and Jews (Sowell 1981; U.S. Congress 1997). Major shopping streets in historically African-American neighborhoods in New York City often have a disproportionate number of African and Afro-Caribbean immigrant entrepreneurs owning and operating small businesses. However, it is methodologically unsustainable to compare these groups of immigrants to African Americans.[6] If some immigrants move up the economic ladder through family accumulation (regardless of access to institutional credit) it does not necessarily follow that there is something "different" and wrong with the values or behaviors of working-class African-American families that cannot do this.

Immigrant families, by definition, are not fully American, but represent a liminal phase in the move from foreign to American (Foner 1997). In the absence of the full moral, social, and legal rights of native born Americans, there is often a shared isolation and socio-emotional dependence that sometimes enables stronger members of families, particularly men, to build businesses and capital networks on the labor of weaker members, usually women, children and newer arrivals. This often makes mutual aid and small business formation a whole family strategy, encompassing extended and mythical kin with geographical or social ties in the sending country. Such a strategy may derive from the "traditional" agrarian families of Arab, Latin American, South Asian, and South European sending countries or may be a return to "tradition" by educated middle classes who lack English fluency or whose job histories and credentials may not be recognized in the United States, as with many Koreans, Chinese, Indians, Israelis, and Columbians. Regardless, for all of these immigrants who must "create their own employers," there are a set of enforced mechanisms for small-scale accumulation and captive markets that neither African-American nor white American families have (Aldrich and Waldinger 1990; Chen 1992; Dasgupta 1989; Park 1997; Sanjek 1998; Young 1983).

When members of such accumulation families become fully American and have access to potentially well paid and secure careers, the persistence of pressures to cling to extended family based, low economic yield small businesses appears "overly traditional" and pathological. This "traditionalism" is often most visible in tensions over changing roles for women in the family, but also surfaces in issues around the personal lives and career choices of young men, who move beyond the confines of "the community."[7]

As the data presented here suggests, African-American kinship norms and behaviors are different from those of immigrants, and probably, as Moynihan suggests, less suited to mutual aid in crisis and poverty. However, the central flaw in Moynihan's model is the implicit assumption, in posing immigrant accumulation families as the norm, that the black family is different from and less functional than the kinship forms and norms of other Americans.

There are few American families that can comfortably incorporate high-functioning socially successful extended kin, much less those who have fallen on hard times and absorbed the quirks and liabilities that come with failure. African Americans, like other Americans, are born with the right to legal regulated employment, public assistance, and social security. They grow up speaking the national language, cannot be deported, and have the expectation (usually unfulfilled) of full citizenship and "equal opportunity under the law." Few American families can count on unpaid labor from wives, sisters, and children after school and, in the absence of significant bank loans, such enterprises are not likely to yield more income per person than wage labor.

Above all, it is not part of the cultural model of the American family to provide such sacrifices for small start-ups that have little chance for growth. The most destructive aspect of the black family is its thoroughly American modernity. It shares the same set of kinship ideals and norms that American families of every descent typically have. The difference is that impoverished regions of urban black America have fewer of the resources for sustaining the neo-local consumption based nuclear families that are the cultural template for American working-class kinship.

The CTI project director was fond of pointing out that with their American citizenship, universal education, and right to government entitlements, if African Americans behaved more like Latin American immigrants and "stuck together," sharing space and capital and donating unpaid labor to family businesses, they would easily outperform new immigrants. His observation is probably true. However, as native born Americans, fully socialized and fully participating in U.S. culture, there is little of the liminal space in which immigrants work to claim a set of roles and places for themselves. African Americans, whether white collar or blue collar, educated and "skilled" or poorly educated and "unskilled," are overwhelmingly urban and working-class and carry the curse and the blessing of the kinship norms that accompany such lives. Their historic role as the lowest paid sector of the American working class has determined that they often do not have the economic, political and social resources that other American families have.

As Bayard Rustin pointed out soon after the Moynihan Report was issued (Rustin 1967: 426), "if millions of Negroes are to change the conditions of their life, it will not be by becoming shopkeepers." Improvements in the economic position of African Americans must come from fundamental changes in the political economy of American society that expand access to the public resources necessary for sustaining private consumption based kinship. Solutions to the problems of African Americans in poverty that attempt to prescribe or impose family values that are not in line with the basic cultural norms of the United States will inevitably reinforce unrealistic expectations by policy makers and sufferers of poverty themselves. Despite much nostalgia for the imagined warmth and security of extended kinship, "family strengthening" measures such as reducing consumption, "delaying gratification," and subordinating the lives and social identities of women, children, homosexuals, and other "junior" family members to the accumulation goals of "senior" members will be experienced by most Americans as an abrogation of their human rights and a violation of consumption family norms that are deeply embedded in U.S. culture.

Notes

1. The phrase "black family" is used because it is and has been the most common descriptive phrase for the debate over African American kinship and economic success in the United States.
2. Throughout this paper, I refer to this comparison as the Moynihan model, despite Nathan Glazer's significant collaboration, as it was Moynihan who gave the model national fame and tied it to public policy.
3. Though Yoon's statistics reveal a clear demographic imbalance in self-employment between African-Americans and Korean-Americans, they do not reveal the full economic weakness of black owned businesses. The 1992 economic census reveals that of total national sales and receipts of $3,324,200 million, African-American businesses captured

$32,197 million or less than 1%. In comparison, Hispanic businesses captured $72,824 or more than twice as much (U.S. Department of Commerce, 1992).

4. The comparison between "consumption families" and "accumulation families" should not be taken as suggesting that American families do not provide any assistance to relatives in crisis. However, with certain exceptions, such as terminal illness and, sometimes old age, assistance is typically provided within a framework in which neo-locality and nuclear residence are normative.

5. Frazier's arguments about the destruction of the black family during slavery rest heavily on W.E.B. Dubois' *The Negro American Family*, first published in 1908.

6. As Stephen Steinberg (1981) has convincingly argued, it is not even fair to measure most immigrant families against the ethnic small business success narrative.

7. Andrew Brimmer has argued that recent increases in white collar professional opportunities for African Americans have also hindered small business creation (Brimmer, 1998).

Chapter 8

HOUSING PANIC
AND URBAN PHYSIOCRATS

It is said that behind every stereotype there is some reality that is either misunderstood or wrongly contextualized. Homelessness also had its poorly contextualized reality. Underneath the discourses of American individualism and race that rationalized and naturalized the categories of poverty studies there was a reality that was related to housing. Numerous scholars, writers, and social critics have documented this obvious connection through work on both underhoused populations and those who researched, designed, and provided services to them (Susser 1996). Up until now, this book has looked at these two categories of people with the goal of deconstructing the seemingly natural connection between homelessness and housing. In this chapter I will attempt to *reconstruct* the phenomenon of "homelessness" as it was viewed by a third category: the 82 percent who told the *New York Times* that they saw homeless people every day.

Kim Hopper (1987) speculated a little about how homelessness was viewed by the larger public, Joel Blau (1989, 1992) raised questions about the public positioning of homelessness, and Christopher Jencks (1994) questioned what it was that policy makers were arguing about. However, there has been little work that has attempted to develop an anthropological view of how the homeless crisis was lived and understood by those who were neither a part of the problem nor of the envisioned solution. This 82 percent saw homeless people every day, despite often having no idea what the housing status was of those who were seen. As with most stereotypes of "exotic others" the homeless trope represented not merely a justification for the political projects of interested actors, but also a psychic lightning rod for a variety of social anxieties, in this case, ones being experienced by ordinary New Yorkers. It is the 82 percent who were the vessel for this trope to which this chapter will turn.

In looking at this group, I will be drawing on fieldwork done between 1989 and 1990 on community activism and civic participation focused on housing, homelessness, and use of public space in New York City's Lower East Side/East Village neighborhood. The research was initiated as part of an attempt to understand the roots of the collective resistance to gentrification and the rioting and street battles between members of the community and police in August of 1988, in and around Tompkins Square Park, which, at the time, was home to a shantytown of over two hundred people, many of whom politically identified themselves as homeless or homeless activists. The neighborhood conflicts that were generated around this encampment provide some insight into the way the 82 percent who saw homeless every day experienced and contributed to the making and unmaking of the homeless crisis of the 1980s and early 1990s.

There was, of course, nothing about this neighborhood or the riots that could be described as ordinary or typical of the United States in the 1980s. In fact, this neighborhood, which provides the backdrop for the hit musical play *Rent*, might well be described as atypical, extreme, or even bizarre, due to its strange mix of anarchists, squatters, long-term heroin users, bohemians, Eastern European immigrants, Newyorikans, recent immigrants from Puerto Rico, and Manhattan yuppies. However, despite the characteristics of this neighborhood that made it unusual, even for New York City, the categories, images, and understandings surrounding housing, homelessness, and community were actually quite typical of New York City at the time. Though many of my informants came at these debates from different perspectives, often believing in radical political solutions, they all shared a common set of categories and assumptions. It is, I believe, the atypically high level of conscious political discussion and the hothouse quality of the debates about housing, homelessness, and community that made this neighborhood, in this particular time, a useful entry point into understanding the social construction of the homeless crisis in the 1980s and 1990s and how the problems of housing and homelessness were popularly understood, as well as larger questions about the political effects of the Reagan Revolution.

Space and Class in Tompkins Square: The Historical Backstory

As the only major open space in an otherwise crowded neighborhood filled with tenements, housing projects, and nineteenth century townhouses, Tompkins Square, with its large elm trees and open airy feel has, for over 150 years, stood as the neighborhood's central locus of conscious community activism and a site of explosive inchoate rebellion, leaving many generations of city officials struggling to impose civic order on unruly mobs making economic demands on the state and democratic claims on park space. The park has its origins in the 1811 City Commissioner's Plan that created Manhattan's grid pattern. However, it did not officially become a park until 1832, when New York City purchased slightly more than ten acres of land on the spot, planted grass and trees and laid out walkways. The square was named for Daniel Tompkins, governor of New York from 1807 to 1816 and vicepresident of the United States from 1817 to 1825.

By the 1850s unruly and impoverished immigrant populations from Ireland and Germany were regularly using the park as an assembly point for early labor demonstrations, food riots, political speak-outs, and other threats to public order. In the wake of the Civil War and the June 1863 draft riots the municipal government attempted to gain greater control over working-class public life, creating drill rooms, military parade grounds, and public armories throughout the city. In 1866 the city government deracinated the trees and grass, removed the walkways and turned Tompkins Square Park into a military parade ground. The military use of the only open space in one of the poorest and most densely populated neighborhoods in the world increased tensions and conflict, culminating in the "Tompkins Square Massacre" of 1874. Finally, in 1879 after both violent and nonviolent protests, the state legislature conceded to the climate of social reform and the discourse of "making citizens," agreeing to turn the square back into a park. In addition, a settlement house, a boys' club, and public welfare facilities were built around the park.

The arrival of Jews, Poles, Hungarians and Irish in the great migrations of the pre–World War I period created terrible overcrowding, as seen in the early twentieth century urban photography that remains popular. There was not enough public or private space and the park was often the site of interethnic conflict, union organizing, and revolutionary violence. Both Emma Goldman and Leon Trotsky are said to have given speeches in the park. In the 1940s and 1950s the construction of vast public housing at the Eastern end of the neighborhood brought in a wave of Black and Puerto Rican migration, and with it new tensions, that, by the mid 1960s found expression in park-based activities by the black power movement and the Puerto Rican nationalist movement. In the late 1960s hippies, antiwar activists, and other counterculture types arrived in the neighborhood, providing an origin for much of the alternative culture that contributed to the riots of 1988 and the mobilizations around housing throughout the 1980s.

The New York City fiscal crisis of 1975 hit the Lower East Side particularly hard. With a population that included many people of color,[1] low-income people who qualified for employment programs, senior citizens on various government programs, charity and community organizations dependent on government support, and public housing (DeGiovanni 1987, Turner 1984), much of the financial base and civic life in the neighborhood nearly disappeared. In the wake of the crisis, the municipal government almost completely disengaged from servicing this neighborhood.

An entire layer of low-capital weekend landlords who owned marginally profitable buildings in such lower-income neighborhoods throughout

New York City was wiped out by runaway inflation, the loss of renters, the OPEC oil shock of 1973 that dramatically raised the price of heating oil for apartment buildings, and strict rent control regulations that narrowly regulated rent increases. Landlords who did not burn down their buildings for insurance allowed the buildings to slowly fall down by ignoring basic maintenance and services and refusing to pay taxes (Barrett & Newfield 1988). I did a brief survey on the Lower East Side in 1990 and Harlem in 1992 that suggested that it was not uncommon for landlords or former managers of buildings that had been abandoned to collect rent long after the municipal authority had seized the buildings for nonpayment of taxes.

This social breakdown in the neighborhood made it a part of New York that was considered dangerous and unlivable for employed middle and working-class New Yorkers. Those who stayed behind watched the neighborhood deteriorate into a drug-riddled urban underground where heroin addicts froze to death in unheated burned-out buildings, prostitutes openly engaged in their business in storefronts of abandoned buildings, garbage piled up on the sidewalks, and streets at the eastern edge of the neighborhood (historically the poorest) often became virtually impassable for cars due to unrepaired pavement. Martin Scorsese's 1976 film *Taxi Driver*, one of a series of urban decay movies set in New York City in the 1970s, was filmed in this neighborhood and depicts the life of those who remained in this decaying city left fallow. As the infrastructure decayed the ideology and civic engagement of anarchists and hippies, along with the demimonde of prostitution, drugs, and teenage runaways increasingly filled the vacuum and defined neighborhood public life.

In the wake of the 1982–83 world economic contraction the city received hundreds of thousands of new immigrants from Latin American, Eastern European, and Asian countries, as well as the professionally oriented recent university graduates from the mainland United States who came to be known as yuppies. Absolute demand for housing and the numbers of people who could afford high rents increased. For much of the 1980s rents rose steadily with the underpaid, unemployed, disabled, and aged losing housing and being forced to move to unfamiliar neighborhoods. Armies of beggars took to the streets and public shelters were full on cold nights. Housing insecurity was the rule, even for the university educated and steadily employed. Neighborhoods all over New York that had previously been poor and working class were deluged by gentrification. Many of my informants who had lived in the Tompkins Square Park area for many years described this as yuppification or yuppie invasion, but many of these "yuppies" turned out, upon inspection, to be new leaseholders in their twenties and early thirties paying 50 percent or more of their income for rent.

One of my informants, a landlord who had managed to salvage a few buildings during the '70s after having lost nearly twenty-five to nonpayment of taxes, received offers during the summer of 1985 of $100,000 for each of these buildings that she had been unable to get $2,000 for in 1977. By 1990, many of these buildings were worth more than half a million dollars. However, the realization of income on these buildings often depended on forcing out long-standing residents with below-market leases. New York City's famous rent control/rent stabilization laws had, for decades, tightly restricted yearly rent increases, except in the case of new leases with "major capital improvements" to the apartment.

In this boomtown atmosphere there were many dramatic excesses. Senior citizens with incredibly low rents, based on long-standing tenure, were being beaten up or thrown down stairs in an attempt to get them out of their apartments. Mentally ill and economically marginal individuals who were often late with their rent payments were suddenly evicted for arrears, after years of tolerance on the part of landlords. When apartments did become vacant, the imperative to raise rents yielded strange, unnecessary, and fraudulent major capital improvements such as surplus double glazed external windows put into walls between rooms in an apartment, sinks, toilets, and stoves exchanged between apartments and buildings; and renovation claims made on apartments that had not been improved since the introduction of hot water and private bathrooms. Despite these efforts to raise rents, many apartments were still far below market rates and landlords, brokers, and supers expected large bribes from new leaseholders or simply granted leases to friends, business associates, the very lucky, and those willing to trade sexual favors for special consideration in obtaining a lease.

The entire process involved mass displacements of those who were unable to pay the new rents and left even those with below-market leases watching their rents rise the maximum amount each year. In some areas of the city poorer residents were driven out entirely, while other areas saw an integration of older neighborhood residents and newly arriving "yuppies" who worked in the financial and other related sectors. Finally, in some neighborhoods there was mass displacement based on price speculation, but few new residents. Nearly everywhere in the city rents were rising, evictions became common, and landlords were exerting pressure on prior residents whose rent stabilized leases were below market prices (DeGiovanni 1987, Barrett & Newfield 1988).

With truly dramatic returns on small investments and folk legends about overnight millionaires, real estate speculation became a central part of New York. However, even many individuals who had purchased apartments in the 1980s found themselves displaced by the stock market crash of 1987. Housing became a virtual obsession on the part of nearly all New Yorkers and it became a constant topic of discussion at social gatherings. Newspapers printed stories about people who had spent two years looking for apartments, and storefront apartment brokerage businesses were opening all over the city, giving old neighborhoods like Hells Kitchen, Loisaida (the Lower East Side), the printing district, West Harlem, and the Bowery the new names Clinton, the East Village, Tribeca, Morningside

Heights, and Noho, respectively. These brokers typically took 15 percent of the first year's rent plus under-the-table bribes depending on the desirability of the lease. It was this 1980s atmosphere of great danger, tremendous possibility, and imminent catastrophe with regard to the basic need of shelter that helped give mass salience to the category of homeless and yielded what I will, in the next section, refer to as housing panic.

Panic in New York: the Raw and the Cooked

On 19 September 1989, in the midst of the homeless crisis the *New York Times* published the following headline on page 2 of their B section, "Woman's Skull Found in Pail at Bus Depot." The story mentioned that the woman was a Swiss dance student and that her lover, Daniel Rakowitz, had given himself up to the police, admitting to having murdered her. The next day on page B 5 the *Times* ran the headline "Accused Slayer of Girlfriend Began a Religion, Police Say," and they described Daniel Rakowitz as a squatter in Tompkins Square Park in New York City and "a marijuana dealer who created his own religion and sometimes said he was God." Wild rumors began to fly around the neighborhood, as reports emerged in the tabloids and electronic media sources that described Rakowitz as a formerly homeless man who, when threatened with being evicted from his apartment by Monika Beerle, the woman he was sleeping with, had killed her, and cooked her in a stew which he served to the homeless in Tompkins Square Park.

The news of Rakowitz's arrest moved like lightning through the neighborhood, with nearly everybody I met in bars, restaurants, community centers, garden and roof parties, and Tompkins Square Park discussing the incident and recalling his unkempt stringy blonde hair, the pet rooster with a sock over its head that he had carried around, his frequent begging for groceries to cook meals for the homeless, and his attempts to start a religion known as "church of 966." The question everybody raised was why a seemingly harmless and gentle neighborhood loony whom everybody knew, would do something so terrible and grisly. The most common explanation offered was some variety of "housing panic": he had been homeless and would do anything to avoid having it happen again.

Within a few weeks of the arrest Hollywood movie actor and neighborhood resident Max Cantor, who later died of a heroin overdose, wrote a long article in the *Village Voice* that drew on interviews with people who had known Rakowitz from the neighborhood. Throughout the winter people continued to discuss the incident and articles and letters appeared in the community newspapers. Rakowitz was eventually tried and found not guilty by reason of insanity. However suspicion hung over the trial verdict, which was rumored to have been the result of one juror trying to drag the trial out because he needed the $15 per day juror remuneration. People in the neighborhood gossiped endlessly about the many irregularities in the investigation and trial, including a first confession that had been ignored by the police and the failure to seal the apartment on 9th Street where the crime had occurred, allowing hundreds of journalists and news crews to ruin the forensic evidence.

At the time, people in the neighborhood expressed much anger at the authorities for what they believed was a cavalier approach to what they perceived as "neighborhood craziness" and a matter involving a "homeless man." The true details of the case will probably never be known and have become more and more interesting and outrageous with each intervening year and each new serial killer cannibal Web site that mentions Rakowitz. However, for the purposes of this analysis, what is important is that newspaper coverage and electronic media reports generally referred to him as a homeless man or a squatter, and the ubiquitous neighborhood discussions were almost entirely focused on his housing status.

There was very little discussion of the themes that have, in the intervening years, made this case part of popular folklore: occult religion, misogyny and sexual obsession, the incompetence of the police, mental illness, and concern for vulnerable foreign students. Even the highly celebrated issue of cannibalism that the case has come to be remembered for seemed to be of only secondary importance. "Daniel," as he was known to neighbors, was identifiable to many who lived in the neighborhood as a homeless man who had lost housing, regained housing, and then been threatened once again with housing loss by a scheming foreign female, using her sexuality to obtain an inexpensive lease. It came down to the argument that he had to kill or be killed. Housing and homelessness had become such a popular obsession that many people came close to arguing for justifiable homicide based on the threat of homelessness or losing a good lease. Several of my neighborhood informants suggested that there was a form of temporary insanity that might be called New York City housing panic.

At a barbecue held after the Gay Pride Day parade in June 1990 in one of the backyards behind a tenement off Avenue C an argument broke out over the Rakowitz case that suggests the surprising degree to which housing panic came to be seen as something real that anybody could have. A Euro-American woman in her late twenties, who worked as a civil servant, forcefully made the comment that, "of course he killed the dancer. She was trying to take his apartment." A man interjected that, "he didn't have to cook her and eat her." The woman continued, "I'm from New York and nobody messes with your apartment here. If they do, they have to expect something bad is going to happen. You don't fuck with somebody's apartment if you want to stay alive. We all used to see that guy begging for groceries in front of the Key Foods. He was disgusting and crazy and fucked up. Who would ever have sex with him, except some scheming Euro-trash who wanted to steal his apartment? Too bad she wound up soup, but you don't fuck with a New Yorker's apartment."

Despite the harshness and seemingly irrational suspension of ordinary norms of humanity and law, the notion of justifiable homicide based on housing panic that this woman was advancing was not immediately dismissed. Somebody pointed out that Rakowitz was actually from Texas to which the woman responded that it didn't matter, being a New Yorker was a matter of attitude not place. Another woman expressed disgust with what the first woman had said, "How can you possibly defend killing someone for a lease?" Someone responded by saying, "The guy was pretty unhinged to begin with, all that stuff about Church of 966 or 1066 or whatever, but I bet the threat of being homeless put him over the edge." There was nobody in the group who was willing to fully support what the first woman had said, yet, there was also a general recognition that an apartment was a life-and-death matter and that it was easy to imagine how crazed and scared Rakowitz might have been when confronted by losing his apartment to a woman he had slept with only a few times.

The second woman jumped in again. "Is everybody in this city crazy? You don't kill someone for an apartment." One man, a gay actor who had lived in the neighborhood for many years, defended the first woman, arguing that "people kill their bosses when they get fired, people kill lovers when they are cheating, why not an apartment? It's better than a job or most of the lovers I've had." The second woman was becoming increasingly frustrated, particularly after the round of joking about bad lovers. She burst out in a slow, deliberate, almost pedagogical tone, "Listen to me, it's crazy. Even in New York, you can't justify murder based on housing." The woman's serious tone had made some nervous and the actor responded with another quip about sex and housing. The first woman reiterated her view that, "It may be crazy, but it isn't stupid. You don't mess with someone's apartment in this city." The second woman excused herself from the group, saying she wanted to get a drink and the first woman muttered off in her direction "go back to Connecticut lady."

The discussion continued in a more friendly way with speculation about why the Swiss dancer was sleeping with Rakowitz, how disgusting that must have been, how much she was having an adventure and how much she was calculating, how Rakowitz must have felt when he found out he was going to be homeless again, and whether he had a good heart deep down since he was always making chicken stew for the homeless. When the stew was mentioned there were nervous jokes about the shocking last meal he cooked for the homeless, but this, like most discussions of the incident, focused mostly on the question of housing, homelessness, and what kind of violence was justifiable to secure an apartment. The views presented by this first woman, suggesting that Rakowitz had an almost customary right to kill Monika Beerle, were certainly not in the majority even in the neighborhood, but they were not uncommon. More importantly, they represented in distilled form the very surprising phenomenon of large numbers of ordinary people identifying with an unkempt, psychotic, cannibal, and murderer.

New Yorkers outside the Tompkins Square Park area were much less likely to be sympathetic to the killer, probably because they had neither met him nor experienced the hothouse world of the East Village, but they also typically focused on housing and homelessness. Regardless of their assessment of Daniel Rakowitz and sympathy for the family of Monika Beerle, the predominant sense was that somehow the New York City housing market had fuelled this tragedy by driving Monika Beerle to move in with Rakowitz, setting off the chain of events that made him explode. In fact, a fund was set up in Monika Beerle's name to help international students who could not afford New York City housing.

The Daniel Rakowitz of Internet lore whose story now sits on Web sites next to Issei Sagawa, Jeffrey Dahmer, Andrei Chikatilo, Armin Miewes "the gay cannibal," and other infamous serial killing cannibals did not yet exist. For most of his East Village neighbors, at the time, he was a tragic and pathetic character who certainly belonged in prison, but more for an irreparable mistake that he had made than for the kind of evil cult activity associated with figures like Charles Manson. The old Puerto Rican woman who adopted his rooster when he went to prison told me in 1998 that she still felt bad about poor Daniel, "He went crazy for the dancer and didn't know what he was doing. He must have been crazy. He named his rooster Daniel."

In a world where landlords wanted high turnover in leases, Europeans, like Monika Beerle, who might only stay a year were often favored as tenants, people were being evicted from longtime homes on technicalities, senior citizens were being thrown down stairs to get them out of desirable leases, and leaseholders throughout New York were facing rapid changes in the availability of affordable housing, the stakes had been raised to the point where it seemed that almost anything was acceptable in the battle for space. It was in this world of individual leaseholders fighting with their landlords, neighbors, and apartment mates over individual leases and apartments that the category of homeless came to be a lightning rod for collective anxieties about financial insecurity, social reproduction, and housing. The ravages of the Reagan Revolution were creating a world that might have been summed up by Margaret Thatcher's famous assertion that "there is no society, only individuals." With no counterhegemonic strong forces presenting viable social housing, employment, health care, or education alternatives the homeless became the helpless, blameless, Christ-like symbols of the best intentions and the worst outcomes.

Homelessness and Urban Physiocrats

In most neighborhoods in New York City the increasing insecurity brought by rising rents and declining housing options for both white and blue-collar working-class people yielded the attitude of "every man against all and the devil take the hindmost." However, in the East Village radical oppositional community organizations, cultural activities, and political struggles emerged around issues of housing and gentrification, culminating in what was probably New York's largest and most destructive urban riot since the 1977 blackout on 6 August 1988 in the area around Tompkins Square Park. Described alternately as "the battle for Tompkins Square Park," "the battle for tent city," and later after the 1989 election, anachronistically, "the battle for Dinkinsville," the riot occurred toward the end of a particularly hot summer and centered heavily on defense of a large homeless encampment in Tompkins Square Park and the right to late-night recreational use of the park.

It was one of those summers when the heat is unrelenting and most people in the Lower East Side, a neighborhood without much air conditioning,[2] stayed out of their often airless tenement apartments until quite late. The 6th of August was a Saturday night, and the neighborhood was filled with out-of-towners, suburban teenagers, and people who lived in and around the neighborhood, enjoying the local bars, nightspots, clubs, inexpensive restaurants, and street culture.

During the previous two weekends, the police department had attempted to break up late-night gatherings in the park.[3] The order had come from the office of then-mayor Ed Koch in response to complaints about noise and radio playing at all hours. Radios had been confiscated and there had been threats from the city that a 1:00 a.m. park closing would be enforced, as per the law. But on the evening of 6 August hundreds of people were congregating in the park and seem to have expected that there would be some trouble.

When 450 police showed up in riot gear and created a police line in the park that sought to drive everyone out, it seemed to many that an army was invading their neighborhood. One informant, an actor who lives in the neighborhood and was near the park when it happened described it as a "police blitzkrieg." Anarchists, squatters, homeless, and other late-night park denizens met the police with resistance, shouting obscenities, smashing empty beer bottles on the pavement, and throwing bottles at the police who were trying to herd the intransigent crowd away from the park. At a certain point the police charged the crowd, covering their badges and swinging clubs. By this time the battle had spilled onto the streets and police on horseback were charging down St. Mark's Place, clubbing everyone from people out walking their dogs to people who were sitting on their front stoops. Senior citizens were knocked over, press photographers were specifically targeted by police who smashed their cameras, and the manager of an upscale cafe who had been known to help homeless people in the park was dragged from her restaurant and beaten.

A helicopter was used to secure the rooftops from people who'd been hurling bottles onto the streets surrounding the park, which had by now been brought under police control. The fire department was called in and escorted into the park by police, because people had returned to the park to set mounds of garbage on fire. In the end, forty civilians and thirteen policemen were injured and there were 121 complaints of police brutality. In the weeks that followed, virtually no police were punished for misconduct. The official report blamed the incident largely on a breakdown of leadership at the command level, because the officer in charge had had a case of the runs and chose to use a precinct toilet blocks away, rather than use the public restrooms in the park after it had been secured. The report also pointed to the deployment of too many "rookie cops" who lost their cool.

In the course of fieldwork, I heard many accounts of why the riot of 1988 occurred and who the main players were. Many people accepted the official reports that pointed to overreaction on the part of police to the instigations of anarchists, squatters, troublemaking teenagers from the suburbs, and groups perceived as everything from outside agitators to inside inflammations. However, few could deny that the battle had involved a very wide cross section of the neighborhood. It was not just that ordinary citizens were being clubbed. The riots were the culmination of years of conflict and struggle within the neighborhood over use of the park, use of the streets and sidewalks, use of abandoned buildings seized by the city for nonpayment of taxes,[4] and conditions produced by a declining social wage. Though the municipal government did manage to clear tent city and bulldoze the shanties, residents soon returned to an uneasy compromise with police where they broke down their tents at 7:00 a.m. every morning.

Most of my informants who were not squatters, anarchists, or community activists affiliated with those groups aggressively stressed the fact that it was not homeless people who battled the police. This sentiment was well put by a university student who lived in the neighborhood who told me that, "It was not the homeless who fought the police. They were too busy trying to protect their stuff. It was the rest of us. It was the whole neighborhood. Why do you think they needed horses? Not to chase a bunch of homeless people with shopping bags. They wanted to teach the whole neighborhood a lesson, so the developers can come in and take over." Another informant who had recently moved to the neighborhood claimed that, "as long as we let the homeless stay in the park nobody is going to invest big money in this neighborhood." This sentiment coming from a waiter at an upscale restaurant in Soho neatly mirrors statements by anarchists and squatters that "this is total war and we need to make the neighborhood unlivable for yuppies."

It is clear from personal reports—as well as newspaper, radio and TV accounts—that those who regularly slept in the park were not among the most fierce combatants, although some did fight the police. The fact that the homeless (who were the main users of the park after midnight) were not the main combatants, and that people in the community were very careful to tell me this, makes one wonder why it was so important for neighborhood residents to declare the homeless innocent of protecting their tent camps. This may have something to do with the need of local residents to view the homeless as passive and truly blameless victims, justifying their continuing presence in the park. However, beyond tolerating the homeless, neighborhood residents tended to see them as symbolic figures in a moral discourse that represented the articulation of fears and insecurities. Like the surprising sympathy for Daniel Rakowitz, the view that many neighborhood people from varying economic and ethnic backgrounds had about the events of 6 August 1988 seemed to be heavily refracted through the lens of housing panic.

Although most residents of the neighborhood were uncomfortable with the anarchist plan to make the neighborhood unlivable for yuppies and unappealing to developers, there was a certain sense in which improvements in the quality and appearance of the neighborhood were seen as signs of creeping gentrification, and not welcomed. As one of my informants who worked as a teacher in a Brooklyn public high school put it, "I never know whether to be happy when the neighborhood gets better or sad. I'm tired of living in a crappy neighborhood where people yell die yuppie scum at me when I go off to work in the morning. I want a neighborhood where there are decent people and nice places to shop, but it's not like I could afford the rent in a nice neighborhood." In many ways the homeless in Tent City had become a kind of stand-in for the displacement anxieties of renters throughout the neighborhood. There was the sense that as long as those "annoying, disgusting homeless people are there we can sleep safely at night. The homeless in Tent City had also become Christ figures for a neighborhood bound together by housing panic and real estate fear.

But the question remains as to exactly who the main combatants were, and why they were willing to risk life and limb for the rights of another group of people. There seems to be general agreement that the major combatants were squatters, anarchists, and other "outside" troublemakers. Both mainstream and alternative news sources suggest a central role for these groups, neighborhood residents agree on this verdict, and police reports tend to blame them, while subsequent battles for the park saw them singled out by the police for harassment and beatings. More importantly, these groups themselves proudly took credit for having been "on the front lines of the battle." This assertion had one major proviso, which is that some homeless did battle the police and that the distinction between homeless people who pitched tents in the park and squatters who occupied buildings seized by the city was a false distinction. Many tent city dwellers were neighborhood residents who had been removed from squats by the city, people on mental or physical disability who lost housing but feared the violence of municipal shelters, aging 1960s/70s hippie residents and youth who were in couples and could not face being broken up by entering the system, and other members of the "community" who had lost housing, but could not imagine life outside their neighborhood.

There was much that united these two groups. On one level, there was the shared ideology of wanting "to free up the land." On another level they worked together in building a counterculture that by the mid 1980s had become almost completely focused on housing. I attended several parties in East Village squats during the late 1980s and early 1990s and spent entire nights listening to people talk about housing and land and play folk songs and rock songs about housing, landlords, squats, and homelessness. Some of the people from Tent City attended squatter parties and the anarchist speak-outs that were held every week in Tompkins Square. Finally, in the winter of 1989–'90 a small army of squatters, homesteaders, tent city dwellers, and various neighborhood characters who often slept in semipublic spaces seized and began the renovation of the ABC community center.

In January of 1990, a group of squatters, anarchists, and tent city residents seized a large turn-of-the-century building on Fourth Street between Avenues B and C. It had once been Public School 105, but had been abandoned due to the city budget cuts of 1975. The group opened the building up under the name "ABC Community Center," named after the three most prominent streets in the neighborhood: Avenues A, B, and C. They started renovations for a multipurpose community center that would provide permanent, semipermanent, and temporary housing for people living on the streets, as well as educational programs such as remedial reading, GED-high school equivalency test preparation, and the ubiquitous carpentry, plumbing, and electrical repair classes for which the squatter movement was famous. Perhaps most threatening to the city government and the community forces aligned with it was the fact that the ABC Community Center was to be a major resource that would have provided the myriad of anti-gentrification/antistate political groups in the neighborhood with a single headquarters and meeting place.

These groups moved rapidly to commit their energies and their meager resources to, as one anarchist put it, "put the state on notice that homeless and poor can free up the land and build communities." The anti-gentrification band known as The Missing Foundation came and gave a concert. This rock band, described by local press as "shadowy and violent" due to its ubiquitous Lower East Side graffitto showing an overturned cocktail glass with the words "the party's over" inscribed below, had caused a stir on local TV news and in newspapers over the previous two summers for its guerilla rock concerts in public places without a permit and its supposed involvement in antipolice action during the "battle for tent city." The anarchist newspaper collective *The Shadow,* which had won the hatred of the local police for publishing pictures of known undercover officers and listing undercover police car license plate numbers was helping to set up literacy and high-school equivalency programs at the ABC community center. A local Tompkins Square based communist organization, known as "The Class War Tendency," whose members were squatting in a "bomb crater" several blocks away attempted to set up political economy classes, and the radical housing activist priest at the local church was involved in helping the homeless to set up a soup kitchen that operated out of the community center.

The Dinkins administration responded with a police mobilization that was the biggest among the many that I had seen up to that point. An artist and housepainter who lived on the block where the ABC had been described it as "bigger than the invasion of Grenada." The police presence was seen by many as an attempt to prevent such things from happening again, and as insurance against a repeat of the 1988 riot. The police sealed off the entire street on which the community center was located and surrounded the building. They brought hundreds of police in on buses and used armored vehicles, tear gas, and attack dogs. The operation took about a week, including a police blockade (broken several times by local clergy, community groups, and squatters); evictions and re-evictions after people re-entered through secret passages; and a room-by-room search, during which people were often holed up behind heavily barricaded fire doors. The entire block was kept sealed off for several days after the building had been cleared and its residents sent back to Tompkins Square Park. A few squatters had use of a van and helped tent city residents, several of whom were in the anarchist movement with them, bring their furniture and personal belongings back to the park. The building was sealed and there was a twenty-four-hour police presence for many weeks afterward.

In the wake of the siege, the city government claimed that this large undertaking was necessary not only because of the criminal nature of what had been done, but because the city was hoping to eventually renovate the building and make it a shelter for homeless senior citizens. However, this lost battle made many people in the squatter community more suspicious and more fearful that they would be next. Although they were far better organized and politically connected than those in tent city, and the duration of their squats (sometimes more than ten years) generally gave them more security and made it harder for the city to evict them, their position was always precarious and seemed to depend on politics, as much as keeping their buildings safe and still standing. Many squats were lost to building inspectors, suspicious fires in adjacent buildings that neighborhood residents claimed the fire department was in no hurry to extinguish, trumped-up police charges, and even the destruction of buildings in the middle of the night. It was therefore seen as a basic necessity for squatters to stick together, work with the homeless, and develop good relations with other neighborhood residents.

There is a story that was told by a close informant from California, who moved to the neighborhood after finishing college in the Midwest. She nicely summed up the relationship between squatters, anarchists, and the residents of Tent City. She described how, on a Sunday in December of 1990, after a demonstration against the war in the Persian Gulf held at the Waldorf Astoria, anarchists held a metal-banging session in Tompkins Square, using pots and pans and sticks. They did this until quite late at night and made a racket that could be heard throughout the neighborhood. Police in riot gear had been making "threatening noises" for some time. About midnight, a group of residents of tent city approached the demonstrators and told them that they wanted to go to sleep. The demonstrators, many of whom were squatters, respected this request and calmly went home.

Sitting on their stoops dressed in their on-the-barricades style pre-grunge clothing and talking of their experiences in terms of "pioneering," "frontier-life," and "fighting housing battles for everyone," they saw themselves as political leaders in a housing movement. At squatter parties, bands played rock, punk, and folk music about killing landlords and abolishing rent; people read poems about housing and homelessness; and one of the most popular topics of discussion was housing. Although it was not that unusual to find a party in New York in the 1980s where everyone was talking about housing, the squatters tended to frame their conversations almost solely in terms of struggle, social change, and confrontation with the state. A prominent graffito around the neighborhood read "total war for space!"

They believed that the 1988 riots represented a major victory against the state. Usually, their confrontations with real estate interests and the state ran the gamut from occupying the waiting room of a corporate office and harassing the receptionist to throwing beer bottles at police. Sometimes they were effective at setting a tone of chaos and antistate, anticorporate conflict that caused others to be brought into a situation in a way that was beneficial to their cause. Very often, little was accomplished, but one always heard them say such things as "it proves what seven people can do for social change." However, as the history of struggles over homelessness and housing in the Lower East Side makes clear, the community of squatters and anarchists could not have done it alone, without ties to their neighbors and an overall climate of housing panic.

Housing: The Tie that Binds

There was a plain, simple fact that constantly emerged in all my research on the neighborhood: housing was an issue that troubled and motivated virtually everyone. There were tenant rights groups; housing activists; radical priests who were arrested over housing struggles; local merchants who helped the homeless; restaurants that provided food for the Tent City soup kitchen; numerous well-organized and successful rent strikes; and multiracial, multiethnic coalitions against real estate speculation. The Lower East Side was a neighborhood in which residence often forced people to develop a high level of political consciousness and awareness of housing issues.

Most residents would not have been living in this neighborhood if they had more money. This applied not only to people living at the economic margins: those in substandard housing, who were doubling or tripling up with other families (DeGiovanni 1987), or who squatted in cold-water flats in abandoned buildings, but also to the many young people working in temporary jobs, living two or three to a one-bedroom apartment. It even applied to yuppies, which on the Lower East Side often meant college-educated entry-level professionals paying half their income in rent and much of the other half in student loans. The fact that these yuppies were usually people who could only afford to get what they regarded as adequate Manhattan housing in the Lower East Side often gave them a keen awareness of the ways in which city policy and real estate development crippled their ability to live the lifestyle of an urban professional. As a result, many people who differed greatly in income level and occupation shared a strong sympathy and empathy for those at the bottom of the housing market hierarchy. The squatters, anarchists, and tent city denizens believed that they were fighting the war for housing for everyone. While this may or may not actually be true, there is a level at which many people in the neighborhood came to accept this to be the case.

The degree to which much of the neighborhood viewed the control of each building and each lot as a struggle with "the powers that be" is suggested by a story that was related to me by an informant who could be considered a yuppie, had little in the way of political beliefs, and had lived in the neighborhood for about five years. The first year she moved in, there were two "bomb craters" across the street from her apartment. One was in the process of being renovated by squatters, and the other, larger one was standing idle. One day, the city sent workmen to put up a scaffolding around the empty building in preparation for demolition. The next day they ran the scaffolding all the way to the building that was being fixed up by the squatters. Late one night, she was awakened by a terrible racket outside her window. She looked out and saw that the squatters were tearing down the scaffolding. People up and down the street stuck their heads out of bedroom windows to scream obscenities at these late-night workmen, but they stopped when they realized what was going on. Within a few minutes there were people all over the block hanging out the windows and cheering. The squatters received an ovation from the neighborhood for tearing down the scaffolding around both buildings. The city eventually evicted the squatters and tore down both buildings, and the lots remained empty for many years. However, this stood as a moment when everyone from urban professionals to the owners of bodegas, who also feared rising rents, united in the middle of the night to cheer on the efforts of people who they believed stood at the front lines of the housing battle.[5]

One Man's Story

A final story that ties together some of these themes is that of Jaime, a homeless man who lived under a pile of cardboard in an abandoned lot next to an apartment building in the heart of Loisaida.[6] Jaime was a well-known neighborhood character who was badly ravaged by alcohol to the point of incoherence. Although he spent most of the winter sleeping in the lot and sitting on the stoop of the building bothering everyone who passed by, on very cold days he would sleep on the top floor landing of the stairs inside the building. Sometimes he would vomit or defecate on the stairs when he was particularly drunk. Although the tenants of this twenty-one-unit tenement did not like this situation, Jaime was a childhood friend of the superintendent, who tolerated and sometimes helped him.

The general feeling among the tenants who were yuppies, working-class whites, Puerto Ricans, NYU and Cooper Union students, and older bohemians was that there was not much to be done and that the least they could do for Jaime was to put up with his occasional drunken accidents. Everyone resented the way he bothered people, leered at women who lived in the building, and always insisted that "Jaime is number one on the block." However, he was always friendly, totally harmless, and ever-present on the stoop. He was a kind of building doorman, and people felt safe coming home and fumbling for their keys when Jaime was on the stoop babbling at them. No one claimed to want him there, and yet if he wasn't there many people would worry about him and no one would feel as safe entering the building at night.

Jaime had lived for twenty-five years, since he and his family arrived in New York from Puerto Rico, in a building that had been where the lot now sat. When it burned down under suspicious circumstances in the '70s, he'd moved into another building on the block, but was evicted as part of recent renovations. After this he moved back to the lot where his home had been. He simply did not want to leave his block, where he knew people and felt accepted. He was living on welfare and, being illiterate, had his forms filled out by an actress who lived in the building, with her carpenter husband.

When spring came, a block committee that had been organized by a group of "homesteaders"[7] undertook a project to build a community garden on the lot. They built a small house in it for Jaime. The community center next door provided the know-how, materials, and student laborers to build him a sturdy six-by-nine foot tar paper shack. He called the garden his "hacienda" and the students who built the shack his "employees." He had keys to the cyclone fence that surrounded the garden and kept many cats to protect him from rats attacking him in his sleep. He became the keeper of the keys and anyone who wanted to join the community garden was expected to walk Jaime over to a hardware store on Avenue C, pay for cutting a key, and buy Jaime lunch at his favorite Puerto Rican *comedor*.

Jaime's life was a very difficult and lonely struggle with displacement, alcoholism, sickness, and the many other problems that are created and exacerbated by poverty and powerlessness. His presence represented a thorn in the sides of the people who lived in the building. Yet many people talked about how they wished they did not have to pay rent, like Jaime. He came to be a symbol of people's fears and insecurities about housing. With housing costs high, public assistance benefits greatly reduced from the 1970s, and the public shelter system a dangerous battle zone, Jaime had no better options. Similarly, the residents of the building lived in tiny apartments in a dilapidated building on a street that was barely paved.

Most of them faced increasingly insecure, temporary, and underpaid employment, longer working hours, and rising rents. In such an environment, they were too defensive to be enthusiastic about trying to evict someone who had a long-standing claim on life in the neighborhood.

In light of the rapidly shrinking social wage and the absence of a satisfactory government housing policy, these neighbors accepted the reality that the best thing they could do to "help the homeless" was to join with others on the block and build a structure that was barely fit for a dog to live in. But a tar paper shack in a community garden was superior to a tent in Tompkins Square Park that must be collapsed every morning at 7:00 a.m. And even this, for many people, was far better than the dangerous, atomized prison-like conditions in city shelters like "the Fort."

Epilogue

In June of 1991, then-mayor David Dinkins announced that the city would no longer tolerate the use of public parks as living spaces. He issued an order giving the residents of Tent City three days to remove themselves and their possessions from the park and announced that the park would be closed for eight months for renovation and modernization. Community meetings were called and angry neighborhood residents vented much frustration at the fact that the city was closing the park at the beginning of summer. Homeless activists, squatters, and others concerned with housing issues organized demonstrations to defend Tent City and keep the park open.

The eviction happened at about 10:30 in the morning, when many of the working residents of the neighborhood were away. A few hundred squatters, anarchists, and people who worked night shifts or were unemployed came out to "defend the park," but to little avail. The roughly one thousand police who were dispatched to the eviction were well disciplined, well coordinated, and heavily protected by armored vehicles, mounted police, and secured rooftops all around the park. Within a few hours the park was entirely emptied of everyone but police. A razor-wire cyclone fence was erected around the perimeter of the park. At key points around the perimeter of the park temporary police command units were set up in trailers and a permanent police office was inaugurated inside the park. During the months that the park was closed there was a twenty-four-hour-a-day police guard at all the approaching streets and constant police activity within the park.

When the reconstruction of the park was completed, the city had, indeed modernized the park, by separating the public spaces, removing the fifty-year-old band shell that had been the site of many historic concerts in the 1960s and 1970s and later hosted the antistate/pro-housing rock concerts of the 1980s. In the summer of 1996 the final nails were put in the coffin of this brief neighborhood social movement of the 1980s as New York City mayor Rudolph Giuliani decided to finally eliminate squatters from the neighborhood. After years of inconclusive battles of position in the courts, between squatters and the city government over the legality of squats, Mayor Giuliani took decisive action. After evicting residents from a few of the isolated, but long-standing neighborhood squats, he ordered police to hit the movement at its strongest point.

In the early morning hours of 13 August 1995 several hundred police with armored cars, tear gas, and riot gear sealed off 13th Street between Avenue A and Avenue B. On this block there was a group of three large tenements that had been home to dozens of neighborhood squatters for over a decade. Police went in and removed men, women, and children, many of whom had grown up in these buildings. There was resistance by the people being evicted, but very little in the way of community support. For the most part residents of the block and the surrounding area were quiet about the whole incident.

The brief moment in which these homeless activists, anarchists, and squatters had been able to articulate the fears and aspirations of a whole community and involve them in a "battle for space" was past. Mayor Giuliani was interviewed that night on the local television news saying, "We had to do this, there is no place for people living in New York City and not paying rent. That just isn't the way life works." While many people in the neighborhood grumbled about the evictions and the mayor's statement and referred to him as "Mussolini on the Hudson," there was little in the way of neighborhood involvement in the protests against this action.

Many of the same anarchists and homeless, who had been able to drag ordinary neighborhood residents into their fights with the state in the period before, during, and after the 1988 Tompkins Square Park police riot, found they were only talking to themselves. Despite housing getting tighter, a persistent problem of people sleeping in public, and many of the former park dwellers, anarchists, and squatters remaining in the neighborhood in basements, communal apartments, and doorways, the struggle for community, social justice, and housing had disappeared along with the housing panic that had spurred it. In its place was a sense of defeat about being able to collectively shape the community. As one person who lived near the 13th Street squats told me, "they were good neighbors, always helping you fix things, always out on the stoop keeping watch, I had no complaints, but you play with fire and you get burned. People just got tired of them fighting the police." Another neighborhood resident, who worked for a national magazine and had been involved in several demonstrations during the late 1980s, said about the housing activists who had once electrified the neighborhood, "you know, there was always trouble wherever they went. For a while it was pretty exciting, but my life is too short to be fighting over falling down buildings. What did they ever do that actually helped this neighborhood? As they say you can't beat city hall." Around the time of these evictions, I was informed by one of the members of the community garden in which Jaime had lived that he had died of tuberculosis and diabetes, after being removed from his garden shack by paramedics and taken to Bellevue Hospital. By this time, it was the late 1990s and both the Reagan Revolution and the fight against it were receding into the realm of distant contemporary history and had been transformed into a Broadway play and social memories of youthful idealism.

Notes

1. According to 1980 Census figures (cited in Turner 1984), the population of the Lower East Side was, at the time, 32 percent White, 8.6 percent Black, 35.3 percent Spanish Origin (mostly Puerto Rican), and 22.7 percent Asian.

2. While many people living in the Lower East Side at the time could not afford either an air conditioner or the greatly increased electricity bills that using one would entail, it is worth keeping in mind that many apartments in the neighborhood simply did not have the electrical carrying capacity for effective cooling. A typical two to four room apartment in a tenement often will have one fifteen amp line. If one assumes roughly two to five amps for a refrigerator and six to ten amps for an air conditioner, it is difficult to imagine even those with the money to pay for both the air conditioner and the additional electricity effectively cooling such apartments.

3. The following account of the riot, the events leading up to it, and the aftermath has been compiled from reports in the *New York Times, New York Newsday,* and the *Village Voice* during the first and second weeks of August 1988, from a documentary audiocassette on the riot prepared by WBAI radio, and from descriptions by informants who were present.

4. According to several of our informants who owned buildings in the 1970's, it was a common practice in periods of high oil prices not to pay real estate taxes for as long as two years. This was not done in preparation for abandonment, but as a kind of low-interest loan to pay for heating oil. When buildings finally were abandoned they often had huge uncollectible tax debts against them. Since these buildings were virtually worthless at the time and the state had little or no efficient apparatus for managing them, much money that was owed to the state was never recouped.

5. I don't mean to suggest that the Lower East Side is a neighborhood in which residents speak with one voice on housing issues. Conflict does occur: such as that between low income minority groups struggling for integrated public housing and the middle-class Orthodox Jews who resisted it during the 1970s. However, the general scarcity of decent, affordable housing in an area with many poor people has provided otherwise diverse groups with a common interest in resisting gentrification and opposing state policies that either ignore or aggravate the current housing crisis.

6. "Loisaida" is the Spanglish word for Lower East Side. It refers principally to the part of the neighborhood that is farthest east and still largely Latino. Unlike parts of the Lower East Side that were being called the East Village, Loisaida had not been gentrified much, the housing stock was poor, and there was very little business catering to tourists and so-called yuppies.

7. Homesteader refers to people who were trying to reclaim abandoned buildings through the continuous occupancy and "improvement of the land" being employed by squatters, but without the resistant antistate antiprivate property ideologies. They were, in fact, attempting legal battles to gain recognized title to the buildings that they lived in.

— *Chapter 9* —

AMERICAN THATCHERISM:
THE MAKING AND UNMAKING OF A CRISIS

From Downing Street Discord
to Washington Consensus

By the end of 1993 New York City had its first Republican mayor in two decades, the Democrats had the White House, and I was finished with my employment as a research associate at the CTI project. Everything was changing, including the homeless crisis. There was talk of closing the Fort Washington Men's Shelter, media coverage of homeless issues was dropping by the day, and it suddenly seemed that everybody, including my employers, was trying to find new areas for research and funding. Some of my colleagues continued with homeless studies, but many realized that it was time to shift directions. Clinton's campaign the previous year had been filled with appeals to "Reagan Democrats." He publicly disrespected prominent African-American Democrat Jesse Jackson and interrupted his campaign to return to Arkansas for a showcase execution of retarded African American Ricky Ray Rector—none of "the usual suspects" in the Democratic Party had raised much protest in response to Clinton's premeditated attempts to marginalize the African American leadership of the Democratic Party. The combination of Clinton's fiscal conservatism as governor of Arkansas, the tremendous sway he seemed to have over the liberals and African Americans, and the weakness of the union movement after twelve years of assault did not bode well for welfare and other social support programs that depended on the support of these sectors.

Long before the sound of Fleetwood Mac filled the streets of Washington on inauguration day, it was clear that there was going to be a new approach to managing the intersection of poverty and race in the United States. The explosion of ghetto riots across the United States, that followed the April 1992 acquittal of four white police officers who had beaten black motorist Rodney King had fatally compromised the Bush presidency. The riots demonstrated the tremendous distance that had developed between the leadership of the nation and people who struggled to survive in Reagan's America. Perhaps believing his own rhetoric about the ghettos, Bush remained in the White House prevaricating and hesitating while Los Angeles burned. Meanwhile, candidate Bill Clinton waded into ghetto crowds amid still-smoldering buildings, shaking hands, smiling and comforting people with his optimistic assurances that nothing like this would happen if he was president. The Willie Horton presidency was over and the sights of everyday life in urban America would change as the words used to describe them changed under this new regime.

However, the homeless crisis was not merely one of the many misunderstandings of the complex American system of caste and class, amplified by Reagan era austerity. It was, instead, a rather predictable outcome of the importation of neoliberal Thatcherite political doctrines to the individualist soil of the United States. The reductions in the social welfare system and the ensuing decline in standard of living for millions of Americans that is generally attributed to the Reagan Revolution and the 1982–83 world recession actually began under the previous president, Jimmy Carter. His time in office could well be characterized by his campaign promise to run the United States as he had run the family peanut business in Georgia: frugally, fiscally cautiously, and with less of the waste that was typically identified with Washington politicians and the tens of thousands of "beltway insiders" connected to the Keynesian New Deal/Great Society federal bureaucracy.

Though much of the fiscal tightening under Carter and his Federal Reserve Bank Chairman Paul Volker had a terrible impact on the lower ranks of American wage earners, Carter's policies were never presented as a fully realized program, an ideology, or a way of life. They were largely one-off measures to fine tune an economy that had only recently exited the post–World War II golden age of economic growth and was almost universally viewed as ailing. They were the practical requirements of running the United States with a small businessman's eye for the bottom line.

It was the arrival of Margaret Thatcher as prime minister of Britain in 1979 and then the inauguration of her political disciple and confidant Ronald Reagan in 1981 that signaled a politico-ideological sea change in the English-speaking world, and beyond. It was Mrs. Thatcher who brought the University of Chicago marginalist school of neoliberal economics that had been used by Pinochet in Chile, into the political mainstream. Moving rapidly to cripple or break powerful trade unions and change the social expectations of British wage earners through radical reductions in funding to social welfare, free market privatizations of public services and infrastructure, conversion of public housing rental units to private ownership, and liberal use of the military at home and abroad, Mrs. Thatcher waged an ideological war for the political soul of society, which unlike the policies of such fiscal conservatives as Jimmy Carter and her Labour Party predecessor James Callaghan, often actually put the creed of neoliberal economic rationalism ahead of the financial bottom line.

It was her program of politico-ideological war against the Labour Party, the idea of the working class, and general notions of social democracy and corporatist or civic belonging that drove her to transform the world into a place where, as she put it in her odd mix of everyday parlance and high social theory, "there is no society, only individuals." Before the much-debated "Washington consensus" that came to define neoliberal economic policy, there was the Downing Street discord, which yielded a decade of social turmoil, massive strikes and political mobilizations, including the great 1984–85 coal miner's strike, in which Mrs. Thatcher pushed the UK to the verge of civil war by using the military to restrict domestic travel; and finally the poll tax riots of 1990 that ultimately removed Mrs. Thatcher, but left Thatcherism firmly in place as the dominant sociopolitical ideology throughout much of the world.

On the other side of the Atlantic the Reagan Revolution was not nearly as well schooled in social theory or able to produce the type of full-blown political program that had led Thatcher to propose the ill-conceived poll tax. Though Reagan had a close collaboration with Thatcher and drew his political vision from the same free-market economists and cold war geo-political theorists, he left behind no enduring ideology, no economic program, or social doctrine. Where Thatcher had theorized about self-reliance, folksy pragmatism and small-town or suburban virtues, Reagan's America often seemed to actually inhabit this imaginary world amidst the fatherly hodgepodge of parochial prejudices, cultural hobbyhorses, and religious fixed ideas that made up the social baggage of an American local Thatcherism. Reagan broke unions Thatcher could only weaken, eliminated social programs Mrs. Thatcher could only "rationalize," and intervened in geopolitics far beyond the cozy confines of the Atlantic.

The fight against American Thatcherism was never able to draw on the same long-standing and historically embedded mass social corporatism of British political life. In the 1980s the United States experienced several major national strikes accompanied by significant labor solidarity campaigns and mass anti-Reaganite social movements such as the decade long Central America anti-intervention struggle. However, the resistance to American Thatcherism was marked by much of the same folksy populism that defined the difference between Mrs. Thatcher and Ronald Reagan.[1]

It was in this individualist and inchoate political culture of the United States that particularist discourses of poverty and difference such as the homeless crisis emerged among threatened sections of the New Deal/Great Society welfare state bureaucracy and other strongly anti-Reaganite political forces and became, for a decade from the world recession of 1982 to the United States presidential election of 1992, the subject of widespread social concern, debate, and urban policy. In New York City David Dinkins had been elected mayor in 1989, based in part on his concern for the plight of the homeless and then in 1993 had failed to gain a second term, as such symbols of the inequities and brutalities of American Thatcherism went from being a shocking attack on a way of life to natural and everyday. In gentrifying neighborhoods throughout New York City and in many cities across the United States the homeless had been a populist lightning rod for many of the social anxieties produced by nearly a decade and a half of American Thatcherism.

All this ended with the election of Clinton. Politicians no longer devoted campaign speeches to the "homeless problem." Human-interest stories about the homeless vanished from the news and those who had passed the 1980s mobilizing political and social organizations on behalf of the homeless suddenly seemed to feel that such public displays of the failure of the social system were either unnecessary or undesirable. All the while many continued without proper housing, new housing loss occurred, and rental costs continued to increase in New York City and other cities that were undergoing similar processes of gentrification in response to the post–cold war boom, the Clinton information superhighway stock price run-up, and the new industrial and special arrangements of late-twentieth-century capitalism (Smith 1996).

The new mayor of New York City, Rudolph Giuliani, reduced the population of the Fort Washington Shelter to two hundred and strictly enforced laws against begging, loitering, and sleeping in public, driving many of my informants out of public sight. New York City public shelters and transitional housing facilities remained grossly overcrowded and people continued to sleep in makeshift housing in the hidden interstices of New York City. Some shantytowns remained in marginal spaces not yet claimed by real estate development. Despite a brief debate about homeless policy raised in the press by Hillary Clinton during the early days of her senatorial campaign against soon to be ex–New York City mayor Rudolph Giuliani, the issue had disappeared. In fact few Democrats or Republicans seemed to have any desire to revisit the homeless crisis and Ms. Clinton moved on to other issues.

Many of the homeless advocacy groups that formed in the 1980s still remain, but their funding and social profile has greatly diminished in the past ten years. The mystery of where the homeless have gone is made all the more curious by the fact that lack of housing for those in extreme poverty in New York City continues and may have actually worsened since the heady days of the homeless crisis. It is always a difficult problem to count those who are most marginal and have no real fixed abode. However the continued rise in rents and reduction in government sheltering and services has clearly not allowed the housing problem to be solved.

Michel Foucault opens his book *Madness and Civilization* by asking what happened to medieval lepers once the leprosariums closed. Clearly he was not primarily concerned with the brute empirical facts of madness or leprosy. He was looking for a broader understanding of how competing social forces appropriate culture, language, and the intellectual templates that we commonly use in order to understand and recreate the world around us. Few scholars, social critics, politicians, or average residents of New York City would disagree that during the 1980s housing densities in New York City increased, people doubled and tripled up, and thousands slept on the streets at night and wandered them by day, looking for change from passersby. In some residential neighborhoods that had previously known little to no begging, going to work in the morning became a frightening and depressing exercise in walking the gauntlet through legions of the "homeless" demanding change or merely lurking around corners and sticking to the warmth of steam grates during winter.

That many New Yorkers descended into deep crisis was not in any doubt. However, such a crisis could have been socially constructed in a variety of ways. The social construction of the homeless in the 1980s, like all social constructions, was the result of a competition for ideological dominance among different social forces in political struggle. It was as much about competing descriptions of society as it was about housing those without a home. The broader struggle over social policy, financial priorities, and cultural meaning in the 1980s was a war of ideas, definitions, and social mobilizations, involving a complex symbolic raising and dipping of battle standards. The homeless was one of these battle standards, used in a variety of ways, by different competing forces to mobilize supporters and intimidate opponents.

Throughout most of the Reagan and Bush years, the crisis of homelessness provided a battle standard for opponents of "leaner meaner" neoliberal economics. This battle standard mobilized the traditional iconography and intellectual methodology of poverty studies and the New Deal public sector wing of the Democratic Party. Former New York mayor David Dinkins's campaign and mayoralty are the archetypal example of this use of the homeless as a battle standard. New York City, with its vast public sector bureaucracy, huge welfare rolls, legendary public patronage networks, and European-style social democratic political culture, was the perfect place for Dinkins's message that society's neediest were all the more needy because of the Republicans in Washington. This was most explicitly stated in his widely distributed and paradigmatic report, *The Way Home: A New Direction in Social Policy* (Dinkins & Cuomo 1992), which Dinkins coauthored with Andrew Cuomo, then head of the New York City Commission on the Homeless (commonly known as "the Cuomo Commission") and director of Housing Enterprise for the Less Privileged (HELP).

The new direction suggested in the subtitle featured a variety of old and uncontroversial suggestions for downsizing the public shelter system. However, at the core of the explanation was the controversial assertion that New York City had so many people without housing because "the federal government, historically the provider of low cost housing, has abandoned the business." Yet, the federal government never played a major role in low-cost housing in New York City, and the same Republican abandonment of low-income housing had not led to the same shortages in all other parts of the country (Jencks 1994; Freeman 2000). In addition, the report did not discuss the role of the majority Democratic Party congress in housing policy in the 1980s. With no attempt to define who the homeless were, little concern for the problems of health care, employment, and overall housing problems in New York City, and no empirical data for the grand assertions about the culpability of welfare-slashing Republicans, the report was nevertheless endorsed by many prominent businessmen, community leaders, and professional politicians, for whom it was simply the common sense of political life in a region that was historically dominated by Democratic Party patronage politics.

Like the Republicans who fought for their vision of social policy by using Mandingo ghetto super-predator Willie Horton as a battle standard for law and order politics,[2] the Democrats also presented the most impoverished African-American men as the symbol of what was wrong with America. A counterpoint to chimerical Nat Turners being turned loose on work release or parole by Democratic Party judicial appointees, the homeless man was the supreme Sambo, created by Reaganomics, ritually humiliating himself in public for food and lodging.

Many authors have written at great length about the 1980s as a time of streamlining the U.S. economy, reduction in public subsidies for social programs,[3] unprecedented expansion of military spending, growth in the public debt, longer work hours, lower standards of living, and greatly reduced job security for millions. Many of them have pointed to the particularly destructive force that these changes exerted on urban African Americans, who in direct and indirect ways depended on welfare and public-sector employment. However, there has been less discussion about the degree to which political discourse about the nation's economic priorities turned heavily on the problems of black America. The 1988 election with all its masculine posturing and hidden affronts to Democratic presidential candidate Michael Dukakis's Greek immigrant background and Jewish wife was probably decided during a debate on national television when it was revealed that Dukakis did not have the masculine force to put Willie Horton to the bullwhip, or more likely give him a lethal injection.

In New York City, only a year later, David Dinkins's mobilization of the homeless showed that there were still parts of the United States that preferred compassion to bullwhips. Dinkins was a black candidate running for election in a union town with a public-sector bureaucracy with agencies that regulate everything from rent and the temperature inside private apartments to conflicts with foreign governments over parking violations and false yellow no parking lines painted on curbs by small business owners who want a clear path to their stores. In 1989, law and order ex–federal prosecutor Rudolph Giuliani campaigned for mayor on the Republican program of fear of crime and disorder, but could not scare New York into electing him. Dinkins was given one chance to make the old welfare system/public sector responsible for the problems of the leaner, meaner, and poorer ghetto. He failed, taking with him the derogatory nickname David (they'll take it from me) Dinkins, and found himself replaced in the subsequent mayoral election of 1993 by Giuliani. In 1997 Dinkins's longtime Democratic Party colleague Ruth Messenger attempted to unseat Giuliani and was easily defeated.

Beyond the Safety Net

We are now in the twenty-first century, the economy has finished an eight-year boom and there has been little public interest in the homeless for over ten years. The trickle down of opportunity to even the hardest cases was substantial. While there is still tremendous misery among tens of millions of Americans,[4] capital did flow into sections of the economy that were formerly left for dead. During the last years of the Clinton boom, unemployment was its lowest in decades, public optimism was high, and there was little sense that poverty was one of the big issues with which America must wrestle (Goode and Maskovsky 2001). There can be little doubt that despite the optimism engendered in financiers and investors by the fall of the Soviet Union and the rise of globalization and the information age, this current contraction in the global economy is not the last one. These contractions will, as always, hit the most vulnerable sectors first and hardest: those who got their piece of the boom late or never found their way in. Now is the time to begin to tackle the difficult issue of social inequality, rather than after the next wave of urban riots.

Like the Bobbitt case alluded to in the introduction, the homeless crisis is no longer publicly important in and of itself. An example of reactive emergency surgery in the face of crisis (the New York City municipal shelter system was actually described in its official charters as an emergency response), most of the patients have either died or disappeared from view. However, even if the provision of emergency shelter and social service intervention for the homeless had been a success instead of a failure, it would have been an example of reactive policy. The point of social policy and administration should be to prevent the conditions for emergency from developing. Just as some authors have used the Bobbitt case as a starting point for discussion of the citizenship and naturalization process for foreign-born spouses of American citizens (Yuval-Davis & Sanson 2000), it is my hope that this manuscript can be more than merely another critique of social policy in the 1980s and can play some small part in the first discussions of poverty and public policy in the new century.

Much was written throughout the 1980s and 1990s about the "disappearing social safety net." As millions of Americans "fell through the cracks" thousands of social scientists weighed in on the declining welfare system. Sadly, far less was written about why there should be any need for a safety net in the first place. A safety net is only as important as the height of a jump and the distance that can be fallen. In a wildly productive society that has achieved exponential increases in productive capacity through technological and work process innovations, the last twenty years have seen housing costs increase dramatically, the average workweek grow by 20 to 30 percent, job security disappear, real wages drop, and the employment market tighten. In addition to all these problems facing all working Americans, the eight years under Clinton saw the United States imprison more people than during any previous period in the nation's history. Only contemporary postcommunist Russia, with its dying industrial economy, imprisons as many people per capita.

Despite eight years of America's greatest economic boom, none of these are signs of social health for the nearly two hundred and fifty million ordinary citizens who comprise the non-Other America. But these developments have been particularly severe for the fifty-plus million Americans at the lower ranges of the wage and skill hierarchy, who remain as poor and miserable as when Michael Harrington wrote his book about them. Though the declining safety net was a problem for most of my informants, it was only one aspect of the bigger problem: the rising bar that they were unable to successfully jump.

Beneath the homeless stereotypes, there was one problem that everybody I met on fieldwork shared: none of them was socially strong. If somebody asked me for a one-sentence summary of what I saw on fieldwork it would be, "I spent five years watching confused, weak, sick, and aged people desperately trying to clear a lofty high jump bar." Some lacked education, some lacked social graces, some lacked job skills, some lacked full mental health, some lacked family, some lacked personality, some lacked friends, and some were just plain ugly looking and had struggled with it their whole lives.

For some of my informants the "straw that broke the camel's back" had been a cusp in the life cycle: a transitional moment when the past is banished and there is not yet an established road to the future. Such points as adolescence, family formation, midlife crisis, job loss, ending a prison sentence, and divorce are too often missed in poverty literature, viewed as a given, or identified as pathological. African Americans in particular, and people in poverty generally are not accorded the same right as "the mainstream" to go through big changes in the life cycle that engender transgression, existential doubt, decision making and transformation. They are not even accorded the right to possess typically American kinship norms.

Such basic rights for the more stable sectors of the American working class as the right to go through a divorce, a period of depression, a period of substance abuse, a period of promiscuity, a period of youthful excess and questioning the social order, or a period of compulsive shopping can be permanently crippling for economically marginal individuals and families that try to participate in American social life. Poverty in an advanced industrial economy is not so much about lack of money, food, or shelter, but about being isolated by a regime of penalty and social denial.

Regardless of which factors came together to create housing loss and underemployment, few of my informants could boast only one major social weakness; most had several, beginning with their caste/color designation. However, since the late 1970s and accelerating after the 1982–83 world recession a good life has required higher and higher functioning of nearly everyone. This diminution of the life chances and social expectations of the socially vulnerable was particularly apparent and particularly acute in New York City, where the country's most comprehensive safety net disappeared at the very moment when the bar for success (or survival) was rising faster and faster. Those that have a few little weaknesses or one big weakness inevitably failed to clear the bar and fell to the ground to become battered social problems.

American Social Zoology

It is said that a scratch can turn into gangrene if not treated properly. The more of the wrong care that is applied, the worse the situation becomes, until amputation is necessary. Likewise with the homeless crisis vast sums of money, millions of hours of labor by well-intentioned professionals, and huge amounts of social concern yielded nothing but deteriorating lives for my informants. The deeper they journeyed into the system that was set up for their care, the more they felt like useless, rotting, gangrenous amputated appendages. At base, these tragic consequences were the result of a deeply flawed method for understanding and responding to the problems that my informants confronted in their daily lives.

This flawed method is the American ethnic model. Similar to Margaret Thatcher's vision that "there is no society, only individuals," it takes groups of people with real or imagined differences from "the mainstream" and reifies those differences into a group social identity that is usually seen to have been self-created rather than the result of participating in collective social existence. A key trait or set of traits that the group is thought to share is identified. These different traits become embodied in their physical selves and are classified in a vast Linnaean social taxonomy based on a reified static morphology and function. Each group in the taxonomy is imbued with its own history; its own culture and kinship; its own strengths and weaknesses; its own successes and failures; and its own distance from the "functional mainstream." This hierarchical human zoology is the measure of all of our sins and shortcomings and defines who is fully human and who is of a lower order.

It is this American social taxonomic logic that provided the foundation for Michael Harrington's mechanical functionalist readings of poverty in America and created the nomenclature to describe and classify it. The rhetorical notion of the United States as two nations, one poor and one not-poor is based in a philosophical particularism that allowed for the discovery of numerous subclassifications such as underclass, inner-city, welfare mother, and homeless. Even the Durkheimian scholars mentioned in Chapter 3 who argue for attributing poverty to "macrostructures" rather than the "faulty values" their Weberian colleagues look to, begin with the notion that there is a speciation of the American population into two, three ... many nations.

Harrington and those who came after allowed that social policy was ultimately the institution for fine-tuning problems in the distribution of resources. However, their unrelenting focus on problematic groups rather than the overall social concerns facing a modern citizenry represented, at best, a progressive era model of "the poor" as loss leaders for proactive social policy. In its more common pedestrian form, it represented a positivist particularism that completely failed to view the parts as a product of the whole, blaming the pinky finger for being small, rather than identifying the hand as determining the morphology and function of the pinky or blaming the black family for being dysfunctional rather than American kinship for producing the black family. Such functionalist and particularist logic has proven a distraction from discussions of how America is coping with the challenges of overall social life.

When social policy is based on this particularist individuated model for the obligations and entitlements of citizenship it inevitably fails. This is because it assumes exactly what needs to be demonstrated: that the challenges being faced by the individual or group of individuals are the result of individual differences of culture, history, temperament, and the like, and not the result of being an identifiable part of a social organism. Solutions, even generous ones like the McKinney Homeless Act, that do not consider the nature of the organism that produced a sick part, but only focus on the section deemed pathological, inevitably involve a form of social excision that is at best provisional.

It is in this particularist ethnic model of American social life that the homeless crisis found its birth. A group of nonwhite urbanites who were often lacking in some combination of proper housing, medical care, education, and employment was reified and ethnicized into "the Homeless." During the 1980s, as the bar for economic survival was raised, those who were unable to jump over it found themselves being sorted out according to designations of difference that were socially endowed in their physical bodies, or the shape of their housing. Rather than identifying a concrete set of needs and life tasks bedeviling all working Americans and destroying the lives of my informants there were two nations that were imagined: those who made it over the bar that separated homeless and homeful and those who did not.

When the homeless research and service industry began its boom period in the late 1980s the logical question should have been, "What went wrong with New York City housing policy?" In less than ten years the city went from having a surfeit of affordable apartments, landlords abandoning valuable real estate, and others offering months of free rent to employed lease signers and virtually nobody sleeping in public to a city plunged into a housing nightmare. Millions of ordinary New Yorkers were wasting months looking for a suitable apartment, often never finding it and struggling to pay grossly inflated rents, while tens of thousands lacked basic amenities. As early as 1983 the New York Times was running regular articles about young urban professionals who had spent months, if not years looking for suitable housing. Dinner party conversations focused on extreme stories about what middle-class people were willing to do to get affordable housing and what landlords would demand for apartments that came under rent stabilization and rent control leases. During my field project on the gentrification of the Lower East Side, a random sample of several dozen of the young professionals living in the area around Tompkins Square Park, who were blamed for gentrification, found that most were barely managing to pay their rent.

However, most social scientists were operating with the ethnicized differencing model and put the majority of the population whom they could not see above the bar into the category of "same America" and the tiny minority who became visible under the bar that made them "other." Those under the bar were called homeless; to be studied and discussed with the goal of discovering exactly what was wrong that they were unable to get over the bar. Those who made it over the bar were excluded from the analysis. Though some homelessologists were conservative in their definitions of the group and demanded proof of sleeping publicly and others like Kim Hopper expanded the group to include "pre-homeless," the methodology was the same: a focus on the species that had missed the jump. The bar remained largely invisible.

As life became more difficult and the pile of problem children grew the discussion inevitably turned to individual zoology and social taxonomy. A debate over the nature of the underclass and its subspecies the crackhead, the ghetto super-predator, the homeless, the working poor, and the welfare mother surfaced at the same time that people began to discuss another poorly operationalized zoological category, the undeserving overclass, with its yuppies, inside traders, corporate raiders, and wealthy black affirmative action benefactors.

Like the allegory of the blind scholars examining different parts of an elephant and arguing about what they were studying, scholarly and popular discussions of poverty and housing loss in the 1980s focused exclusively on particularistic problems facing ethnicized groups with exotic problems like shelterization, deinstitutionalization, working poverty, homeless specific behavior, the rust belt, and so on. They rarely ever reached toward discussions of what kind of an overall society America is and was becoming that it should spawn these problematic new social identities with their disturbing problems and behaviors.

Social Policy for High-Wire Artists

As early as 1974, there were visible signs that the golden age of high employment, copious leisure time, a growing standard of living, and steadily rising social indicators was disappearing. Oil shocks, inflation, governments defaulting on loans, and tight capital flows caused by high wages, aging infrastructure, obsolete productive machinery, and economic instability suggested that the golden age was over. Despite wage and price controls during the Nixon/Ford presidency, "stagflation" and cuts to the state sector under Jimmy Carter, and the crushing of the Professional Air Traffic Controllers Organization (PATCO) strike by Ronald Reagan in 1981, it wasn't until the world recession and Mexican currency collapse of 1982 that people throughout the Americas found themselves forced to confront the long term prospect of lower real wages and different economic expectations. For Latin America, the 1980s was called the lost decade, because every country south of the Rio Grande (with the exception of Cuba, which continued the postwar progress until 1987) saw the improvements of the post–World War II era disappear.

In the United States this change in the economics of society was first fully articulated in the contest between Ronald Reagan and Walter Mondale for the U.S. presidency in 1984. Both candidates recognized that the "easy ride" was over and that if the United States was going to keep investment flowing and the economy competitive, Americans would have to cut down on some of their consumption and jump higher and farther to get the things they wanted in life.

Reagan defended the Republican Party vision of social policy as founded on the abstract ideals of citizenship and equality of opportunity. To this end he argued against affirmative action for black people, women, and historically underrepresented minorities and intensified the assault on public assistance that had begun under Jimmy Carter. He argued against privileging a "lazy" caste of the population over a "hard working" one. His argument reflected an almost purely social Darwinist belief in abstract equality of opportunity, what Anatole France had described as "the law, in its majestic equality" forbidding "the rich as well as the poor, to sleep under bridges, to be in the streets and to steal bread."

Walter Mondale in turn defended affirmative action and the Great Society antipoverty programs, arguing that there was a responsibility we have for taking care of our neighbors. Mondale posed the economic environment in a far more fatalistic way, more like a game of musical chairs, where somebody would not get a seat. He argued for a European-style solution, where austerity would involve increased taxes on those who worked to support those who did not. He also defended affirmative action arguing, in effect, that some small section of the groups designated as underrepresented should be given seats at the expense of groups not designated as such. Not surprisingly, many of the steadily employed and threatened members of the majority who were not part of the Great Society bureaucracy that administered public assistance voted for Reagan.

Once again the speciation of American social policy yielded an environment where high-wire artists could sweep gracefully over all the jumps and hurdles and other economic struggles of life and everybody else was left fighting over the crumbs. Families were divided over support for so-cial programs, often based on how connected they were to the sectors be-ing cut, how many public housing projects were in their neighborhoods, and other such circumstances. Neighbors were divided over affirmative action by how many points their children could count on getting on their standardized college entrance exams, or where they expected to study. As the economy became more efficient and lean, the high-wire act continued, while people tore each other apart in a ruthless war of every man against all. It was out of this increasingly harsh and competitive world of the Rea-gan revolution that the homeless bureaucracy surfaced.

Economy and Society in an Orectic Era

The arrival of the post–cold war boom in the early 1990s and the rise of the orectic era of the Clinton presidency made these conflicts and questions less important as some opportunity began filtering down to the bottom. Even the people who lived in the Single Room Occupancy near where I lived during fieldwork saw improvements. They were suddenly described as those people at the SRO, rather than "those homeless people." Though many of them no longer received public assistance, the booming economy was providing more low-skill jobs and the level of despair had dropped. Some of them had purchased automobiles and engaged in optimistic future-oriented personal activities such as decorating their rooms and buying new furniture.

Despite the improved opportunities that arose during the Clinton years there were thousands who still had no housing and continued to sleep in public. However, there were no longer dance songs, movies, and magazine articles about these people. "Who are the homeless, really" was no longer an important question. If anybody raised the issue of homelessness, it was more likely to involve a new question: "where have all the homeless gone?"

With the party of the New Deal/Great Society anti-poverty bureau-cracy in the White House, many of the displaced workers of the Reagan Revolution were absorbed by the booming private sector. Child poverty levels dipped under 20 percent of the population for the first time in nearly two decades, and an expansive optimist in the White House made the moral discourse on homelessness obsolete. There was nobody who needed to raise the homeless banner. The arrival of tighter economic times has not brought these discourses back. The optimism and complacency of the Clinton years that hid vast seas of unvocalized misery among over-worked, underpaid working-class people in post-Reaganite America has given way to the ultimate silencing: the endless war on terror. However, the bar remains high, the speciation of America is firmly imbedded, and the extent of planning for a rainy day is massive growth in police forces and prisons throughout the United States. The crisis remains well man-aged, but the future is not bright.

I recently ran into an old colleague whom I had not seen since we were both studying homelessness in the early 1990s. He had moved on to many other things, as did I during the years between my fieldwork and my first attempts to write this manuscript. When I told him that I was trying to pull together the lessons I had learned during my fieldwork with the homeless in the early 1990s, he laughed and said, "The homeless? That's so twentieth century." As a former homeless researcher who had focused primarily on immediate policy recommendations, "soft money," and articles in public health journals, he could not imagine why I would want to tackle the homeless stuff. "Nobody is interested in the homeless anymore. It's a dead letter. Besides I thought you were the guy who said the homeless don't exist." He told me that I'd be better off working on drugs, HIV, or the falling crime rate, where there is research money. I joked with him that I wanted to write the last homeless book.

The Last Homeless Book

As Ida Susser recently observed (2001), "the poor, the homeless, and the hungry have dropped off the political agenda." However, in arguing for a last book on the homeless and for a new set of policies to resolve the problems of poverty in America, one of the key questions that is rarely ever addressed directly is the one that my colleague was indirectly posing: "the homeless, so what." Why should anybody care about this group of people, who I have spent nearly two hundred pages attempting to deconstruct? If they never really existed for the twelve years of the Reagan/Bush revolution, why should anybody care about them now, in this current period, where the general feeling about poverty could be characterized in terms of the SUV ethos:[5] "the poor ... fuck 'em." The traditional response to this question has usually connected in some way to the Western religious ethos of the Judeo-Christian-Islamic tradition that claims a godliness to doing good works for those in need. However, both the religious imperative of good works and the "SUV ethos" are somewhat abstract and voluntaristic foundations for social policy.

Nineteenth-century social critic Jacob Riis asked us to feel shame in his title; Michael Harrington immediately asked us to feel shame for the poor in our midst; and Kim Hopper and Anna Lou DeHavenon asked us to be guided by our sense of compassion for "the homeless." All of these pleas draw on these traditional Christian religious notions of shame, guilt, and compassion directing voluntary good works that, in some way are part of bearing witness.

The multitude of homeless advocacy groups that emerged in the 1980s took a slightly stronger approach, mixing their calls for compassion with a dagger directed at the heart of the orectic SUV mentality claiming that we were "all only two paychecks away from homelessness." During the lean mean economically difficult 1980s, this scare tactic was of only marginal value, even in the historically immigrant and bohemian East Village. However, during the Clinton years, it was laughable. At present it might be seen as unpatriotic or somewhat unrealistic. Scaring people is no better a basis for rational and humane social policy than shaming them.

The project that I worked on generally presented the issue of caring for the homeless in terms of reducing the public expense, public nuisance, and public health threat posed by homelessness. Though much of their presentation was grounded in compassion, the practical value that they proposed for their intervention was directed at the quality of life for everybody else; a much more compelling justification than sentimental claims on people's sense of shame and far more realistic than trying to convince people who have the social resources to avoid housing loss that they are likely to lose housing.

The cleanliness, safety, and appearance of the streets is an important part of what New York City mayor Rudolph Giuliani famously referred to as "quality of life." However, as Giuliani proved during his two terms in office, it is not necessary to have a housing policy, a homeless policy, or any social services to reduce the danger, spectacle, and harassment caused by homelessness; all that is needed is vigilant police force, some prisons, and a little elbow grease. His campaign to recategorize formerly "homeless beggars" and "homeless window washers" as trespassing criminal extortionists and "squeegee pests" accomplished much of what the CTI project claimed as its "public good" component.

In most books about poverty and social policy, the answer to the question, "why should I care" is put up front. I have put it last, because I believe that it is a much more important question than who is poor, why they are poor, or what can be done to help them. It is more than a question of anthropological inquiry. It is a question of social priorities that must be answered through discussion, debate, and action. It goes to big questions about the nature of society and the meaning of life.

If we look at society not as composed of weak and strong, black and white, poor and non-poor, inner city or suburban, homeless or homeful, or "other America" and "same America," but rather, in a Durkheimian way, as a living organism composed of many different connected pieces and parts, morbidity in one place does not bode well for the rest of the organism. When conditions are good there is plenty of room for weakness, pathology, and systemic imbalance. When conditions become more difficult and more is demanded of the organism for survival, breakdown in one place presages systemic failure.

The people we saw running around the streets in rags during the 1980s need to be viewed in this larger systemic light. If we take society's weakest members not so much as objects to be helped, locked away, or ignored, but as indicators of who we are and where we are going, we are faced with much deeper questions than what to do with those who are unable to meet the basic level of social survival and citizenship. The weakest members of society become social barometers or canaries in a coal mine.

They measure the amount of competition, the level of functioning that is necessary to survive, the displacement of those who must labor to live, and the degree of comfort and security that we can claim for our own lives. If they are drowning from the high price of housing, declining real wages, rising costs for education, declining public health, and the revival of nineteenth-century diseases, then the rest of us are probably "up to our necks in it."

Competition breeds excellence say some, competition creates waste say others, and still others point to the damage it does to the social fabric upon which our lives are based. The question that the existence of poverty raises is: do we really want to live in a society based on such severe economic competition? Do most people really enjoy the daily battle with co-workers, friends, family, and all the strangers out there for who gets a job, a house, a raise, a good word from the boss? How many people really enjoy the extra five to fifteen hours a week that Americans work as compared with Europeans? Can we as a society really justify commodifying and parceling out such huge rewards and such stern punishments for social accomplishment and social failure?

If instead of taking a Durkheimian approach, we take a Marxian one and examine the many attempts to make economies more competitive by adopting the "American model" of pure competition with less social support, fewer guarantees, and a higher level of commodification, we must necessarily be confronted with the specter of a global "race to the bottom" for wages, standards of living, and the overall quality of life for all working people. Countries around the world talk about the need to adopt the American model or lose the competition with the United States for investment and markets. However with its vast wealth and unparalleled productivity the United States could be at the leading edge of reversing this three decade trend of an ever-rising bar that must be jumped to survive. The homeless crisis and all its preceding crises of "other Americas" and all the crises yet to come for newly imagined problematic groups are administrative tasks that are expensive, difficult, frustrating, and ultimately tragic. But worse than that, they are intimately tied to the task of keeping the rest of us running full speed to the morning commute.

Notes

1. In much of the advanced industrial world, the fight against neoliberalism has often been confused by the fact that social corporatism, and traditions of working-class political organization have often been so powerfully embedded that it was often only possible for social democratic heads of state to implement Thatcherite programs. France, for instance, is one of the many European countries where Thatcherism was never able to fully transform national politics. Though largely defensive, the battles waged against economic rationalism have often been fiercer than even the 1984–85 coal mine strike or the poll tax riots. The French national strike wave of late 1995 is an example of this.

2. Willie Horton politics were more than merely campaign rhetoric. In 1990 the percentage of the population engaged in law enforcement employment increased 5.4 percent, the largest yearly increase since 1975. During the twelve years of the Reagan/Bush presidency, the federal and state prison population increased by 267 percent. During February 2000, the United States celebrated the incarceration of its two millionth prisoner, giving the United States 25 percent of the world's prison population.
3. With the exception of law enforcement and tax subsidies for real estate ownership.
4. A largely uncontroversial measure of continuing levels of poverty among a population that cannot take any responsibility for its own misfortune is child poverty. Despite a small, but steady decrease in poverty for Americans under eighteen years old beginning with Bill Clinton's inauguration in 1993, at the end of the decade the official national and New York State percentages remained 18.7 percent and 24.2 percent respectively, placing over thirteen million American children in poverty. These numbers are dramatically higher than they were prior to the beginnings of American Thatcherism during the last two years of the Carter administration in the 1970s.
5. There is a whole literature in the field of marketing on the product niche of the Sport Utility Vehicle. It is not generally a group that is identified with social conscience and concern for neighbors both abstract and real.

BIBLIOGRAPHY

Abelmann, Nancy and John Lie. 1995. *Blue Dreams: Korean Americans and the Los Angeles Riots*. Cambridge: Harvard University Press.

Aldrich, H. and Roger Waldinger. 1990. "Ethnicity and Entrepreneurship."*Annual Review of Sociology* 16: 111–135.

Anderson, Nels. 1923. *The Hobo: The Sociology of the Homeless Man*. Chicago, Ill.: University of Chicago Press.

Aschenbrenner, J. 1975. *Lifelines: Black Families in Chicago*. NY: Holt, Rinehart & Winston.

Auletta, Ken. 1982. *The Underclass*. New York: Random House.

Barak, Gregg. 1991. *Gimme Shelter: A Social History of Homelessness in Contemporary America*. New York: Praeger.

Barrett, Wayne and Jack Newfield. 1988. *City For Sale: Ed Koch and the Betrayal of New York*. New York: Harper & Row.

Baxter, Ellen and Kim Hopper. 1981. *Private Lives/Public Spaces: Homeless Adults on the Streets of New York City*. New York: Community Service Society, Institute for Social Welfare Research.

Bennett, Neil, David Bloom and Patricia Craig. 1989. "The Divergence of Black and White Marriage Patterns." *American Journal of Sociology* 95, no. 3: 692–722.

Billingsley, Andrew. 1968. *Black Families in White America*. N.J. Prentice Hall.

Blassingame, John W. 1972. *The Slave Community: Plantation Life in the Antebellum South*. New York: Oxford University Press.

Blau, Joel. 1989. "The Limits of The Welfare State: New York City's Response to Homelessness." *Journal of Sociology and Social Welfare*, 16, no. 1.

———, 1992. *The Visible Poor*. New York: Oxford University Press.

Bogard, Cynthia J., J. Jeff McConnell, Naomi Gerstel, and Michael Schwartz. 1999. "Homeless Mothers and Depression: Misdirected Policy." *Journal of Health and Social Behavior* 40 (March): 46–62.

Brecher, Jeremy. 1997. *Strike!* Boston, MA: South End Press.

Brimmer, Andrew. 1998. "Long Term Trends and Prospects for Black-Owned Businesses." *Review of Black Political Economy* 26, no.1: 19–36.

Butler, John Sibley. 1991. *Entrepreneurship and Self-Help Among Black Americans: A Reconsideration of Race and Economics*. Albany, NY: SUNY Press.

Chayanov, A.V. 1986. *Chayanov on the Theory of Peasant Economy*. Daniel Thorner, Basile Kerblay, R.E.F. Smith, eds. Madison, WI: University of Wisconsin Press.

Chen, Gavin and John Cole. 1988. "The Myths, Facts, and Theories of Ethnic, Small Scale Enterprise Financing." *Review of Black Political Economy* 16, no. 4:111–123.

Chen, Hsiang-shui. 1992. *Chinatown No More: Taiwan Immigrants in Contemporary New York*. Ithaca: Cornell University Press.

Cherry, Robert. 1990. "Middleman Minority Theories: Their Implications for Black-Jewish Relations." *Journal of Ethnic Studies* 17, no. 4: 117–138.

Coontz, Stephanie. 1992. *The Way We Never Were: American Families and the Nostalgia Trap.* New York: Basic Books.

Culhane, Dennis P. and Randall Kuhn. 1998. "Patterns and Determinants of Public Shelter Utilization Among Homeless Adults in New York City and Philadelphia." *Journal of Policy Analysis and Management* 17, no. 1: 23–43.

Dasgupta, Sathi Sengupta. 1989. *On the Trail of an Uncertain Dream.* New York: AMS Press.

Davis, Mike. 1990. *City of Quartz: Excavating the Future in Los Angeles.* New York: Verso.

DeGiovanni, Frank. 1987. *Displacement Pressures in the Lower East Side.* New York: Community Service Society of New York.

Dehavenon, Anna Lou. 1995. *Out in the Cold: The Social Exclusion of New York City's Homeless Families in 1995.* New York: Action Research Project on Hunger, Homelessness, and Family Health.

D'Emilio, John. 1988. *Intimate Matters: A History of Sexuality in America.* NY: Harper & Row.

DeOllos, Ione. 1997. *On Becoming Homeless: The Shelterization Process for Homeless Families.* Lanham, MD: University Press of America.

diLeonardo, Micaela. 1998. *Exotics at Home: Anthropologies, Others, American Modernity.* Chicago: University of Chicago Press.

Dinkins, David N. and Andrew M. Cuomo. 1992. *The Way Home: A New Direction In Social Policy.* Report of the New York City Commission on the Homeless.

Dubois, William Edward Burghardt. 1970. *The Negro American Family.* Boston: MIT Press.

Fantasia, Rick and Maurice Isserman. 1994. *Homelessness: A Sourcebook.* New York: Facts on File.

Feagin, Joe and Nikitah Imani. 1994. "Racial Barriers to African American Entrepreneurship: An Explanatory Study." *Social Problems* 41, no. 4: 562–584.

Fitch, Bob. 1991. "What a Friend We Have in Dinkins: The Left Vs. the Democrats." *Against the Current* March/April 1991.

Fogel, Robert William and Stanley Engerman. 1974. *Time on the Cross: The Economics of American Negro Slavery.* Boston: Little Brown.

Foner, Nancy. 1997. "The Immigrant Family: Cultural Legacies and Cultural Changes." *International Migration Review* 31, no. 4: 961–974.

Fraser, Steve and Gary Gerstle. 1989. *The Rise and Fall of The New Deal Order, 1930–1980.* Princeton: Princeton University Press.

Frazier, E. Franklin. 1948. *The Negro Family In The United States.* New York: The Citadel Press.

Freeman, J. 2000. *Working Class New York: Life and Labor Since World War II.* New York: New Press.

Furstenburg, F., T. Hershberg and John Modell. 1974. "The Origins of the Female-Headed Black Family: The Impact of the Urban Experience." *Journal of Interdisciplinary History* 6, no. 2: 211–233.

Gans, Herbert. 1967. "The Negro Family: Reflections on the Moynihan Report." In *The Moynihan Report and the Politics of Controversy; a Trans-action Social Science and Public Policy Report.* Lee Rainwater and William Yancey, eds. 445–456. Cambridge: M.I.T. Press.

George, Henry. 1879. *Progress and Poverty: An Inquiry Into the cause of Industrial Depressions, and of Increase of Want with Increase of Wealth.* San Francisco: W.M. Hinton & Co.

Gerstel, Naomi, Cynthia J. Bogard, J. Jeff McConnell, and Michael Schwartz. 1995. "The Therapeutic Incarceration of Homeless Families." *Social Service Review* 70: 543–72.

Ginzberg, Eli. 1956. *The Negro Potential.* NY: Columbia University Press.

Glazer, Nathan & Daniel Patrick Moynihan. 1963. *Beyond the Melting Pot; The Negroes, Puerto Ricans, Jews, Italians, and Irish of New York City.* Cambridge, MA: M.I.T. Press.

Goffman, Ervin. 1961. *Asylums.* Garden City, NJ: Doubleday.

Goode, Judith and Jeff Maskovsky (eds.). 2001. *The New Poverty Studies: The Ethnography of Power, Politics, and Impoverished People in the United States.* NY: New York University Press.

Gordon, Linda. 1994. *Pitied But Not Entitled: Single Mothers and the History of Welfare, 1890–1935.* New York: Free Press.

Gould, Mark. 1999. "Race and Theory: Culture, Poverty, and Adaptation to Discrimination in Wilson and Ogbu." *Sociological Theory* 17, no. 2:171–200.

Gounis, Kostas. 1990. " Shelterization." *Hospital and Community Psychiatry* 41: 1357–1358.

———, 1992. "The Manufacture of Dependency: Shelterization Revisited." *New England Journal of Public Policy* 8: 685–693.

———, 1993. "The Domestication of Homelessness: the Politics of Space and Time in New York City Shelters." PhD dissertation, Columbia University.

Gregory, Steven. 1998. *Black Corona: Race and the Politics of Place in an Urban Community.* Princeton, NJ: Princeton University Press.

Grunberg, Jeffrey and Paula Eagle. 1990. "Shelterization: How the Homeless Adapt to Shelter Living." *Hospital and Community Psychiatry*, 41, no.5 (May).

Gutman, Herbert. 1976. *The Black Family in Slavery and Freedom, 1750–1925.* New York: Pantheon Books.

———, 1987. *Power and Culture: Essays on the American Working Class.* New York: Pantheon Books.

Handlin, Oscar. 1957. *The Uprooted: The Epic Story of the Great Migrations That Made the American People.* New York: Grosset & Dunlap.

———, 1959. The *Newcomers: Negroes and Puerto Ricans in a Changing Metropolis.* Cambridge MA: Harvard University Press.

Hannerz, Ulf. 1969. *Soulside: Inquiries into Ghetto Culture and Community.* New York: Columbia University Press.

Harrington, Michael. 1962. *The Other America: Poverty in the United States.* New York: Macmillan.

———, 1984. *New American Poverty.* New York: Holt, Rinehart, and Winston.

Harvey, David. 1990. *The Condition of Post-Modernity: An Enquiry into the Origins of Cultural Change.* Cambridge MA: Blackwell.

Hays, Samuel P. 1957. *The Response to Industrialism, 1885–1914.* Chicago: University of Chicago Press.

Hoch, Charles. 1989. *New Homeless and Old: Community and the Skid Row Hotel.* Philadelphia: Temple University Press.

Hoff, Joan. 1994. *Nixon Reconsidered.* New York: Basic Books.

Hofstadter, Richard. 1955. *Age of Reform: From Bryan to F. D. R.* New York: Knopf.

Hogan, D. and Evelyn Kitagawa. 1985. "The Impact of Social Status, Family Structure and Neighborhood on the Fertility of Black Adolescents." *American Journal of Sociology* 90, no. 4: 825–855.

Hopper, Kim. 1987. "The Public Response to Homelessness in New York City: The Last Hundred Years." In *On Being Homeless: Historical Perspectives.* ed. Rick Beard. New York: Museum of the City of New York.

———, 1990. "Shelterization." *Hospital and Community Psychiatry.* 41: 1357.

———, 1991. "Homelessness Old and New: The Matter of Definition." *Housing Policy Debate* 2: 757–813.

———, 1992. "Counting the Homeless: S-Night in New York." *Eval. Rev.* 16, no. 4: 376–88.

———, 1995. "Definitional Quandaries and Hazards in Counting the Homeless: An Invited Commentary." *American Journal of Orthopsychiatry* 65: 340–365.

Hopper, Kim & Jill Hamberg. 1984. *The Making of America's Homeless: From Skid Row to New Poor 1945–1984.* New York: Community Service Society of New York.

Hopper, K., E. Susser and S. Conover. 1986. "Economics of Makeshift: Deindustrialization and Homelessness in New York City." *Urban Anthropology* 14: 183–236.

Hunter, Robert. 1904. *Poverty.* New York: The Macmillan Company.

Jackson, Kenneth. 1985. *Crabgrass Frontier: The Suburbanization of the United States.* New York: Oxford University Press.

Jencks, Christopher. 1994. *The Homeless.* Cambridge, Mass.: Harvard University Press.

Katz, Michael B. 1990. *The Undeserving Poor: From the War on Poverty to the War on Welfare.* New York: Pantheon Books.

———, 1993. *The Underclass Debate: Views From History.* Princeton, NJ: Princeton University Press.

———, 1996. *In the Shadow of the Poor House: A Social History of Welfare in America*. New York: Basic Books.

Kim, Claire Jean. 2000. *Bitter Fruit: The Politics of Black-Korean Conflict in New York City*. New Haven: Yale University Press.

King, Martin Luther Jr. 1967. "An Address by Dr. Martin Luther King Jr. Delivered on October 29, 1965." In *The Moynihan Report and the Politics of Controversy; a Trans-action Social Science and Public Policy Report*. Lee Rainwater and William Yancey, eds. 402–408. Cambridge: M.I.T. Press.

Kirby, John B. 1980. *Black Americans in the Roosevelt era: Liberalism and Race*. Knoxville: University of Tennessee Press.

Leacock, Eleanor B., ed. 1967. "Distortions of Working-Class Reality in American Social Science." *Science and Society* 31, no. 1:1–21.

———, 1971. *The Culture of Poverty: A Critique*. New York: Simon and Schuster.

Leuchtenberg, William. 1963. *Franklin D. Roosevelt and the New Deal*. New York: Harper & Row.

Lichter, Daniel. 1988. "Racial Differences in Underemployment in American Cities." *American Journal of Sociology* 93, no. 4: 771–792.

Link, Bruce G; Ezra, Susser, Ezra, Ann Stueve, and Jo Phelan. 1994. "Lifetime and Five-Year Prevalence of Homelessness in the United States." *American Journal of Public Health* 84: 1907–1913.

Lovell, Anne M., Susan Makiesky Barrow and Elmer Struening. 1992. "Between Relevance and Rigour: Methodological Issues in Studying Mental Health and Homelessness." In R.I. Jahiel ed. *Homelessness: A Prevention-Oriented Approach*. 272–295. Baltimore: John Hopkins University Press.

Mackenzie, William. 1967. *Politics and Social Science*. Baltimore: Penguin Books.

Marable, Manning. 1983. *How Capitalism Underdeveloped Black America*. Boston: Southend.

Marcus, Anthony. 2001. "The Good, The Bad, and the Ugly: Negotiating Ghetto Role Models." *Focaal—European Journal of Anthropology* 38, no. 1: 41–64.

———, 2003. "Shelterization and the Homeless: Some Methodological Dangers of Institutional Studies." *Human Organization* 62, no.2: 134–142.

———, 2005. "The Culture of Poverty Revisited: Bringing Back the Working Class."*Anthropologica* 47, no.1.

Marx, Karl. 1954. *Capital*. Moscow: Foreign Languages Publishing House.

Maxwell, Andrew. 1993. "The Underclass, Social Isolation and Concentration Effects: The Culture of Poverty Revisited." *Critique of Anthropology* 13, no. 3: 231–45.

McAdoo, H.P. 1980. "Black Mothers and the Extended Family Support Network." In *The Black Woman*. L.F. Rodgers-Rose, ed. 125–144. California: Sage.

McNulty, Thomas. 1999. "The Residential Process and the Ecological Concentration of Race, Poverty, and Violent Crime in New York City." *Sociological Focus* 32, no. 1: 25–42.

Minehan, Thomas. 1934. *Boy and Girl Tramps of America*. New York: Farrar and Rinehart.

Mitchell, Don. 1997. "The Annihilation of Space by Law: The Roots and Implications of Anti-Homeless Laws." *Antipode* 29: 303–335.

———, 2001. "Postmodern Geographical Praxis? The Postmodern Impulse and the War Against the Homeless in the Post-Justice City." In *Postmodern Geography: Theory and Praxis*, Claudio Minca (ed.). 57–92. Oxford: Blackwell.

Moody, Kim. 1988. *An Injury to All: The Decline of American Unionism*. New York: Verso Press.

Moynihan, Daniel P. 1965. *The Negro Family: The Case for National Action*. Washington D.C.: U.S. Government Printing Office.

Myrdal, Gunnar. 1964. *An American Dilmma: The Negro In a White Nation*. New York: McGraw-Hill.

Nash, June. 1989. *From Tank Town to High Tech: The Clash of Community and Industrial Cycles*. Albany, NY: State University of New York Press.

Nash, June & Maria Patricia Fernandez-Kelly, eds. 1983. *Women, Men, and the International Division of Labor*. Albany, NY: State University of New York Press.

National Law Center on Homelessness and Poverty. 2004. "Homelessness and Poverty in America."(accessed September 20, 2004) http://www.nlchp.org/FA_HAPIA/

Niemonen, Jack. 2002. *Race, Class, and the State in Contemporary Sociology: The William Julius Wilson Debates*. Boulder, Colo: Lynne Rienner.

Oliver, Melvin and Thomas Shapiro. 1995. *Black Wealth/White Wealth: A New Perspective on Racial Inequality*. NY: Routledge.

Orr, Marion. 1999. *Black Social Capital: The Politics of School Reform in Baltimore, 1986–1998*. Lawrence: University Press of Kansas.

Park, Kyeyoung. 1997. *The Korean American Dream: Immigrants and Small Business in New York City*. Ithaca, N.Y.: Cornell University Press.

Park, Robert Ezra. 1925. *The City*. Chicago, Ill: The University of Chicago Press.

Park, Robert Ezra, Ernest W. Burgess & Roderick D. McKenzie. 1967. *The City*. Chicago: University of Chicago Press.

Patterson, Orlando. 1998. *Rituals of Blood: Consequences of Slavery in Two American Centuries*. Washington, D.C.: Civitas/Counterpoint.

Peletz, Michael. 1995. "Kinship Studies in Late 20th Century Anthropology." *Annual Review of Anthropology* 25: 343–372.

Phelan, Jo and Bruce Link. 1999. "Who Are the Homeless? Reconsidering the Stability and Composition of the Homeless Population." *American Journal of Public Health* 89: 1334–1338.

Piven, Frances Fox. 1971. *Regulating the Poor: The Functions of Public Welfare*. New York: Pantheon Books.

————, 1997. *The Breaking of the American Social Compact*. NY: New Press.

Reissman, Frank. 1967. "In Defense of the Negro Family." In *The Moynihan Report and the Politics of Controversy: A Trans-action Social Science and Public Policy Report*. Lee Rainwater and William Yancey, eds. 474–478. Cambridge: M.I.T. Press.

Riis, Jacob A. 1890. *How The Other Half Lives: Studies Among The Tenements of New York, by Jacob A. Riis: With Illustrations Chiefly From Photographs Taken by the Author*. New York: C. Scribner's Sons.

Rochefort, David A. and Riger W. Cobb. 1992. "Framing and Claiming the Homelessness Problem." In *Homelessness: New England and Beyond*. Padraig O'Malley ed. New England Journal of Public Policy. 49–66. Amherst, MA: University of Massachusetts.

Roscigno, Vincent. 2000. "Family/School Inequality and African-American/Hispanic Achievement." *Social Problems* 47, no. 2: 266–290.

Rossi, Peter Henry. 1989. *Down and Out in America: The Origins Of Homelessness*. Chicago: University of Chicago Press.

Rustin, Bayard. 1967. "Why Don't Negroes ..." In *The Moynihan Report and the Politics of Controversy; a Trans-action Social Science and Public Policy Report*. Lee Rainwater and William Yancey, eds. 417–426. Cambridge: M.I.T. Press.

Ryan, William. 1967. "Savage Discovery: The Moynihan Report." In *The Moynihan Report and The Politics of Controversy; a Trans-action Social Science and Public Policy Report*. Lee Rainwater and William Yancey, eds. 457–466. Cambridge: M.I.T. Press.

Sampson, Robert. 1987. "Urban Black Violence: The Effect of Male Joblessness and Family Disruption." *American Journal of Sociology* 93, no. 2:348–382.

Sanjek, Roger. 1998. *The Future of Us All: Race and Neighborhood Politics in New York City*. Ithaca: Cornell University Press.

Sawhill, Isabel, ed. 1988. *Challenge to Leadership: Economic and Social Issues for the Next Decade*. Washington, D.C.: Urban Institute Press.

Sheldon, Sam and Henry Walsh. 1994. "The Old Homeless." In *Paths to Homelessness: Extreme Poverty and the Urban Housing Crisis*. Doug Timmer (ed.). Boulder: Westview Press.

Shinn, Marybeth. 1992. "Homelessness: What's a Psychologist to do?" *American Journal of Community Psychology* 20: 1–24.

Sinclair, Upton. 1904. *The Jungle*. New York: Doubleday.

Sitkoff, Harvard. 1978. *A New Deal for Blacks: The Emergence of Civil Rights as a National Issue*. New York: Oxford University Press.

Small, Mario and Katherine Newman. 2001. "Urban Poverty After the Truly Disadvantaged: The Rediscovery of Family, the Neighborhood, and Culture." *Annual Review of Sociology*: 23–46.

Smith, Gavin. 1985. "Reflections on the Social Relations of Simple Commodity Production." *Journal of Peasant Studies* 13, no. 1: 99–108.

Smith, Neil. 1979. "Gentrification and Capital: Theory, Practice and Ideology in Society Hill." *Antipode* 11, no. 3:24–35.

——, 1982. "Gentrification and Uneven Development." *Economic Geography* 58:139–155.

——, 1996. *New Urban Frontier: Gentrification and the Revanchist City*, New York: Routledge.

Snow, David, Leon Anderson, and Paul Koegel. 1994. "Distorting Tendencies in Research on Homelessness." *American Behavioral Scientist* 37: 461–75.

Solenberger, Alice. 1911. *One Thousand Homeless Men: A Study of Original Records*. New York: Charities Publication Committee.

Sowell, Thomas. 1981. *Ethnic America: A History*. NY: Basic Books.

Stack, Carol B. 1974. *All Our Kin: Strategies for Survival in a Black Community*. New York: Harper & Row.

Stark, Louisa R. 1994. "The Shelter as 'Total Institution': An Organizational Barrier to Remedying Homelessness." *American Behavioral Scientist* 37: 553–562.

Steffens, Lincoln. 1904. *Shame of the Cities*. New York: McClure, Phillips & Co.

Steinberg, Stephen. 1981. *The Ethnic Myth: Race, Ethnicity and Class in America*. Boston: Beacon Press.

——, 1995. *Turning Back: The Retreat from Racial Justice in American Thought and Policy*. Boston: Beacon.

Susser, Ezra and Kostas Gounis. 1990. " Shelterization and Its Implications for Mental Health Services." In *Psychiatry Takes to the Street: Outreach and Crisis Intervention for the Mentally Ill*. N. Cohen, ed. 231–255. New York, NY: Guilford Press.

Susser Ezra, Eliecer Valencia, Sally Conover, Alan Felix, WY Tsai, Wyatt. 1997. "Preventing Recurrence of Homelessness Among Mentally Ill Men: A Critical Time Intervention After Discharge From a Shelter." *American Journal of Public Health*, 87: 256–262.

Susser, Ida. 1982. *Norman Street*. New York: Oxford University Press.

——, 1993. "Creating Family Forms: The Exclusion of Men and Teenage Boys From Families in the New York City Shelter System, 1987–91." *Critique of Anthropology* 13, no. 3: 267–85.

——, 1996. "The Construction of Poverty and Homelessness in U.S. Cities."*Annual Review of Anthropology* 411–435.

——, 2001. "Preface." In *The New Poverty Studies: The Ethnography of Power, Politics, and Impoverished People in the United States*, Judith Goode and Jeff Maskovsky (eds) NY: New York University Press.

Susser, Ida and Alfredo Gonzalez. 1992. "Sex, Drugs, and Videotape: The Prevention of AIDS in a New York City Shelter for Homeless Men."*Medical Anthropology* 14: 307–22.

Sutherland, Edwin Hardin and Harvey J. Locke. 1936. *Twenty Thousand Homeless Men: A Study of Unemployed Men in the Chicago Shelters*. Chicago, Philadelphia: J.B. Lippincott Company.

Tabb, William & Larry Sawyers eds. 1984. *Marxism and the Metropolis: New Perspectives in Political Economy*. New York: Oxford University Press.

Timmer, Doug A., Stanley Eitzen and Kathryn D. Talley. 1994. *Paths to Homelessness: Extreme Poverty and the Urban Housing*. Boulder, CO: Westview Press.

Tomlins, Christopher. 1985. *The State and The Unions: Labor Relations, Law and The Organized Labor Movement In America, 1880–1960*. New York: Cambridge University Press.

Tonry, Michael H. 1995. Malign *Neglect—Race, Crime, and Punishment in America*. NY: Oxford University Press.

Toro, Paul & Melissa Warren. 1991. "Homelessness, Psychology, and Public Policy." *American Psychologist* 46: 1205–07.

Turner, Joan. 1984. *Building Boundaries: the Politics of Urban Renewal in Manhattan's Lower East Side*. City University of New York Graduate Center doctoral dissertation.

Unger, Irwin. 1996. *The Best of Intentions: The Triumph and Failure of the Great Society under Kennedy, Johnson, and Nixon*. New York: Doubleday.

United States Census Bureau. 2004. "Housing Affordability 1995."(accessed September 20, 2004). http://www.census.gov/hhes/www/housing/hsgaffrd/afford95/afford95.html

United States Census Bureau. 2004. "Historical Census of Housing Tables: Crowding." (accessed Sept. 20, 2004). http://www.census.gov/hhes/www/housing/census/historic/crowding.html

United States Congress. 1987. Stewart B. McKinney Homeless Assistance Act, United States Public Law 100-77, U.S. (July 22, 1987) URL:< http://thomas.loc.gov/cgi-bin/bdquery/z?d100:HR00558:ITOM:/bss/d100query.htmlI > (December 12, 2002).

United States Congress/Senate, Committee on the Judiciary, Subcommittee on Immigration. 1997. Immigrant Entrepreneurs, Job Creation, and the American Dream. Hearing Before the Subcommittee on Immigration of the Committee on the Judiciary, United States Senate, One Hundred Fifth Congress, First Session. Washington, D.C.: U.S. G.P.O.

Valentine, Charles A. 1968. Culture and Poverty: Critique and Counter-Proposals. Chicago: University of Chicago Press.

Washington, Booker T. 1907. The Negro in the South, His Economic Progress in Relation to His Moral and Religious Development: Being the William Levi Bull Lectures for the Year 1907. Philadelphia: G.W. Jacobs and Company.

Weinberg, Arthur. 1961. The Muckrakers: The Era in Journalism that Moved America to Reform, The Most Significant Magazine Articles of 1902–1912. New York: Simon and Schuster.

Weinstein, James. 1968. The corporate Ideal in the Liberal State, 1900–1918. Boston, Beacon Press.

Weir, Margaret, Ann Orloff & Theda Skocpol. 1988. The Politics of Social Policy In The United States. Princeton: Princeton University Press

Weiss, Nancy J. 1983. Farewell to the Party of Lincoln: Black Politics in the Age of FDR. Princeton, N.J.: Princeton University Press.

Wiebe, Robert H. 1962. Businessmen and Reform: A Study of The Progressive Movement. Cambridge, MA: Harvard University Press.

———, 1967. The search for Order, 1877–1920. New York, Hill and Wang.

Wilson, William J. 1978. The Declining Significance of Race: Blacks and Changing American Institutions. Chicago: University of Chicago Press.

———, 1987. The Truly Disadvantaged: The Inner City, The Underclass, and Public Policy. Chicago: University of Chicago Press.

———, 1989. "A Response to Critics of The Truly Disadvantaged." Journal of Sociology and Social Welfare 16, no. 4: 133–148.

Wolters, Raymond. 1970. Negroes and the Great Depression: The Problem of Economic Recovery. Westport, Conn.: Greenwood Pub.

Yoon, In-Jin. 1997. On My Own: Korean Businesses and Race Relations in America. Chicago: University of Chicago Press

Young, Phillip. 1983. "Family Labor, Sacrifice, and Competition: Korean Greengrocers in New York City." Amerasia 10: 53–71.

Yuval-Davis, Nira & Jo Sanson. 2000. "Citizenship." In Routledge International Encyclopedia of Women. NY: Routledge.

Zinn, Howard. 1995. A People's History of the United States: 1492–Present. New York: Harper Perennial.

INDEX